AN INTRODUCTION TO SOUTH ASIA

Second edition

B.H. Farmer

London and New York

318184

UNIVERSITY OF BRADFORD
LIBRARY

2 2 AUG 1995

ACCESSION No.	CLASS No.
034104446X	C954 FAR
LOCATION	

First edition published in 1983
by Methuen & Co. Ltd

© 1983 B.H. Farmer

Second edition published in 1993
by Routledge
11 New Fetter Lane, London EC4P 4EE

Simultaneously published in the USA and Canada
by Routledge
29 West 35th Street, New York, NY 10001

© 1993 B.H. Farmer

Typeset in Garamond by
J&L Composition Ltd, Filey, North Yorkshire

Printed and bound in Great Britain by
TJ Press (Padstow) Ltd, Padstow, Cornwall

All rights reserved. No part of this book may be reprinted or
reproduced or utilized in any form or by any electronic,
mechanical, or other means, now known or hereafter
invented, including photocopying and recording, or in any
information storage or retrieval system, without permission in
writing from the publishers.

British Library Cataloguing in Publication Data

A catalogue record for this book is available from the British Library

Library of Congress Cataloging in Publication Data
Farmer, B.H.
Introduction to South Asia. – 2 Rev. ed
I. Title
954

ISBN 0–415–05695–0
ISBN 0–415–05696–9 (pbk)

CONTENTS

TABLES AND MAPS

TABLES

MAPS

PREFACE TO THE SECOND EDITION

In the preface to the first edition of this book, published in 1983, I thanked, and still thank, a number of ladies who had typed a fair manuscript. It is a measure of the changes in technology over the intervening years that the text of this second edition has been produced on a word processor and printer. These were provided by my college. I would like to express my gratitude for them and to those who gave invaluable help with the new technology. These were Dr M. Richards, who advised me and installed it; Miss S. Smith, Mr J.M.S. Doar and Dr D.J. Greaves, who taught me how to use such of it as I needed and dealt with early difficulties; and Mr J. Warbrick, who helped greatly with later stages of the work.

I would also like to thank the many friends, too numerous to mention here, who have helped with information, references and comments; and Mr Tristan Palmer and his colleagues at Routledge for much help.

A necessary condition for my work on this book has been the skill of Mr J. Keast-Butler, consultant opthalmologist, without which I should not have been able to see; another necessary condition has been the support of my wife.

I have added two maps to this edition, though the reader should still have access to an atlas or to other maps of South Asia.

Finally, I have generally used 'Russia' for Imperial Russia, 'the USSR' or 'Soviet Russia' for the Communist successor to that empire, and 'Commonwealth of Independent States' or 'CIS' for the immediate successor to most of the former Soviet Republics.

B.H. Farmer
St John's College, Cambridge

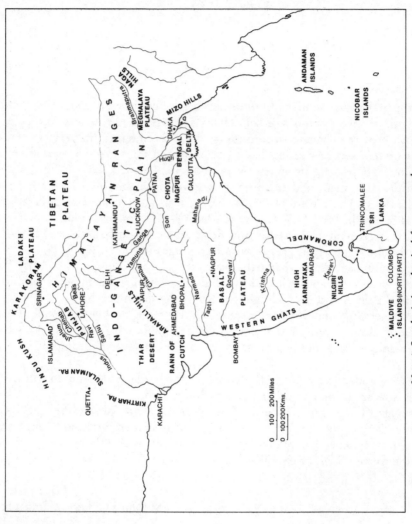

Map 1 South Asia: physical features and towns

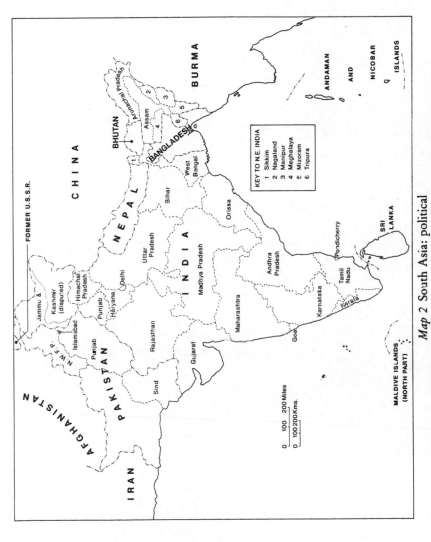

Map 2 South Asia: political

Note: Some boundaries are necessarily somewhat generalized at this scale. The dotted line in Jammu and Kashmir shows the 'Line of Control' (see text).

1

INTRODUCTION: THE DEFINITION, IMPORTANCE AND INTEREST OF SOUTH ASIA

Of every five people in the world, one is a South Asian. That is, in terms of the definition adopted in this book, one of the over 1000 million residents in the vast subcontinent that covers 1,725,000 sq. miles (4,468,000 sq. kilometres) and that includes Bangladesh, Bhutan, India, the Maldive Islands, Nepal, Pakistan and Sri Lanka. On grounds of size and population alone, then, South Asia cannot fail to be of importance in the world scene; and the problems faced by its people, or created in the region for the rest of us, must be of the widest interest.

Perhaps the term 'South Asia' does, however, still call for explanation. That it is unfamiliar is clear from the fact that the Centre of South Asian Studies in the University of Cambridge has become inured to the receipt of mail addressed to 'The Centre of Starvation Studies', or of 'Salvation Studies', and of enquiries about Indonesia or Vietnam. In imperial days the region (plus Burma until 1935) could have been referred to as 'The Indian Empire', though that, strictly, is a term that certainly recognizes the dominant position of India in both area and population (some 80 per cent of South Asians live in India), since the partition of the Indian Empire it is apt to give offence to Pakistanis and to Bangladeshis (I heard a speaker at a conference in Dhaka in 1976 refer to the 'Bangla–Pak subcontinent'). 'South Asia', then, may be unfamiliar, but it is neutral and inoffensive.

The peoples of South Asia differ greatly between themselves. The reasons for this are rooted in the history of their origins and ancient civilizations (themselves of absorbing interest) and of external impact. The consequences of social differences, whether of religion or of caste or of some other source of division, may readily be traced into contemporary politics. The difficulties of achieving and preserving national unity and of maintaining stable international boundaries are, of course, all too familiar in the post-colonial world. But in South Asia these difficulties have had a particular cogency, and have from time to time excited the attention of the world at large – as when, for example, communal violence has erupted in India, or when India and Pakistan went to war over the emergence of an independent Bangladesh.

1

It is also pertinent to ask, again in the context of post-colonial politics more generally, why some countries in South Asia have managed to change their governments by 'democratic' means, or at any rate by the use of the ballot box, while others, notably Pakistan, have frequently found themselves under autocratic rule, usually by the military.

South Asia, I have said, has vast populations. In many parts of the subcontinent these are packed tightly into the countryside (though, for reasons to be explored, much more so in some areas than in others), and unbelievably crowded in some of the cities. The average density of population in this predominantly-rural subcontinent is, for what it is worth in this varied terrain, some 580 per sq. mile (224 per sq. kilometre).

South Asia, in fact, provides instances of that kind of less-developed economy (China is another) with generally severe pressure of population and low standards of living. Since data on South Asia are both more available and more reliable than those for China (though not without their pitfalls), and since there is a relatively free interchange of research workers between South Asia and other parts of the world, they have proved highly attractive to students of development, both South Asian and foreign. Some of the latter have, rightly or wrongly, been especially interested in government policy and planning in South Asia in general, and in India in particular, as a 'democratic' alternative to the methods that have been pursued in China. One can also see foreign aid policies, with their mixed motives, at work over time in South Asia.

Turning to international relations, the most spectacular and newsworthy events since independence have so far been internal to the subcontinent, in the shape of recurring conflict between the two main successors to the British Indian Empire, India and Pakistan. But India has also had a border dispute with, and suffered invasion from, China, and long tended to be friendly to the USSR, while Pakistan has built up links with the Islamic countries of the Middle East, with China, and at times (for the relationship has been a somewhat chequered one) with the United States. But action and interest have not solely depended on conflict or alliances against possible conflict: India, and at times Sri Lanka, have been prominent in the non-aligned movement, with its declared aim of steering clear of involvement with the superpowers. More specific has been the aim of converting the Indian Ocean into a lake of peace from which superpower rivalries would be excluded. Events in Iran and Afghanistan, to say nothing of the oil that lies on some of that ocean's shores, increasingly made that pacific solution unlikely. But, with the collapse of the USSR, a new situation, not without its uncertainties, has arisen.

These, then are some of the main characteristics of South Asia and its people, and some of the principal issues that these peoples face: issues of national unity and types of government, of economic development and social change, of the reciprocal impact of South Asia and the wider world.

INTRODUCTION

This little book will try to provide its reader, in non-technical language, with ideas and information to enable him to reach sensible conclusions on these and other issues, many of which have been the subject of controversy. Its author's hope is that, while it cannot hope to be completely comprehensive, it will demonstrate how interwoven and interacting are environment, society, economies and politics in South Asia; and also succeed in conveying something of the fascination of the subcontinent, something of the character and humanity of its diverse peoples, something of their poverty and hardships, but also of their achievements; for all of these things have kept him in the spell of South Asia since he first set foot there close on fifty years ago.

2

THE ENVIRONMENTS OF SOUTH ASIA: NATURAL AND SOCIAL

THE NATURAL ENVIRONMENT AND ITS MODIFICATION BY HUMAN AGENCY

The density of rural population in South Asia is largely explicable in terms of the varying fertility of the natural environment, as modified during the millennia of its human occupance. There is a great arc of dense population (more than 200 persons per sq. kilometre) stretching with few interruptions from the Punjab to West Bengal and Bangladesh: over considerable areas the density rises to more than 500 per sq. kilometre, notably in north Bihar, West Bengal and Bangladesh.[1] Patches of similarly dense population are to be found down the east coast of India, over most of the southern states of Tamil Nadu and Kerala, in south-western and central Sri Lanka, and between Bombay and Ahmedabad on the west coast of India. At the other extreme there are sparse populations, down to 100 persons per sq. kilometre in Baluchistan, on the north-west frontiers of Pakistan, in the higher Himalaya, in the hills of the Indo–Burmese border, and in the driest parts of the Thar Desert (shared by India and Pakistan). Intermediate densities prevail elsewhere.

The population map is not completely explicable in terms of varying environmental fertility, for two broad reasons. First, the South Asian rural population is not, so to say, in equilibrium with its 'natural' environment, in spite of the long history of settlement. Some areas like northern Bihar and Bengal are manifestly overpopulated; others, like parts of the desert now being irrigated, or the Dry Zone of Sri Lanka, are still receiving new settlers.

The second reason is that South Asia is not entirely agricultural, nor are all of its towns and cities 'country towns' which, like Thomas Hardy's Casterbridge, are 'but the pole, focus or nerve-knot of the surrounding country life': for then urban population would vary with rural population. Quite apart from ancient temple, craft and palace towns, there are great metropolitan cities like Bombay, Calcutta, Madras, Karachi and Colombo, grown from ports established by the British, and each causing a penumbra

4

of denser population in its hinterland. And the same effect springs from newer industrial cities and administrative centres.

The 'natural' environment, comprising interrelated elements of physiography, soil and climate, constitutes natural fertility which has been heavily modified by man. The physiography of South Asia falls into three zones: plateau, plain and mountain. Indeed, so much seems evident from the 'glance at the map' which is all that most people take. One has, however, to be careful about the ascription of such simplicity to landscapes that may be very differently perceived by those who live and work in them. South Asians may turn out to have as detailed a set of names for small regions, perceived as differing, *inter se*, as the British have bestowed on, say, the parts of the Weald or the French on their *pays*. And the plains dweller may see the edge of a plateau as a range of hills.

The plateau is the dominant landform in peninsular India, the 'Deccan': over 600 feet (183 metres) in elevation in the Nagpur area, over 1600 feet (488 metres) in the Bombay Deccan, over 3000 feet (914 metres) in high Karnataka and Chota Nagpur. There are also, however, coastal plains: narrow on the west, broadening out on the east into the great deltas that carry a very high population density. The principal rivers, moreover, have broad valleys. The plateaux are cut, for the most part, in very ancient crystalline rocks such as granites, gneisses and quartzites, which do not furnish rich soil-forming material and tend not to bear such dense rural populations as more favourable bedrock. The exceptions in the Deccan are of considerable human significance. They are:

1 The coastal, fluvial and deltaic plains, with their alluvia: often rich soil-formers, though much depends on the precise material – for instance, coarse sands, not infrequent along coasts, spell soil poverty (it is an unscientific perception that all alluvium is fertile).
2 The area of over 500,000 sq. kilometres in the hinterland of Bombay covered by outpourings of basalt, the 'Deccan Trap'. This, in broad valley bottoms, weathers to give a deep, black soil, regur or 'black cotton soil', which is water-retentive and classed as 'good' or 'very good'; but difficult because it flows under irrigation or heavy rainfall.
3 Down-faulted basins in the north-east Deccan preserve remnants of Gondwana sediments which contain South Asia's only really important coal seams.
4 The Aravalli Hills running out from the northern Deccan are true ridges, not plateaux; they tend to have repelled settlement and forced movement between the plains of the Indus and the Ganga round their northern extremity – hence the historical importance of the site of Delhi.

Outside the areas just enumerated, the natural resources of the crystalline plateaux of the Deccan and their outliers in Sri Lanka and Meghalaya are also best put in negative terms: not only not very fertile, but also limited coal; no hope of onshore oil (though very different geologial conditions offshore yield oil, as in the Bombay High); only sporadic opportunities for the deep tubewells that have proved so important in the Indo–Gangetic Plain.

This plain, one of the world's really great plains, rests on a broad arc of alluvia all the way from Karachi to the Punjab and, past Delhi, down the Ganga and its tributaries to the Bengal delta; a narrower belt runs up the Brahmaputra valley into Assam. Most of the alluvia, to a depth of several thousand feet, have been brought down through geological time and into the present by the erosion of the plateaux to the south and, even more, of the mountains to the north: a reminder that, much as men have contributed to the erosion of hill areas, they are, on a geological timescale, relatively puny accelerators of a long-continuing process.

But the alluvia, physiography and soils of the great plain are by no means uniform. Quite apart from the transition from extreme aridity in the desert to extreme humidity in Bengal, and remembering the importance of the local scale to the cultivator, there are these contrasts:

1 The contrast of older and newer alluvium: the latter still being actively laid down in the floodplains of the rivers; the former at a somewhat higher level, and often terminating in a bluff overlooking the floodplains. The older alluvium tends to be more weathered and less fertile, and is often dissected, sometimes into a fantastic network of gullies, like those that form the haunt of dacoits along the River Chambal.

2 The different contrast of the old and new deltas in Bengal: the former in the west moribund, not being actively built but pitted with ponds and swamps; the latter in the east (and covering much of Bangladesh) still being flooded, still accreting silt, still growing at its seaward margin. Many human phenomena from land use to the distribution of endemic malaria, reflect the contrast of moribund and active deltas.

3 The contrast between well-drained pebble fans at the foot of the mountain wall, and the Tarai and Duars of the low-lying lands, formerly flood-prone and malarial, to plainward. The latter have been the scene of very recent pioneer settlement in both India and Nepal (whose southern frontier runs significantly through the Tarai').

4 The contrast between all of these and the deserts of both India and Pakistan, where the stark arid landforms of sand-dune and alkali clay flat take over from the gentle contours of the greater part of the plains.

The mountains on the north-western, northern and north-eastern margins of the South Asian subcontinent basically owe their formation, still continuing and accompanied by earthquakes from time to time, to the meeting of the Indian and Eurasian tectonic plates, the former being subducted under the latter. The mountains to the north form a region of great physiographic complexity. They are often shown as parallel or subparallel ranges with names like 'Inner' or 'Great Himalaya'. But what appears as a range on a small-scale map is, to the local inhabitants, a row of high peaks with radiating spurs, separated by deep valleys, with high passes at intervals. There are also interior valleys, of great human importance, as in Kashmir and around Kathmandu. The closest approach to a continuous range, and even then cut at intervals by the rivers debouching on to the plains, is provided by the southernmost hills (locally called the Siwaliks). Northward, beyond the highest Himalaya (the 'abode of snow'), lie the great high plateaux of Tibet and Ladakh.

The north-western mountains and hills are very different: a series of ranges arranged like the loops of a theatre curtain gathered together by cords at intervals. Some ranges are physiographically relatively simple and built mainly of sandstones and limestones, others are more complex and volcanic. Between the ranges lie high plateaux, and across them are historic passes like the Khyber.

The north-eastern hills, on the borders between India and Bangladesh on the one hand and Burma on the other, are geologically not dissimilar from those of the west, with parallel ranges gathered in a great knot at the hairpin bend in the Brahmaputra. But whereas the western hills are largely arid or sub-arid, here in the east the monsoon rainfall is very heavy indeed, so that there has been much more dissection.

Difficult though these hills, and indeed most of the mountain belts outside the larger interior vales may be, they form the homeland of a whole number of peoples, from the Pathans of the North-West Frontier through the Paharis of Himachal Pradesh and the Gurkhas of Nepal to the Nagas and Mizos of the eastern hills. Often these hill peoples straddle political frontiers.

A number of points need to be emphasized about *average* climate in South Asia: first, the importance of seasonal rhythm, not that of summer and winter (though hot and cold seasons can be recognized in the north) but that of a wet south-west and a dry north-east monsoon, or, in terms of the crop seasons, *kharif* and *rabi* respectively. Over much of South Asia 70 to 90 per cent of the annual rainfall arrives in the former season, roughly from June to September; leaving the rest of the year as a dry season, or one of minor rains. The impact of this seasonal rhythm on the agricultural calendar need not be laboured. There are three variants of this simple pattern:

1 In the north-west of the subcontinent there is precipitation from depressions in 'winter'. In Peshawar more rain falls between January and March than between June and September. Significant *rabi* rains are felt down the plains to western Uttar Pradesh, and are useful for wheat and other crops.
2 In Tamil Nadu and in the 'Dry Zone' (the north and east) of Sri Lanka there is a dry season in the south-west monsoon, and a rainfall maximum somewhere in the months October to January which provides the main rice-growing period, *samba* in Tamil Nadu and *maha* in Sri Lanka.

7

3 In the Wet Zone (south-west) of Sri Lanka and in southern Kerala there is rain at all or most seasons, with a dry season creeping in as one moves north. Here is the film-maker's ideal tropical paradise, in verdure clad all the year round and with romantic palm-fringed beaches. The climate suits tea, rubber and coconut, but it is far from ideal for rice cultivation[2]; photosynthesis, other things being equal, is less under cloudy, rainy conditions.

Secondly, whatever the rainy season, mean rainfall totals vary greatly from place to place, from the aridity found in Baluchistan and the Thar Desert to over 200 inches (5080 mm) in parts of the Western Ghats and in Meghalaya south of the Brahmaputra valley. The contrast between seasonally wet and always relatively dry areas has been a recurrent theme in Indian history and lies behind many regional variations in the contemporary economic map. Thus there is an axis of near-aridity running south from the Thar Desert through the western Deccan to the 'burning sands of Ramnad' on the coasts of Coromandel and into northern Sri Lanka. This axis, with dryness reflected in relatively light and open forest, provided a path for the north-south movement of peoples and armies, whereas the region of heavier rainfall and denser jungles to the east long remained little penetrated, the homeland of tribal peoples. The axis was, however, a belt prone to famine when the exiguous rains failed.

For variability of rainfall is to be reckoned with in many parts of South Asia, particularly in light rainfall areas where less-than-average rainfall is apt to spell crop failure: it is not surprising that an Indian Finance Minister described his budget as 'a gamble in rain'.

Now, an inch of rain is usually far less effective in South Asia than in temperate latitudes with their 'small rain'. This arises largely from high intensity: the mean amount of rain per rainy day in the subcontinent is over 0.8 inches (20 mm), more than six times the corresponding figure for Cambridge, England. And very high daily rainfalls and extremely high intensities for shorter periods are frequently recorded. Much rain is lost by rapid run-off, which may be accelerated by deforestation and lead to floods and soil erosion. Effectiveness of rainfall is also diminished by high evaporation and transpiration.

Very little natural vegetation remains in South Asia. What passes for 'forest' or 'jungle' has been degraded by the action of people or by their cattle and goats over the millennia, a process accelerated more recently. This applies to much 'forest' legally classified as 'reserved' or 'protected'.

Soils have been mentioned in passing but a further point must be made. Over much of the great plains it is often held that the alluvia have been degraded in fertility or structure, or both, by long cultivation without adequate manure to produce Kipling's 'used-up, overhandled earth'.[3] It is possible, however, that the ascription of loss of fertility to these soils derives from Englishmen's mistaken perceptions, with Fen peat and Romney marsh

8

in mind, of a pristine fertility that these tropical and subtropical deposits never had.

To conclude this outline of South Asian 'natural' environments, our subcontinent is one in which disasters can and do overwhelm societies through no fault of theirs, for instance, through earthquakes of the kind that wrought death and destruction in Himalayan areas north-east of Delhi in October 1991, or through inroads of the sea, caused by severe tropical cyclones, such as brought utter devastation and the reported loss of some 150,000 lives in deltaic islands of Bangladesh in April and May 1991.[4]

But in other cases 'natural' disasters may be brought about or accentuated by human action. In particular, landslides and severe river flooding may be associated with enhanced run-off attributable at least in part to deforestation in mountainous areas, following very heavy rainfall, as in Kashmir, Punjab and Sind in September 1992, with devastating effect and severe loss of life.

Now one of the strands in an increasing concern for the South Asian environment has been a perceived need to strike at the causes of such disasters. This strand tends to be interwoven with a regard for 'natural' vegetation, whether or not its degradation or destruction may be associated with these disasters, for instance, 'natural' vegetation for its own sake, or seen as an amenity or as a source of genes worth building into crop plants, or as a habitat for wild life (notably now-rare creatures like the Indian tiger and rhinoceros). Concern of these divers kinds tends to be found amongst the intelligentsia, though not exclusively so. With some of its members, as with the distinguished official from the Indian Department of Agriculture, B.B. Vohra, there is a related advocacy for a more conservational attitude to water resources, including the use of small irrigation reservoirs and of groundwater rather than gigantic dams. Vohra has in fact been very actively associated with a number of organizations involved in these matters.[5]

But other conservational strands have origins that lie farther afield, notably in anxieties about man's actual or potential damage to his environment in a broader, indeed global sense, and especially in the need for sustainable development, whether agricultural or otherwise (not that cultivation in perpetuity, even under tropical conditions, is a new concept);[6] and in the perils threatened by man-made global warming and an associated rise in sea-level (which could make the Maldives disappear altogether and grievously affect low-lying areas elsewhere in South Asia. When the writing of this book was in its final stages, the related problems of environment, population growth and sustainable development were brought to the fore by the UN Conference on the Environment and Development held in Rio de Janeiro in June 1992, though there were sharp differences of opinion between 'advanced' and less-developed countries. There has been a welcome addition to the literature on these and related matters.[7] It is too early to assess the likely consequences of all this for policy and practice.

It must be strongly emphasized, however, that the modern environmental movement, with its attempt to reconcile conservation and development, is not entirely a matter of the local intelligentsia, of high-level global states-manship, or of expatriate 'experts'. In Chapter 6 I shall recount a notable Indian case of continuing opposition to a gigantic dam project from a combination of local people and members of the intelligentsia. Then there is the Chipko movement among local women who hug Himalayan forest trees in an attempt to prevent felling. And a recurrent theme in this book, explicit or implicit, will be ITK, the Indigenous Technical Knowledge which, except when swamped by circumstances or overruled by 'experts' and officials blinded by urban bias, does act to conserve the ecosystem and other aspects of the environment. Again, Chapter 6 holds an example, largely in terms of terrace construction, which may well have prevented the degradation of slopes in Nepal from turning so far from crisis to catastrophe.[8]

THE SOUTH ASIAN SOCIAL ENVIRONMENT APPROACHED THROUGH THE CASTE SYSTEM

To approach the South Asian social environment through the caste system is useful, but does not imply that to explain caste is to explain South Asian society. Anyway, caste is a phenomenon that many find fascinating, yet intensely puzzling. I shall begin by dissecting a dictionary definition. The third edition of the *Concise Oxford Dictionary* defines caste thus:

> Indian hereditary class, with members socially equal, united in religion, and usually following the same trade, having no social intercourse with persons of other castes.

Is caste, then, restricted to India? Some go further and see it as a cultural trait necessarily linked to Hinduism. The relationship of caste with both India and Hinduism will become clearer as we proceed. The word 'hereditary' does convey something of the essence of caste, which is indeed inherited. A member of the relevant South Asian societies is inescapably a member of a caste, and this is, with few exceptions, that of his parents, who are both of the same caste (or subcaste, or even segment of a subcaste). And caste endogamy tends to survive even when other caste restrictions drop away.

The word 'class' is, however, not without difficulty here. Some sociologists argue that the caste system is not only more rigid, but also more elaborately hierarchical than any class system. Others argue that such perceptions of caste embody an ascription of oddity, of the kind often made by products of one civilization when confronted by another, and point to flexibility as a result of caste mobility and sanskritization, of which more later. It is also often pointed out that caste and class in South Asia are, while often related, not identical.[9] The dominant landowners are generally of high caste. The landless are for the most part of low caste. In between come castes that have increasingly struggled, odd as this may seem, to be defined as 'backward' or 'lower backward' castes, the former middle farmers, the latter mainly small farmers and artisans – the purpose being to improve their status and in particular to secure the benefits, especially job reservation, mentioned in the Indian Constitution, but a major political issue.

Now, in spite of what will be said about caste amongst Muslims, class stratification is a more adequate key than caste to social structure in Pakistan. This is closely related to one of the most unequal landownership patterns in South Asia. Pakistan is indeed a landlord's country.

That caste is related to Hindu religious ideas is generally recognized (though their force and relevance is a matter for argument). One such idea is *karma*, often translated 'fate'. The belief is that a person's actions in one of his successive reincarnations and the extent to which he fulfils his *dharma* (right behaviour given his place in society, itself largely caste-related) will determine his circumstances, including his caste, in his next reincarnation. Another religious idea is that of pollution, or loss of ritual purity: a matter of much more moment the higher a caste's position. Pollution may come about for a whole host of reasons: for a Brahmin, for example, by eating meat, or by undertaking a whole range of jobs, from fishing (which takes life), through toddy-tapping (which produces alcohol), to washing clothes (which may be stained with polluting exudations of the human body) and to handling animal carcases or dead bodies or human excrement. The higher, 'clean' castes will not do polluting work. Most Brahmins will not put a hand to the plough, though this, like distaste for manual work generally, is not entirely a matter of caste status (nor confined to South Asia). A lower caste does some polluting work according to its ritual status; thus its members may catch fish, but not handle dead bodies. The lowest castes of all do the most polluting work, such as the handling of human excrement. Pollution also comes about through certain intercaste relations like accepting food from, or eating with, members of a lower, polluting caste; or sexual relations with a person of such a caste; or through contact with someone of an 'untouchable' caste. If a Hindu of a 'clean' caste becomes polluted there are rites of ritual purification or, in what are seen as more extreme cases (such as marriage out of caste), a sentence from a caste council of loss of caste status.

Dharma and *karma* and concepts of ritual purity and pollution clearly give caste a flavour quite different from that of class in a western society. Louis Dumont went further, seeing the opposition pure/impure as 'the very principle' of caste hierarchy.[10] The application of these concepts varies from place to place; they are most strictly applied in South India. Some aspects of pollution have diminished with 'modernization'.

Returning to the dictionary definition, are members of a caste 'socially equal'? One can find apparent simplicity in a complex scene by thinking in terms of the four *varnas*, broad, apparently universal and supposedly original caste groups: Brahmins (priests) at the top, then Kshatriyas (warriors),

11

then Vaishyas (cultivators, cowherds and others), and fourthly Sudras, manual workers serving the first three 'clean' *varnas*. This leaves the Untouchables outside the four *varnas* altogether (Gandhi, who renamed them 'Harijan', 'sons of god', held that originally they were Sudras). The four *varnas* have some place in rationalizations of the caste system, and there are cases in which a caste claims the status of a particular *varna*, generally one of the uppermost. But what matters in everyday life is not *varna*, or usually even caste as a first-order subdivision of *varna*, but a second- or lower-order subdivision, usually called *jat* or *jati*. This, in British days, often corresponded, especially for census purposes, to a 'subcaste'. It is at this level that, in some sense, 'social equality' in terms of status is to be found. (A complication is that the group a man calls his *jati* may vary according to the purpose for which he is relating himself to it.)

But social status by caste and economic status need not be identical. Under some modern conditions, especially in towns and in the bureaucracy, the two may be wide apart. Thus I remember a government officer's *chaprassi* (messenger) in Madhya Pradesh who was a Brahmin. He carried his officer's files in the office and in the field. But at mealtimes in the field he ate first and apart.

Or there is the case of three coastal castes in Sri Lanka: Karava, originally fishermen; Durava, originally toddy-tappers; and Salagama, originally weavers, later cinnamon-peelers.[11] Many, though by no means all members of these castes rose to affluence under western impact and with the coming of a plantation economy, especially in the nineteenth century, as carters, traders, and eventually plantation-owners and businessmen. All three were relatively low in the hierarchy as it was perceived by the dominant inland cultivating caste, the Goyigama, with whom they came into conflict, particularly in the 1890s. It is significant that newly-affluent and aspiring members of the coastal castes did not invoke western liberal ideas about the equality of man but, instead, sought to establish themselves higher in the status hierarchy provided by caste. This applied especially to the Karava, some of whom produced genealogies to support their claim to be of Kshatriya status, and thus superior to the Goyigama. But, whatever the caste status of the aspiring groups, their rise in terms of economic status is clear, and that is the point here.

In fine, membership of a common *varna* or of a common caste will not guarantee social equality with other *varna* or caste members. Membership of a *jati* may well do so in terms of ritual status, though not necessarily in economic terms (see also remarks on *gotra* (lineage) on p. 15).

What of 'united in religion'? Since *karma*, *dharma* and ritual purity are Hindu concepts, is caste peculiar to Hindus? Some would aver that, given the syncretic and variable nature of Hinduism, it is impossible to define a Hindu *except* as a person enmeshed in the caste system. But castes, or some of their features, are not confined to Hindu society. In spite of the original professions of the Sikh *gurus* about the desirability of a caste-free society, there are endogamous groups among the Sikhs that are often described as castes. Islam is, in theory, even more caste-free than pristine Sikhism, yet a Muslim edited a book on *Caste and Social Stratification among the Muslims of India*.[12] There are Muslim Jats as well as Sikh and Hindu Jats cultivating in the two Punjabs and in Uttar Pradesh (UP). Other Punjab castes are also represented among all three religions.

The Buddhist majority in Sri Lanka have a recognizable caste system, though one with a number of peculiarities. There are no Brahmins or Kshatriyas. The Goyigama, inland at any rate, are both the majority and the dominant cultivating caste, but are divided into subcastes: there is a great social distance between the Radalas, the village aristocrats of the Kandyan areas and the village cultivator with only a little land, or none at all. There are also no Untouchables, for no Buddhist is unclean in the ritual sense; but there is a caste, the Rodiya, who are largely outside the system and who traditionally lived by begging. There is caste endogamy and a caste hierarchy, disputed and locally variant though it may be. South Asian Christians, too, may preserve caste: in some places there is a high caste church and a low caste or Harijan church.

Caste, then, is not an exclusively Hindu phenomenon, though one may suspect that among non-Hindus it is peculiar to areas influenced by Hinduism in the past. Many contemporary Muslims, Sikhs and Christians are the descendants of converts from Hinduism who carried their caste with them into the new religious community.

A definition of caste in terms of a common religion raises particular problems when one turns to the 'tribal' population of India (and to some extent of the hill areas of Bangladesh). (The 'tribes' of the North-West Frontier of Pakistan are, of course, almost all Muslims.) Indeed, to use the term 'tribal' is also to run into problems of definition: it usually carries the meaning primitive, or aboriginal, or jungle- or hill-dwelling, and often too the implication of distinct language and animist religion, of being outside Hindu civilization. The term *adivasi*, meaning original inhabitant, is now also often used with the same connotations. But when one seeks to decide whether a given group of people are 'tribal', or a caste or groups of castes within Hindu society, difficulties arise. Thus the Nagas, Khasis and Mizos of north-east India are indubitably hill-dwellers, some of them jungle-dwellers, with languages unrelated to Indo-European tongues like Assamese or Bengali. But many of them are Christians, and some behave more like modern economic man than many an Assamese plains-dweller. Again, the large group in central India known as Gonds are often classed as 'tribal', for forest-dwellers many of them are. But they speak a Dravidian language, and are recognizably Hindu (they formerly had their own powerful kingdom and were driven into the hills in historical times). It is clear, too, that many present castes represent former 'tribes' which entered the Hindu fold by the process known, following M.N. Srinivas, as 'sanskritization'[13] – the process by means of which a group take on the rituals, customs and lifestyle of a caste in the Hindu hierarchy, including the absorption of the sacred literature in Sanskrit (hence the term), in order to claim higher ritual status (they may none the less retain earlier practices). Some former 'tribes' have succeeded in establishing themselves with relatively high status, but many Harijan castes are probably former 'tribals' who were less successful. Some 'tribals' are former castes who became cut off in the forest. Yet others, like some of the Khasis, became westernized and Christianized before they could be sanskritized. So when, with all these possibilities, is a 'tribal' group a non-Hindu 'tribe' and when is it a Hindu caste? F.G. Bailey resolved the problem by postulating a spectrum with indubitable caste at one end and indubitable tribe at the other, further groups coming somewhere in between.[14] The Government of India adopted another solution. Under the Constitution a list of peoples are designated Scheduled Tribes, and accorded certain privileges and benefits: the Scheduled Tribes numbered some 52 million, according to the 1981 Census. But a number of groups, some of which appear to be towards the tribal end of Bailey's spectrum, are excluded, and clamour to be included in order to share in the benefits. There are also under the Constitution Scheduled Castes (Harijans, with 105 million members in 1981); and Backward Classes (see above), whose inclusion is likewise subject to argument.

The penultimate part of the dictionary definition is the phrase 'following the same trade'. One sees lists ascribing specific occupations, sometimes very narrowly defined, to particular castes or subcastes: for example, to take three beginning with 'B', Bhangi, sweepers; Bharbunja, grain-parchers; Bhats (of UP), hereditary genealogists and heralds. There certainly are, in South Asia today, connections between caste and occupation. In the past, over parts of the subcontinent at any rate, and to some extent today, division of labour has been expressed in the *jajmani* system, under which each caste in a village society fulfilled a specific ritual function and alone undertook specific jobs, under a higher caste patron, with the priestly Brahmin overall. In many ways, however, the patron-client connection involved in, or surviving from the *jajmani* system is a more important key to contemporary social and ritual relations than minute division of labour. For it must be remembered that the primary occupation in rural South Asia is (as indeed it always was) the cultivation of the land: albeit subject to caste restrictions and with very unequal access to the means of production: indeed, much landless and dependent, and formerly bonded or enslaved, labour. And the occupational functions of the several castes and subcastes have been eroded and complicated by western impact: there was, after all, no hereditary caste of railway-engine drivers, or of university dons. But pollution remains pollution: so, in the village as elsewhere, the Bhangis and other Harijans continue to sweep, the Chamars to work in leather, the Dhobis to wash clothes.

And so to 'no social intercourse with persons of other castes'. Here much depends on the meaning attached to 'social intercourse'. The *jajmani* system, like patron–client relationships generally, involves a certain stylized system of social intercourse, with heavy emphasis on hierarchy, on ritual status and function; superficially a system of co-operation, though sometimes involving conflict between castes or between factions. We have also seen that concepts of pollution imply a bar on some kinds of social intercourse, for example, on dining together. But they tend to be weakening, especially because of the mobility brought by train and bus (not even a Brahmin wants to starve on a long train journey): so do complex rules about who may sit, or wear particular clothes in whose presence. But, it must be emphasized, this does not mean that the caste hierarchy is necessarily less marked in more fundamental ways (there are still upper-caste patrons and low-caste clients), or that deep-seated features like caste endogamy are significantly weakening.

'No social intercourse with persons of other castes' may be taken to imply that there is freedom of social intercourse *within* a *jati* in a village, or even that such a *jati* is an indivisible social unit. But this would be to ignore the variable importance of *gotra* (lineage), those persons who trace their descent from a real or mythical common ancestor. For there may be great rivalry between lineages within a *jati*, especially among dominant castes who strive for village leadership; political factions may be based on rival lineages. All this is well brought out in M.N. Srinivas's masterpiece, *The Remembered Village*[15] (a desire to promote the interests of one's family or lineage is often, and sometimes hypocritically, construed in the West as nepotism).

I hope that it is now clear why the Indian villager (and not only the villager), enmeshed in *jati* and *gotra*, has been said to live in a 'cellular society'.

But there are, finally, a few important points about caste that fall outside the dictionary definition, or need to be drawn out of the foregoing discussion for separate treatment. The first is caste mobility. It is important not to overemphasize the rigidity of the caste hierarchy, either historically or in modern South Asia. We have seen how tribes may become castes, with luck well off the bottom rung of the ladder, all too often not even on a rung; and mentioned the rise in economic status, and in the claimed caste status of certain coastal castes in Sri Lanka. The study of South Asian social history makes it clear that castes, or some caste members, have climbed in the hierarchy by sanskritization; or by pioneer settlement leaving lowly status behind; or by migration into the subcontinent and subsequent validation by the Brahmins as, say, a caste within the Kshatriyas; or, today, by moving to the cities and claiming a new caste status. By seeking to climb within the system, such groups affirm it. There can also be downward mobility. For example, desanskritization when a caste was dragged down in ritual status by a less sanskritized dominant caste; and Brahmins may fail to show their *gunas* or appropriate qualities by lack of learning and ritual purity, and so lose status relative to other local Brahmins. For South Asian society was not, and is not, without regard for moral qualities or for those qualities in action. It is not all a matter of status and of dominance by powerful groups, as anyone who has felt the force of South Indian (or Islamic) puritanism is aware, while *ahimsa* (non-violence) is very much a Buddhist and Hindu concept. Clearly such features as the occupational mobility and the urbanization of modern life can give a great fillip to caste mobility, just as it can weaken the joint family system.[16]

Now a particular caste hierarchy, with a number of *jati* in a particular order, often is, or was, a very local phenomenon. The same *jati*, or a *jati* with the same name, may be at different places in the hierarchy in two villages not very far apart, and may, in pre-British days, have had no contact except, perhaps, at great centres of pilgrimage.

With the British there came, not only modern transport, a new urbanization, and new space relations, but also the census, which sought to record each person's caste and subcaste. The inclusion in the same census subcaste of *jati* formerly out of contact and at different places in local social and economic hierarchies sometimes meant that the unity of the group concerned was a census construct. In visual terms, for the local caste pyramid (or, better, irregular tower-block) was substituted a horizontal stratum covering a wide area, and tending to be mapped by the unwary as a unity. As political interactions developed between the Raj and its Indian subjects, the identity and apparent validity given to region-wide caste by the census, and by officials who leant on it, reinforced the effects of new modes of transport and trade, and was seized on by a novel social grouping, the caste association. There arose in UP, for example, associations of Kayasths (a 'writer' caste) who agitated in the interest of their newly-identified caste fellows. At the same time, and for similar reasons, came a greater consciousness of *varna*.

André Béteille has emphasized that too much must not be made of the domination of South Asian society by an ideology of hierarchy, or to imagine that equality as a principle is to be found only in other societies.[17] After all, Sikhism was originally a revolt against the rigours of caste; and, in theory at any rate, caste is repugnant to Islam. However caste-based Sinhalese Buddhist society may be, the Buddha himself disapproved of caste and sought escape from domination by the Brahmins, replacing priests by monks. And a number of movements within Hinduism have, over the centuries, attacked at least some aspects of caste hierarchy and privilege.

British rule brought a new power situation that weakened some of the forces that had kept castes in their unequal places (though it also, as in recognizing princely rule in the 'Native States', and in attempts to unify Hindu law, in some cases ossified the hierarchy). With the impact of the West came, as a reaction, not only Hindu and Buddhist revivalism but also movements, like the Brahmo Samaj founded by Ram Mohan Roy, whose aims included the removal of the extremes of caste. The later Arya Samaj went further and envisaged a caste-free society. Later still, Mahatma Gandhi and his followers sought to improve the lot of the Harijans, believing that untouchability was a late and pathological growth on the caste system. One not infrequently meets good, sincere Gandhians engaged in voluntary welfare work for the benefit of Harijans or tribals. We have seen that the Indian Constitution contains provisions designed to improve the condition of Backward Classes; while an Act of 1955 declares illegal the enforcement of disabilities on grounds of untouchability. Indeed, there is a strand of sincere egalitarianism running through South Asian social history, owing nothing for long centuries to western liberalism, sometimes faint and hidden from view by the strong fabric of a status-ridden caste society, sometimes much clearer and more evident. But a different view, shared by many Indians, is that this same strong fabric has kept society together in spite of incursions from outside and drastic changes in internal rule.

There is today a good deal of humbug and of political expediency about calls for greater equality. Some of the most strident advocates of equality are ambivalent or hypocritical where caste is concerned: and Harijans and tribals generally remain the most disadvantaged strata in India's complex society, still refused temple entry and access to village wells, still (in the south at any rate) living in hamlets away from the villages of the 'clean' castes.

In those villages, and in most Indian villages, local power is still held, because the largest landholdings are still held by members of the locally dominant caste or castes. Power and dominance over others, though here enmeshed with caste status, are of as great significance as in other 'traditional' agrarian societies. These relationships, agrarian change or lack of it, and related politics and government action, will have to be explored later in this book.

It used to be fashionable to see in South Asian villages, or in many of them at any rate, self-sufficient and self-governing 'village republics', each ruled by its *panchayat* or council, surviving as empires rose and fell and dynastic conflicts washed to and fro across the face of the subcontinent. This was the view of early nineteenth-century British writers like Sir Henry Maine, who made comparisons with a Europe that had lost the primitive communism and self-sufficiency that they thought had survived in these 'republics'. Marx knew the work of some of these authors, and gave the picture a new colour with his writings on the unchanging village and its 'Asiatic mode of production', about which he wrote with something less than consistency.[18] The notion of village republics was taken up with enthusiasm and idyllized by Indian nationalists, including Gandhi; and there were prescriptions for communal tenure and for a restoration of *Panchayati Raj*, rule by village councils (as will be seen later). How does all this square with village caste hierarchies, their interaction with economic status, and the model of the dominant caste, even if the *jajmani* system is seen as implying a functioning village community, albeit a very unequal one? It is clear that the Englishmen who identified 'village republics' were smitten with a certain romanticism, and resurgent nationalism is often romantic; while Marx, so far as he relied on apparently empirical evidence, was misled by the British authors he read. Further, the operation of the British legal and revenue systems in the Indian Empire tended to give some preference to what had survived, or was seen as surviving, of corporate land tenures (though this is a thorny thicket not to be entered here). But there have not been lacking those who have stressed, not co-operation and idyllic harmony in the village community, but bipolarity between dominant and suppressed, exploiter and exploited. Notable among these was B.R. Ambedkar, himself an Untouchable and a doughty opponent of Gandhi (although an author of the Indian Constitution), who saw village unity as a myth and the village as a cesspool of iniquity.

What of society in South Asian towns? First, is there is a sharp break, a dichotomy, between urban and rural? or do rural and urban settlements alike lie on a continuum? Weber contrasted 'traditional' rural society and 'rational' urban society (a distinction that lingers on). Perhaps Marx was a dichotomist, with his misplaced strictures on 'the idiocy of rural life'. There have certainly been dichotomists among students of South Asian society. It is, however, possible to see in some of these the bias in urbanites' perceptions of the superiority and modernity of urban life, just as there may be an opposite bias in some who see rural life and society as idyllic. As for theories of a continuum, a gradual transition from village to city, it is certainly true that in many smaller towns and cities, and on the fringes of larger ones, are to be found 'urban villages', sometimes with their fields intact, and still preserving the caste structure of village society. In some cities too, especially ancient ones, particular castes tend to cluster in specific *mohallas* (wards) or *thoks* (subdivisions of *mohallas*), as (on a smaller scale) in villages; sometimes there are caste *panchayats* with administrative and judicial functions. But most larger towns and cities consist of a mixture, in varying proportions, of 'traditional' social groupings on this basis, or a modification of it, and of what may be called 'the new elites', the whole governed under western-style municipal institutions tending to supersede, in whole or in part, caste *panchayats* and other 'traditional' bodies.

By the 'new elites' one means those groups who, in contrast to the 'traditional elites' which held power over wide areas in pre-British days, or which still dominate village or local society, have had a western-style education, can (and sometimes habitually do) speak English, and have adopted at least some of the insignia of the western middle classes.[19] These groups grew in numbers and influence in British days and after, while remaining a small proportion of the total population. In contemporary South Asia they dominate, to a greater or lesser extent, the professions, the universities and the higher ranks of the public service (civil and military), and play a varied role in national politics. For the most part, and to a greater extent in some spheres than others, they have a class base. Some of them are the products of expensive local equivalents of the English public schools and of the more socially-esteemed universities. Caste throws a shadow, however, for few Harijans (or for that matter tribals) can aspire to the requisite education. Caste is also evident in the business sectors of the 'new elites': members of *bania* (trader) castes, for example, are still prominent in industry and commerce in Bombay, though the more modern sectors of industry appear to have a wider base for recruitment.

Cosmopolitanism is also a characteristic of at least some of the 'new elites' in India and Pakistan: members of them in a big city will be drawn from all over the country, though not necessarily proportionally to population in the source areas. Some of their members, among administrators and politicians at any rate, operate at national level. Such city-dwellers seem a far cry, in location, in occupation, and in attitudes, from society in the villages or ancient towns from which their ancestors came, though not to such a great extent as in the case of the imitation Englishmen, the 'brown Sahibs' who passed into the Indian and Ceylon Civil Services towards the twilight of British Rule. Today one meets people who, wherever they may be serving, retain roots in their home regions and pride in its culture.

I now turn to religions in South Asia.[20] (all statistics are for 1981 unless otherwise stated). Hinduism is, of course, numerically the most important religion in the subcontinent. Over 80 per cent of Indians are Hindus, *sensu lato*; there are important minorities in Sri Lanka and in Bangladesh (fewer now, and far fewer in Pakistan); and Hinduism, alone or in a syncretic amalgam with Buddhism, is significant in Nepal. It will be clear by now that it is not easy to define a Hindu, particularly amongst tribal people (and what of the Harijans, as seen by 'clean' caste Hindus?), and that it is also not easy to define Hinduism which may, to different individuals, mean anything from animism to atheism, from polytheism to monotheism (not mutually exclusive, for a number of gods may be seen as manifestations of one god), from simple village cults to the higher flights of philosophy. Hinduism has, over the centuries, absorbed deities and ideas from the myriad peoples of the subcontinent, and from time to time seen attempts at purification by reformist sects, some of which survive within it. Absorptive syncretism and the schism of sects, together with the absence of a unifying creed, spell complexity and the proliferation of cults. Some have suggested that a Hindu is a man who accepts the religious authority of the Brahmins, perhaps with, though not always with, acceptance of the caste system and of such observances as the prohibition on cow slaughter. Beyond this it is hard to go for present purposes. What is clear, however, is that Hinduism has over the millennia created common cultural traits all over India:

19

through sanskritization, and indeed through the existence of Sanskrit as a common sacred language which is the vehicle for the transmission of ancient literature, the common heritage; through the great centres of pilgrimage; through the conferment of legitimacy on a single all-India political power, the heir of the *Chakravarti Raj* of ancient tradition and the provision of a generally-understood Hindu idiom in which Indian nationalism could express itself (though the last two features have tended to alienate Muslims, increasingly of late when Hindu chauvinism has been propagated by the Bharatiya Janata Party (see Chapter 4).

Islam obviously contrasts strongly with Hinduism. It is, of course, not without its divisions. But its unyielding monotheism has set it strongly apart from Hinduism and made it generally incapable of compromise, still less absorption. Muslims look to Islamic countries of the Middle East, whereas there are relatively few Hindus outside India. Muslims form 97 per cent of the population of Pakistan, and some 87 per cent of the population of Bangladesh. In India, in spite of partition in 1947 and the separation of Pakistan, they still numbered 75.5 million in 1981: more than in all but three Muslim countries, and some 11 per cent of the total Indian population. But they are very unevenly distributed. The strongest concentrations are in Kashmir (disputed with Pakistan), on the borders of Bangladesh, and locally in Kerala, with lesser concentrations spreading from Delhi down into UP and Bihar. The Maldives, like the Indian islands of Lakshadweep, are overwhelmingly Muslim.

Sikhs cluster most strongly around their sacred city, Amritsar, in Indian Punjab, and spread out into adjacent states and areas. With a reputation for enterprise, they are to be found in relatively small numbers in towns all over India except the south. They total 13 million, some 2 per cent of the Indian population. In their homeland in Punjab they are, to put it mildly, strongly assertive politically.

In Sri Lanka most of the majority Sinhala community are Buddhists of the Theravada or Hinayana persuasion. Resurgent Buddhism, intertwined with strong feelings about language and political identity, has been a major political force. In Nepal, Bhutan, Sikkim and other northern hill areas, it takes the more syncretic Mahayana or lamaistic form, which is in fact the state religion in Bhutan. After independence in India a large number of Harijan followers of Dr Ambedkar expressed their discontent with their lot by declaring themselves Buddhists. This movement was particularly strong in Maharashtra, Ambedkar's home state, where 4 million people were returned as Buddhists.

Jains, who arose as a Hindu reformist sect, are effectively confined to India and number some 3.2 million, with highest concentrations in Maharashtra, Rajasthan and Gujarat. They are mostly urban businessmen with a reputation for shrewdness.

Finally, Christians in India number 16 million, with strong concentrations in the north-eastern hill states, and also in Kerala and adjacent parts of Tamil Nadu. Christian missionary activity has made some headway amongst tribals and Harijans, who have nothing to lose but their lowly status in the caste hierarchy.

I now discuss some aspects of the position of women in South Asia.[21] Comments are often made on the fact that women became the Prime Ministers of Sri Lanka, India, Pakistan and Bangladesh. But this singularity arises not from any dominance of women in South Asian society but rather from what are sometimes called 'dynastic considerations': or, more accurately, the desire by politicians to profit from the name and reputation of a deceased father or husband. Humbler women may be locally dominant, as in the case of the woman of Shamlegh so memorably depicted by Kipling in *Kim*. If it is urged that she lived in a polyandrous hill society very different from the male-dominated lands to the south, then let me cite a redoubtable Hindu widow whom I encountered in the course of fieldwork in Madhya Pradesh and who ran the family and its lands with firm autocracy.

But the vast majority of South Asian women live a life of subordination, if not subjection, most of all in Muslim societies, especially where purdah is strictly enforced and Islamic fundamentalism and legal disabilities are evident. Here very few women are to be found in the professions or, indeed, in paid employment of any sort. Women's place is very definitely in the home, or at any rate in the compound, where they may undertake tasks connected with agriculture. But one rarely sees them working in the fields. Relatively few girls attend schools and female literacy is low. At the other end of the spectrum lie certain tribal societies and, in odd juxtaposition, some highly-westernized members of 'new elites' (not that they are to be seen in the fields either). In intermediate parts of the spectrum women are still subordinate, but they are to be seen in the fields (for example, in Maharashtra and Sri Lanka), often doing back-breaking and poorly-paid, or unpaid, work like transplanting paddy. Small boys are firmly taught to avoid 'women's work', as was one I saw in Tamil Nadu happily playing with his sisters and pretending to cook some rice in an old tin, only to be scolded by his mother for simulating 'women's work'. Women's tasks such as collecting firewood and water from far away can be very heavy indeed. Moreover, women and their daughters outside the 'new elites' may usually only eat when their menfolk have finished and nothing but inferior food may be left. This, with other forms of neglect of female children or even infanticide, and with sick and worn-out mothers, helps to explain that curiosity of South Asian demography: that women are in a minority in the population. However, in Sri Lanka by the early 1980s the life expectancy of females at birth was somewhat higher than that of males.

There are also abuses of the dowry system, particularly (or most noticeably) in the urban 'lower middle classes'. The custom is for a bride to take her dowry to her husband's family home, where she usually lives after marriage. Threatening demands may be made on the poor woman; and murder or apparent suicide are not unknown – it was reported that there were 11,000 cases of the two combined in India in the three years to 1991.

But also not unknown are women's movements, spontaneous or inspired by voluntary or foreign aid workers or by feminists. I have already mentioned the Chipko movement among women in the hills. By way of further instances, there is the Septagram Women's Self-reliance Movement started in 1976 in Bangladesh, the Self-employed Women's Association in Ahmedabad (Gujarat) and a Working Women's Forum in Madras. It remains to be seen what permanent effect such movements may have on the status and welfare of women, especially the millions of poor women. But one thing is clear: that improvements in the status and education of women are crucial to family planning and to efforts to tackle the population problem.

South Asian languages, to which we now turn, fall into well-marked families and branches[22] (approximate numbers speaking each major language as their declared mother tongue in 1981 are indicated in brackets). Languages of the Iranic branch of the Indo-European family, notably Pushtu (11 million) and Baluchi (3 million), are spoken on the North-West Frontier of Pakistan and in Baluchistan, stretching into Iran and Afghanistan. A great swathe of tongues of the Indic branch of the same family occupies the Indo–Gangetic Plains and the northern and central Deccan: Sindhi (15 million in Pakistan, with some in India), Punjabi (51 million), Kashmiri (3 million), Hindi (defined in the broadest way, 250 million), Urdu (40 million), Nepali (perhaps 14 million in Nepal and eastward), Bengali (160 million), Assamese (12 million), Oriya (24 million), Gujarati (33 million) and Marathi (50 million): and, literally isolated, Sinhala (perhaps taken to Sri Lanka with Buddhism: 12 million) and, related to Sinhala, Divehi, spoken in the Maldives (0.2 million). Sanskrit is an ancient member of the branch and the parent of at least some of the languages just enumerated. To the north and east are spoken a whole congeries of Tibeto–Burman languages, with outliers in Meghalaya. A Tibetan dialect, Dzongkha (possibly 0.7 million) is the official language of Bhutan. The southern Deccan is the homeland of the Dravidian languages: Tamil (50 million) (also spoken in parts of Sri Lanka), Telugu (52 million), Kannada (57 million) and Malayalam (25 million), with Gondi in northern Deccan outliers; and, far away in Baluchistan, Brahui. Finally, some tribal peoples of the north-east Deccan and into Meghalaya and eastward speak tongues unrelated to any of these.

In Pakistan the existence of Punjab and Sind as separate provinces recognizes the linguistic and cultural differences between them, though only some 60 per cent of people in the latter are Sindhi speaking. Baluchistan and the North-West Frontier Province only partially cover the area in which

Baluchi and Pushtu are spoken. Bangladesh is overwhelmingly Bengali speaking, except for the hill tracts and adjacent areas. In Sri Lanka language is a main factor in the trouble-torn communal division between Sinhala Buddhists and Tamil Hindus.

A word must be said on the nature and relations of Hindi and Urdu. There developed in the Delhi region under the Moguls a lingua franca, based on local Hindi with many additional Persian words, which in due course came to be known to the British as Hindustani (which was taught to me in Roman script in the army in 1943). During the nineteenth century Hindustani had bifurcated: 'Hindi' for Hindus dropping Persian words and gaining others of Sanskrit provenance, and using the related Devanagiri script. Hindi 'in the broadest sense' remains a lingua franca superimposed on a multitude of local dialects. Urdu for Muslims gained words from Persian and Arabic and uses Arabic script.

In the Republic of India language has been a most potent factor in shaping and activating the political map. The Republic inherited from the Raj a patchwork quilt of British provinces and of princely states. By stages, and not without hitches, the latter were absorbed into a system of States federated to the Indian Union (see Chapter 4). But the resultant map at first bore little relationship to the linguistic pattern. Bombay State, for example, included Gujarati, Marathi and Kannada speakers. Madras State included Tamil, Telugu, Kannada and Malayalam speakers as well as peoples using Gondi and other tribal tongues. It was Telugu speakers who first successfully agitated against this state of affairs. In 1953, despite the initial opposition of Nehru, they won an overwhelmingly Telugu-speaking State, Andhra Pradesh, carved out of Madras and Hyderabad States (the latter identical with the old princely state). There followed in 1955 a States Reorganization Commission whose recommendations, such as were accepted, formed the basis for redrawing the internal political map of India primarily on a linguistic basis. Madras State was limited, by and large, to Tamil speakers (and later became Tamil Nadu). Kerala and Mysore (later Karnataka) were respectively dominated by Malayalam and Kannada speakers. Bombay State at this stage remained unified, but in 1960 split on a linguistic basis between Gujarat and Maharashtra (respectively speaking mainly Gujarati and Marathi). The Punjab of the Commission also later split between a largely Punjabi-speaking Punjab and a Hindi-speaking Haryana; though here the assertivenes of the Sikhs in the former was an active force. Orissa speaks Oriya (with many tribal languages), West Bengal speaks Bengali, truncated Assam speaks Assamese: 'truncated' because of the eventual excision from it of a series of mini-states, partly on a linguistic basis (again, see Chapter 4). The rest of India is the 'Hindi belt' divided between Bihar, Uttar Pradesh, Madhya Pradesh (which also has many tribal languages), Himachal Pradesh, Rajasthan, the Union Territory of Delhi and Haryana.

Under Schedule VIII of the Indian Constitution fifteen languages are given the status of 'Languages of India': they are, in alphabetical order, Assamese, Bengali, Gujarati, Hindi, Kannada, Kashmiri, Malayalam, Marathi, Oriya, Punjabi, Sanskrit, Sindhi, Tamil, Telugu and Urdu. The 'Official Languages of the Union' are Hindi in Devanagari script and English. In them most business by and with the Government of India and between States is done. English might have been abolished years ago but for what the non-Hindi belt States (particularly in the south) see as 'Hindi imperialism'. (But only some 200,000 people record English as their mother-tongue). Most States do their own business in the locally dominant tongue, and in English. Rajasthan and Bihar prefer to cite the former in their case as respectively 'Rajasthani' and 'Bihari'. It will be noted that Urdu, though a 'Language of India', has no corresponding State; and the same applies to many tribal tongues.

Now, as W.H. Morris-Jones has said, 'language is perhaps the most important mark of group identification' because 'a means of communication is inescapably a delineator of group boundaries'.[23] Literature, newspapers, the understanding of the radio, political propaganda, and in India some at any rate of the caste and other associations, necessarily stop at regional boundaries. Not surprisingly, regional politicians, skilled at working in the local language and sometimes knowing no other, cannot readily operate beyond the language frontier, and are in favour of including all who share their tongue in the same political unit, their State. They can rely on strong emotions. In Europe similar considerations are associated with nationalism, with powerful movements for the identification of nation with language group and for the political independence of that group. Yet in India, so far at any rate, and with exceptions to be discussed in Chapter 4, politicians and others have been content to work for Statehood within the Union, albeit with greater local autonomy and not without hostility to the Centre and its policies.

In conclusion, and returning to the local scale, B.S. Cohn has made it clear that the speech used by a man in any given village has an extremely local range (like a *jati*) and changes gradually as one moves from village group to village group across country, but our man will find the regional dialect comprehensible for most purposes across a wider area (though there may be turns of phrase confined to his caste). This is not peculiar to India, and was common in Europe in the past. In the last two centuries or less there have developed standard regional languages over a wider area still through the growth of literature, newspapers, education, communications and so on. It is these that we know by such names as Gujarati or Telugu, and these that form the vehicle for linguistic separatism. Many Indians, including some of the humblest, are able to speak in the standard regional language, or in some sort of Hindi (which can be understood over a far wider area than the 'Hindi' belt), while reverting to a very local dialect in their village and its environs.

The approach in the next chapter will be mainly historical. It will be concerned with the impact of Europe, and particularly Britain, on South Asia, with reactions to that impact, and with the coming of independence and partition. Such a concentration on modern history is appropriate for this book.

But I do not wish to ignore the importance to South Asians of their earlier history or of endogenous historical processes in the development of their economy, society and polity. That history stretches back a very long way, for the Indus civilization was flourishing some 4500 years ago, and those processes were at work, in spite of, or in association with, dynastic changes, over an equally long period, for all Marx's 'unchanging' villages. This chapter has shown what deep historical roots lie beneath, or are perceived as lying beneath the features and processes of contemporary society, for instance, the four *varnas*, the processes of sanskritization and caste mobility, the antiquity and caste-structured nature of urban life (and, of course, of the village), the absorptive syncretism of Hinduism, the coming of Islam and Sikhism. The student of South Asia must, indeed, be constantly aware of the length of, and the continuities in the history of, the subcontinent.[24]

If he is himself a South Asian, he will recognize the force of this long history, of perceived tradition, in his daily life, even if he rejects some of it as myth. It is one of many paradoxes in at least Hindu society that this force is so strong, in spite of the absence until very recently of the recording of history, of the chronology of events as these are understood in other societies. The Sinhala Buddhists have their monastic chronicles, the *Mahavansa* and *Culavansa*, recording (in a manner reminiscent of the biblical books of Kings and Chronicles) the acts of good kings who were pillars of Buddhism, of bad kings who were not, and very potent influences these have been in the triple intertwining of language, religion and state in modern Sri Lanka. The Muslims of the subcontinent, particularly in the period of the Mogul emperors and their successors, have left rich historical sources, and these have assuredly had their influence on modern Muslims. It is not so with the Hindus. But they rely, with tremendous effect, on their ancient writings, the Vedas (hymns going back to 1000 BC and earlier, preserved first in oral tradition and written down in Sanskrit centuries later), with the associated Brahmanas, Upanishads and Sutras, all eventually held to be sacred; and the later Epics, the Mahabharata and Ramayana. It is not easy for critical scholarship to disentangle myth from history in these writings, or in later genealogies and stories of heroes preserved in oral tradition. But something coming down from remote time forms part of the heritage of all contemporary Hindus, whatever their origin and whatever otherwise divides them. Let us not neglect, then, however contemporary our study, the sense of history and of tradition that is so alive to them as to other communities in South Asia.

3

THE BRITISH PERIOD, THE COMING OF INDEPENDENCE AND PARTITION*

The European impact was only the last in a long series of external influences on South Asia. By sea came, for example, voyagers from ancient Middle Eastern and Mediterranean civilizations. Later, Arab traders brought Islam to western and southern India, to Ceylon, and to the Maldive Islands; and founded communities that are Muslim still. By land, over the great north-western passes, poured wave after wave of invaders, from the early Aryans who brought Indo–European languages, to the ancestors of the Mughal emperors, while with Turki invaders Islam came to the northern parts of the subcontinent.

But South Asia was drawn into a new age with the arrival of European voyagers who had discovered the long sea route round the Cape of Good Hope and who sought the precious spices of the Orient. The first of these was the Portuguese Vasco da Gama, who landed in 1498 at what is now Kozhikode (Calicut) in Kerala. In spite of conflict with local rulers and Arab traders, the Portuguese soon set up a chain of sea-linked forts in South India and Ceylon, made converts to Christianity, and intermarried with local people. Later they brought a number of crops from the New World, for example, maize, potatoes, manioc, chillies and tobacco. Goa, their head-quarters, remained a Portuguese possession until annexed by independent India in 1962, and, with several smaller former Portuguese colonies, is still a Union Territory, ruled directly from New Delhi. On the heels of the Portuguese came the Dutch, who ruled the Low Country of Ceylon for 137 years; continued the process begun by the Portuguese whereby that area was differentiated from the up-country, Kandyan area; and had a lasting effect on law. But India they quickly left for a richer source of spices in the East Indies.

The British East India Company established itself at Surat in 1608, at Madras (mainly to buy textiles) in 1641, and at Calcutta in 1691 (Bombay grew to importance later), and rapidly dominated the Portuguese at sea.

The French Compagnie des Indes Orientales founded Pondicherry, south of Madras, in 1674, but was relatively inactive till the 1720s. By 1740 it had a number of additional posts on the east coast of India, and one at

Chandernagore, north of Calcutta, and was the only serious rival to the British. The clash of the two companies in India was brought about, not so much by rivalry in trade, as by the wars between Britain and France in Europe. The French were defeated by Clive at Plassey in Bengal in 1757, and in South India at Vandivasi (Wandiwash) in 1760, while the Dutch were ousted from Ceylon in 1795–6, basically in order to deny the splendid natural harbour at Trincomalee to the French during the wars. Thereafter the British were the only European force to be reckoned with in South Asia, until the Russians began to peer over the northern mountains in the 1860s, though the French continued to hold Pondicherry, Chandernagore and other small establishments until they were amicably ceded to independent India and became Union Territories.

Thus far in the narrative the British agent was not the government in London but the East India Company, though the newly-won territories in Ceylon, at first administered by the Company, became a Crown Colony in 1802; colonial rule was extended to the whole island in 1815. The Company's main motive was profit through trade, which was also the private motive of its servants. Political activities by the Company were occasioned by, or sought justification in, the protection of trade. Interest lay not so much in spices as in indigo, sugar and, above all, textiles, the silk and cotton products of long-standing and high-quality handloom industries. Some of the textiles were exchanged for spices in South-East Asia. Local agents were essential: so arose, slowly at first, an element in a 'new elite'. Trade was at first carried on through coastal posts, often fortified, built on land held from local rulers, with some of whom alliances were forged. There was, in the earliest phase, no question of wide territorial conquest or of sovereignty.

In time, the Company's servants went further and sponsored rulers of their choice, as when Clive after Plassey installed Mir Jafar as the Mughal Emperor's Governor of Bengal. But soon the Company's servants had made themselves the rulers of Bengal and Bihar. Some historians see these servants as 'the real founders of empire', like the conquistadors.[1] The acquiescence of the Company back in London was purchased by promise of rich land revenue. By 1805 rule had been extended to the Satluj (Sutlej) in Punjab, to much of what was to become the Madras Presidency, and to patches north of Surat. So did trading posts become territory and so was British influence extended to ever-widening areas of India. So, too, did higher administration pass into the hands of the Company's officials.

However, the British Government had already stepped in to curb and control the powers of the Company and its servants. Parliament was in particular alarmed by the near-bankruptcy that resulted from political adventure in Bengal; for much of the promised revenue had run into private pockets, and expansion was costly. A Regulating Act was passed in 1773, while the India Act of 1784 made the Company responsible to Parliament and declared 'that to pursue schemes of conquest and extension of dominion in India are measures repugnant to the . . . policy of this nation'. Nevertheless, further acquisitions were made in the remaining years of Company rule, that is, until the rebellion of 1857. Notably, the rest of Punjab and Sind were added.

In 1858 the British Crown assumed the government of the Company's territories and suzerainty over the princely rulers. By 1914 the Indian Empire had grown to its full territorial extent.

I now turn to some of the more important economic and social consequences of British rule, especially to ways in which they help to explain patterns and processes in contemporary South Asia, our prime concern, while recognizing that many of the effects of imperialism are the subjects of controversy, and that some will remain for examination in later chapters.

THE ECONOMIC IMPACT

Some of the concrete economic effects of British rule are obvious enough. Thus by independence undivided India had some 45,000 miles of railways: 29 miles per thousand sq. miles of area, 132 miles per million population, both high figures for a colonial territory.[2] The corresponding figures for Ceylon are 898 miles; 36 miles per thousand sq. miles; and 135 miles per million population. There were, however, substantial gaps in the Indian network, notably in the north-eastern Deccan, Rajasthan, Baluchistan and the North-West Frontier Province.

Roads existed in India long before British days. But the British extended the network (at first largely for strategic reasons) until at independence there were 130,000 miles of surfaced roads in India and nearly 11,000 miles in Ceylon. The density of the network was relatively high in such areas as the Madras Presidency and the Wet Zone and hills of Ceylon, but was low in many others, and villages innumerable remained without all-weather roads.

Irrigation, again, is by no means a British or a modern invention, though evolving technology under the Raj was able to achieve engineering feats beyond the ken of ancient constructors, skilled though they were. These feats included major canal works in the Punjab and in Sind (turning deserts into granaries) and in the Doab between the Ganga (Ganges) and Yamuna (Jumna), also taking off from the lower reaches of east coast rivers, and in the Bombay Deccan. In Ceylon restoration of ancient tanks and of their dependent channel systems began in the 1850s, and there was some new construction.

The railways had much to do with the spreading of a money economy and with increasing the output of existing non-food crops (for example, cotton, oil seeds and spices). They also made it possible to switch food grains from surplus to deficit or famine areas (though they did not enable the poor to purchase).

Irrigation works brought new lands into cultivation and gave at least the potential for surpluses both on them and on lands already cultivated. There has been much argument as to whether the British achieved the right mix of railways and irrigation works. Indian 'nationalist' historians and others are apt to argue that, judged by economic criteria, too much was invested in railways because of their strategic significance, and that the cost to the Indian economy was high. For a long time, too, irrigation works were not initiated unless they were expected to be commercially viable as judged by rather narrow criteria. There has also been controversy, not untinged with ideology, on the costs and benefits, merits and demerits of irrigation works constructed or restored in the British period. Thus Elizabeth Whitcombe, in an exhaustive survey, highlighted, *inter alia*, waterlogging (accompanied by debilitation and mortality), unsatisfactory returns to government, low cultivated proportion of theoretically-irrigable area, and the inflexibility of giant canal systems.[3] She concluded that the canals proved 'a costly experiment'. On the other hand, Ian Stone, in a detailed study of the Ganges Canal in the Ganga-Yamuna doab concluded, in what was in part a rejoinder to Whitcombe, that it was the canal which was the primary source of 'the dynamism and prosperity' shown by western Uttar Pradesh (UP) following its construction.

In aggregate, and viewing the British period as a whole, the Indian cultivated area increased. Though in some regions and at some periods the waste crept back, and though areas of jungle remained available for agricultural colonization schemes after independence, 'there came, at a different date in different regions, a critical point in time beyond which rural settlement advanced strongly into the waste, no longer to relapse into major phases of retreat'.[4] In most regions this advance was a matter of piecemeal encroachment, but there were government-organized colonization schemes, notably in Punjab; and in Assam and Kerala tea and other plantations were established, serving an export market. What is more controversial is the trend in agricultural production and productivity. G. Blyn concluded, after patient analysis of elusive data, that over the period 1891–1947, at any rate, per capita agricultural output declined.[5] There were, however, substantial differences between crops (wheat doing better than rice) and between regions, Bengal tending to drag down the all-India averages. Later work by M.M. Islam reached conclusions for the period 1920–46 less adverse to Bengal than Blyn's, and suggested that trend rates for Bengal proper were in turn dragged down by Bihar and Orissa, included in Bengal in early statistics. More recently A. Heston has concluded that

there was very substantial growth in foodgrains and total output during the period from 1860 to 1920, both growing more rapidly than population. After 1920, however, growth in foodgrain output appears to be less, and of non-foodgrain output more, than the growth of population.

In this whole context (and indeed in the study of contemporary South Asia) aggregate statistics often conceal great regional and other disparities, while temporal trends mask violent fluctuations due to the vagaries of the monsoon; and the inaccuracies and complications of the underlying official data are legion.

On the question of the complex changes made by the British to the related subjects of land tenure and land revenue there is a constantly growing body of literature of which the paragraphs that follow can only convey some of the main points. First, the British inherited a situation already of great complexity, though it usually reflected adaptation to the local situation, and the principle that revenue was due to the ruler, 'a wage for a protector' according to Hardy.[6] The revenue might be collected by an intermediary *zamindar*. The British reaction to this situation in the Bengal of the 1790s was to make a permanent settlement for the revenue with the *zamindars* and to empower them to transfer their rights. They in fact became landlords, though not of the improving sort for which the British had hoped. The status of the actual cultivators tended to be depressed. Permanent settlements were not made in other areas. But revenue settlements with *zamindars* of varied provenance were widespread in the plains west of Bihar, in the Central Provinces, and in parts of the south, and led to a growing market in revenue-collecting rights and to sales of land by revenue defaulters. In the 1890s Congress began to agitate against *zamindars*, seen as lackeys of the Raj, and, in power after independence, abolished them.

In Bombay and Madras Presidencies and in the plains of Assam the dominant form of revenue settlement eventually made was *raiyatwari* (*ryotwari*), that is, the government collected the periodically-adjusted revenue itself, theoretically from the actual cultivator, though in most *raiyatwari* areas there was a pyramid of holders of rights, varying from area to area in nature and character. As Dharma Kumar has said, 'the village was not always and everywhere a simple community of peasant proprietors; often it was far more differentiated and complex', as, indeed, the visitor to a present-day South Indian village finds when invited 'to meet the *raiyats*'. When a land market developed and land came to be pledged as a security for loans, the registered *raiyat* was often a landlord, not the actual cultivator. The network of village-level officials required to keep records and to collect *raiyatwari* revenue provided ready-made dramatis personnae in politics. The weight of the revenue assessment, under whatever system, often fell heavily on the actual cultivator. After 1900, however, political pressure saw to it that land revenue was of decreasing relative importance to the Raj. From about the same time the benefits of government-organized research in plant breeding and agronomy have to be set against the depressing effects of the revenue system.

It has been a prominent part of charges against the British that they vastly increased, if they did not bring into being, the class of landless labourers whose plight is now so prominent a part of the Indian village scene and of this book. Dharma Kumar, however, convincingly showed that, for the Madras Presidency at any rate, such labourers, and for that matter agrestic servitude, antedate the British impact, and estimated that they formed some 10 to 15 per cent of the population in the early nineteenth century and 15 to 20 per cent in the period 1871–1901, hardly a catastrophic increase.[7] Again, H. Fukazawa, in a study of western India, concluded that there was little support for the view that there was widespread 'pauperization' of rural labour during the British period, though change there was; but that there was so much regional variation that further studies are needed.[8] No doubt similar considerations apply to other regions that cannot be covered here.

Finally, agrarian revolt, at any rate partly arising from grievances about land tenure and revenue, has been a recurrent event in the Indian countryside, especially in some Districts.

The princely states lay outside the British land and revenue administration and were in theory at any rate free to levy land revenues as their rulers pleased. Sometimes, however, the British leant on the ruler.

In Ceylon, as early as 1802 *rajakariya* tenures involving labour service to the government were abolished and 'peasant proprietorship' instituted, coupled with a tax on paddy land (abolished in 1892, whereafter there was no land revenue in the colony). More controversially, an enactment of 1840 declared waste land to be Crown property, enabling plantations up-country to be established with great rapidity but depriving villages of land they had customarily used for shifting cultivation, pasture and other purposes (the economic effects of this measure have, however, probably been exaggerated, and certainly over-simplified).[9]

Argument over the effects of British rule on industry have also waxed warm. M.D. Morris contested the once familiar view that the British found a society ready for an industrial revolution and prevented its development.[10] He saw the growth of manufacturing impeded amongst other things by low incomes (and so low demand), paucity of relevant skills, and limited entrepreneurship. Far from textile handicrafts being exterminated by imperialism (as Marx had predicted), they survived and may even have grown as cheap imported yarn benefited the handloom weavers (though what of the spinners? and some recent research has shown that survival was only after severe initial decline and with a reduction in the number of weavers).

Some support for the general Morris thesis comes from work by A. Heston from which there emerges a picture, albeit shadowy and tentatively sketched, of a small rise in real per capita incomes during the British period; a picture that contrasts strongly with that drawn by other authors, notably Jawaharlal Nehru, who held that foreign political domination led to a rapid destruction of the economy that India had built up, the result being 'poverty and degradation beyond measure'.

Indian economic historians and others have not been slow to challenge Morris's conclusions on a number of scores. Thus it is held (with reason) that in some respects, notably in terms of pre-industrial textile technology, India was in advance of most other countries; while it has been shown that inland trade is of long standing (though limited and local in its effects). Indeed, marked interregional disparities characterized the 'traditional' economy, and exist today. It is, again, argued that even if the handicrafts survived the flood of cheap Lancashire cotton (as undoubtedly they did, in some areas at any rate), then the weavers must have become much worse off as prices tumbled.

Now, in spite of the handicaps urged by Morris, India did see factories set up in the British period: jute mills at Calcutta, cotton mills along the Bombay–Ahmedabad axis, at Nagpur, and in the south (especially Madras and Coimbatore). The earliest of these textile ventures date from 1854, but the fastest growth was in the 1870s (except in the south, whose boom period came between the two World Wars). Meanwhile, coal- and iron-ore mining were becoming firmly established; and in 1911 the Tata iron and steel plant at Jamshedpur, in south-eastern Bihar, began production. By 1941 India was producing annually a million tons of steel, three-quarters of its requirement. There also grew during the days of the Raj many sugar and some cement factories, and a number of minor consumer-goods industries. Selective protection came after 1917, and is held responsible for considerable growth between the wars in steel, sugar, cotton and match production. At independence 50 per cent of India's exports were of manufactures.

However, throughout the British period India remained heavily dependent on imports of manufactures, mainly from Britain, where the government bought most of its stores. Before independence modern factories never played more than a small part in the economy; never employed more than about 2 per cent of the work-force; made but few machines; and failed utterly to penetrate most regions. In fact, the industries just mentioned were, with few exception, located in or near the three great company ports, or within their penumbra. One exception was the textile industry of Kanpur (UP); another was the sugar industry with its dependence on fresh cane supplies. Indian historians, whatever their parent school of thought, stress the regional insignificance of industrialization in the British period.

The legacy of the British to independent India, Pakistan and Bangladesh is, then, clear in terms of concrete construction like railways, roads and irrigation works; and also, one must emphasize, in terms of a modern commercial infrastructure, a 'steel frame' of administration, and a framework of law (with an independent higher judiciary) lacking in many other developing countries. The countries of the Raj entered independence with rapid increases of population, with agriculture barely able or unable to keep pace with those increases; with a complex and inequitable agrarian structure; and with sizeable, but relatively insignificant and regionally non-existent factory industries. What remains controversial is the extent to which agriculture and industry might have been more developed (and, indeed, the economies transformed) if British policy had been different, or if imperialism had never penetrated the subcontinent.

In many ways the imprint of Britain on Ceylon is clearer and heavier.[11] The economy of an island which was sixth-sevenths forested towards the end of the eighteenth century, but producing rice to feed itself as well as spices, was transformed into an export economy producing tea, rubber and coconut products for an overseas market from foreign- and locally-owned plantations and from small-holdings; and importing great quantities of rice. Population trebled between 1872 and independence. Industries were largely confined to the making and mending of machinery for the plantations. Economic activity centred on the Wet Zone and the Hills; the Dry Zone, apart from surviving rice-growing villages and a few modern irrigation and colonization schemes, lay under a heavy pall of malaria.

The baseline from which the development of the independent South Asian countries started, including some reference to Nepal, Bhutan and the Maldive Islands, will be delineated in a little more detail in Chapter 6.

THE SOCIAL IMPACT

Deliberate efforts by the British to change South Asian society tended to be confined to the abolition of customs repugnant to them, such as *satti* (suttee), the burning of the living Hindu widow with the corpse of her husband, declared illegal in 1829; or *rajakariya*, partly because of the hindrance that it offered to the mobility of labour, judged necessary for the plantation economy. Indeed, the most important changes in society brought about in both India and Ceylon by the British were the result of measures instituted with other purposes in mind. Some of these have already been discussed. Others were the effects of the concept of equality before the law, and of educational activity.

As early as 1835 it had been 'declared that the content of higher education [in India] should be Western learning, including science, and that the language of instruction should be English'.[12] Slowly schools were started, and Christian missions took educational initiatives. But it was not till 1857 that the first three universities, those in Calcutta, Bombay and Madras, were founded, and a grant-in-aid system for private schools and colleges was introduced. Early effects of the new education were largely concentrated in the Presidencies (of which Bengal led) and especially in the three port cities, though Poona became a secondary centre in the Bombay Presidency.[13] British territories elsewhere, and even more the princely states, lagged behind, in most cases till well into the twentieth century; though the Anglo-Oriental College at Aligarh (UP), later to become Aligarh Muslim University, was founded in 1875, and Allahabad University and Punjab University, Lahore, in 1887.

In Ceylon western-style education made relatively little headway before 1870.[14] Thereafter there was rapid development with concentration in two areas: around Colombo, and in the Ceylon Tamil-settled Jaffna Peninsula.

In nineteenth-century India those in the Presidencies who benefited from the new education came from highly restricted social groups: in Bengal from upper Hindu castes such as Brahmins, Kayasthas (writers) and Baidyas (traditionally physicians); leaving the Muslims well behind; in Bombay from Brahmins, Gujarati trading castes, Prabhus (writers) and Parsis (again, Muslims were less affected, especially in Sind); in Madras, Tamil areas were ahead of Telugu areas, and Brahmins at first held a position of overwhelming strength, though towards the end of the nineteenth century the share of Vaisya and Sudra castes in the secondary schools was increasing (as it did later in the universities). In nineteenth century Ceylon members of the Low Country Goyigama, the three coastal castes (see Chapter 2), and upper caste Jaffna Tamils, benefited most.

In the twentieth century western-style education gathered momentum in India, here through official action, there through missions, but increasingly through indigenous effort, often as a Hindu or Buddhist reaction to Christian missions. Only four more universities were, however, founded between 1900 and 1920; though nine appeared between 1920 and independence (including Dacca, now Dhaka University in 1922). On the eve of independence there were still great blanks in Rajasthan and Gujarat, and in central and south-central India. In the future West and East Pakistan Punjab University (Lahore) and Dacca University respectively stood alone, as did, in Ceylon, University College, Colombo, founded in 1921. Some of the spaces on the map of India were at least partially filled by colleges affiliated to universities in other areas, or by various technical institutions. And schools of many kinds were creeping steadily over the map, though very unevenly. In fact, literacy grew steadily in both India and Ceylon from the 1880s until independence,[15] but at that point still tended in India to be highest in coastal areas of the three Presidencies and in Travancore-Cochin (now Kerala), though even there it touched only some 10 per cent of the population. Literacy remained very low (under 5 per cent) in much of Rajasthan, in Hyderabad, and in the east central Deccan; and was almost non-existent in Nepal, Bhutan and the Maldives.

Many nineteenth-century writers, from Karl Marx to James Mill and to British administrators, were in broad agreement that Indian society had been historically resistant to change (nowadays we know more about social change in pre-British days). Marx attributed this to 'the dissolution of society into stereotyped and disconnected atoms'; but claimed that the British conquest was bringing about rapid alteration in society. Not surprisingly these authors differed sharply between themselves. To Marx the British impact was destructive of 'village republics'(see Chapter 2) yet he saw colonialism as a modernizing force which would lay 'the material foundations of western society in Asia'. James Mill also envisaged rapid transformation, while criticizing British administrators.

Controversy also surrounds the nature of the social changes that accompanied economic and tenurial transformation during the British period. Eric Stokes opposed the view that for most of India social stagnation rather than revolution was the hallmark of the British period.[16] He was primarily concerned with the century ending in 1857, but also looked ahead to later phases of British rule. In the decades that immediately followed Plassey, he says, the social and cultural impact was indeed small. The East India Company, though it introduced English-style high-level administrative and judicial institutions, still behaved like an Indian ruler in other respects, and upheld Hindu and Muslim law and religious practice. But after the 1800s ideology at any rate was couched in the language of evangelicalism, utilitarianism and 'improvement', and was accordingly censorious about local society and culture, especially religion. However, there was a great gulf between ideology and achievement (a gulf not unknown in contemporary South Asia). Indigenous cultures prevailed in 'the interior' and still more so in the princely states. Indeed, the work of some historians had laid bare the British officer in the countryside, not as the fountainhead from which change flowed, but 'as a prisoner if not a puppet of local social forces': of hereditary administrators (Brahmins, Kayasths or Muslims), of equally hereditary and caste-determined village officers who came from the same group whatever paper reforms might be made in land revenue systems. Again, 'although rural society must have undergone a profound change by the suppression of open violence and the turning of individual and group struggle into a battle for land rights through the courts, there was no complete structural change'. Careful local research shows that old elite castes held their own on the land or appeared in a new guise; or that changes thought to have been due to the Company and the Raj had already been seeping through the social fabric; or that the decay of old elites was relatively slow.

In short, in the countryside by 1857 neither Marx's prognostications of decay and resurrection into westernization, nor the hopes of some British officials and writers that 'progress' would bring 'improved' capitalist agriculture were fulfilled. However, the grip of the traditional administrative castes on government offices was to some extent to be weakened by the institution in 1860 of open competition based on educational qualifications, and the associated rise of western-educated administrators.

So much for Stokes's invaluable work of 1978, with some glosses on it, in part with the benefit of hindsight. One may also add here that latter-day Marxists, unlike their founding father, have thought in terms of the stagnating rather than the revolutionary effects of colonialism, for example, through its alliances with the landlords and through the supposed comprador-like quality of the bourgeoisie.

A different conspectus on the social effects of British rule covering broadly the same period as that treated by Stokes emerges from a masterly survey by C.A. Bayly, which hinges largely on more recent research, much of it still in progress.[17] This survey also illuminates a good deal that has gone before in this book. Bayly emphasizes a point earlier cited from Stokes: 'the suppression of open violence', and hence the diminishing role of warrior groups. Because of this, and also because of the effect of deforestation as felt in the decline of nomads, pastoralists and some tribals, there came 'the formative phase' in what was to be the dominance of settled peasant farming, with its poverty. (For deforestation see also Chapter 2, and for the advance of rural settlement see also above.) This scenario is clearly far removed from Marx's unchanging village, and equally from reliance on a thesis of the imperialist dual economy, which in fostering 'cash crops' left the peasantry in primeval neglect. Equally clearly the context in which local power was operating had suffered a sea change from that of former times, and, startlingly, the familiar 'traditional' village was virtually a creation of colonial rule, while the settled peasantry may be seen as a 'creative adaptation' to changed conditions. Also radical is the suggestion that a more rigid and stratified caste structure owed much to the defeat of the warriors, nomads and tribesmen. Bayly concedes, however, that much is still unclear, and subject to regional variation (and that is almost a leitmotif of parts of this book, as, for that matter, is creative adaptation by the peasantry to later agrarian changes such as those associated with the 'Green Revolution').

During the British period Ceylon saw more rapid social change than many parts of India because of the rapid establishment of a plantation economy, with which came an influx of Indian Tamil labour and a new dimension to the Sinhala/Tamil plurality that was such a long-standing feature of the island society and polity.[18] With the new economy, too, came a rapid commercialization and a great deal of economic individualism, with social effects working through land tenure and the rise of a new urban and English-speaking elite including, in prominent positions, the members of the coastal castes (see Chapter 2).

Nepal is a very different case, at the opposite end of the spectrum in terms of the pace of westernization. Cut down in size by the British after the Gurkha War of 1814–15, but never in the Empire, its buffer-state function and almost complete isolation in the days of the Raj preserved its fossil status, an exaggeration of that of some princely states within the Indian Empire. However, in the nineteenth century the Ranas succeeded in establishing themselves as hereditary prime ministers and effectively the rulers under a figure-head king. And peace after a long period of wars resulted in relatively rapid population change, with pressure on land resources, the transmutation of pastoral peoples into settled agriculturalists, increasing concentration of land in the hands of upper castes, and the growth of landlessness,[19] while Gurkhas serving in the Indian Army and Nepalis more generally migrating to work in India began to generate a 'remittance economy'.

Bhutan, though like Nepal a part of the northern buffer-zone of the Raj, was even less subject to social change during the British period. The Maldive Islands did not become a British Protectorate until 1887, and were never subject to colonial occupation.

THE POLITICAL IMPACT AND POLITICAL CHANGE

The story of political change during the British period has been told in a number of different ways. First, in terms of concentration on the Indian National Congress as the premier 'nationalist' institution, founded in 1885, its roots were in the three Presidency cities and in Poona. In early years its members came principally from the English-educated elites: it had no permanent organization; it passed resolutions, and tried to impress its policies on the Government of India and on opinion in Britain. It remained relatively weak up to the end of the nineteenth century. In the twentieth century the pace of political change quickened markedly. In 1905 Curzon, the Viceroy, announced the partition of the Bengal Presidency into a new Province of Eastern Bengal and Assam (which had a Muslim majority), and Western Bengal (comprising the rest of Bengal with Bihar and Orissa). This inflamed Bengali opinion, and terrorist movements appeared, not only in Bengal, but also in the Bombay Presidency and Punjab; while Congress split into moderate and extremist wings. In 1906 the All-India Muslim League was founded. The First World War and the Russian Revolution respectively shook credit in western superiority, and raised hopes that, if Russian despotism could fall, so could the British.[20] There followed the arrival of Gandhi; the launching of a great movement of protest; and, in the Punjab, the Jallianwallah Bagh massacre when troops fired on a prohibited meeting, leading to a mood of deep resentment. Soon Gandhi became a major influence in the Congress, and established links with the masses, later in somewhat uneasy partnership with Nehru. Events moved on until Britain conceded independence after the Second World War, and partition became inevitable given the intransigence of Jinnah and the Muslim League.

But the tale can also be told in terms of British reactions to an ever-strengthening national movement and to various forms of unrest by means of successive constitutional devices to give Indians more power. Such historiography also emphasizes the differing policies of Conservative, Liberal and (later) Labour governments at Westminster. Thus, a Liberal government which came to power in 1905 produced the Morley–Minto reforms and the India Act of 1909: Indians were admitted to executive offices, and the Imperial Legislative Council was enlarged to sixty members, twenty-seven of them indirectly elected, and its powers broadened. Six of the new constituencies were for Muslim landholders. In 1917 it was proclaimed that the policy of H.M. government . . . is that of the increasing association of Indians in every branch of the administration, and the gradual development of self-governing institutions, with a view to the progressive realisation of responsible government in India as an integral part of the Empire.

There followed the India Act 1919 and the Montagu–Chelmsford reforms which, *inter alia*, enlarged the central legislature and introduced 'dyarchy' and ministerial responsibility in the provinces. Dyarchy (which operated from 1921 to 1937) was seen by Spear as a first step towards the federation that is independent India.[21] In each province the governor's executive was responsible to him only, whereas ministers were responsible both to him and to the largely elected provincial legislature. The principle of communal electorates was extended. This cumbrous system was boycotted by Congress, worked by other parties in Punjab and Madras (where the Unionist and Justice parties, the latter a development of the anti-Brahmin movement, respectively took office), and elsewhere depended on shifting coalitions of elected members. The 1935 India Act further extended the features of the 1919 Act, especially in terms of popular representation. Dyarchy was abolished in the provinces, but retained at the Centre. The federal principle was also extended: notably, the princes were given an opportunity to adhere (which they eventually declined). Congress took part in elections, won clear majorities in five out of eleven provinces, and became the largest party at the Centre. Then came the Second World War, the resignation of Congress ministries (because the Viceroy declared war on behalf of India), and the complex of events leading to partition and independence on 15 August 1947.

The corresponding Ceylon story can be told similarly, though it moved at a slower pace. As early as 1835 two Ceylonese members, one Sinhala and one Tamil, were nominated to the Legislative Council, which was reformed in 1912 and again in 1921. On both occasions officials remained in a majority, and there was communal representation; on the earlier occasion the franchise for Ceylonese was restricted to the English-educated. It was not until 1919, in the wake of communal rioting in 1915, that the Ceylon National Congress was formed in emulation of the Indian Congress. A constitutional commission reported in 1931, and was followed by the introduction of universal suffrage, territorial (not communal) electorates, and limited ministerial responsibility. Hard on the heels of a further commission (1944–5) and of Indian independence came Ceylon Independence Day, 4 February 1948.

Both of the modes of narration just followed have value as a chronological framework and as partial unearthings of the roots of politics in contemporary South Asia, especially if they disclose the ideas and ideals of the prominent characters. Thus Gandhi may be seen as a shrewd politician with great mass appeal because of his thoroughly Indian framework of reference and because of his concern for the poor generally and for the Harijans in particular, and with a strong desire that India should avoid what he saw as the social miseries of the industrial revolution in the west – hence his espousal of decentralized cottage industries. And Nehru may be seen as a thoroughly westernized figure, an ardent modernizer, deeply impressed with the industrialization of the Soviet Union, but charged with a fervent love of his country that he was able to convey to mass audiences and, like other prominent Congressmen, a firm proponent of secularism in politics. Again, supporters of Congress were a diverse group: Congress was indeed a movement, even a bandwagon, not a political party with a single ideology Jinnah is far too enigmatic, aloof and ambiguous a character for his ideas and ideals to be encapsulated here in a few lines. This, indeed, will appear shortly, as will the nature of the Muslim League as an essentially communal organization.

But to tell the story of pre-independence political change in these ways is, first, to convey an impression of almost unhindered forward progress towards independence; and, secondly, to risk placing undue emphasis on the role of Congress, of the Muslim League, and of the English-educated elite – an elite that was wafer-thin even in the Presidency cities, and still more attenuated, or absent altogether, elsewhere in the subcontinent, even though it long had a near-monopoly of the new legislative bodies. And it is to think too much of ideals rather than of interests, of dedicated and self-sacrificing personalities rather than of self-seeking pressure-groups.

To obtain a more balanced judgement questions like the following need to be asked. What of political moment was happening in Indian society at large? Were there links between the politics of Congress, the Muslim League and other 'national' bodies and those of regional and local levels? Were caste and other associations a means of exerting pressure upwards from these levels or was the countryside inert and inactive, except for acts of occasional though spectacular rebellion like those of 1857? In the last twenty years or so a number of scholars have addressed these questions and found a great deal of local variety.[22]

One answer to the first question just posed is that, apart from many princely states (where British rule fossilized dynasties that might otherwise have gone the way of Nineveh and Tyre), the establishment of the Raj meant the extinction of the old rulers, the old 'first-line elite': gone were the Sikh lords of the Punjab, the Nawabs of Awadh (Oudh) in the north and of Arcot in the south, and many another ruler in between. In some areas they were followed into limbo by what Stokes called 'the second line of the political elite', the former rural magnates who could not successfully transmute themselves into the revenue-collecting *zamindars* required by the British.[23] But under the old rulers there had also been an elite derived from Brahmin, writer and other upper castes and literate in the local languages or in Persian. Some of these became early members of the new English-educated elite. On one view of Indian political history, Indian 'nationalism' was a matter of the pressure exerted on the British by the English-educated elites, which were divided, self-interested and intensely competitive; and which drew their power from an ability to understand and to utilize the pressures coming from other elements in rural and urban society and to convert them into pressures on the Raj. Thus some of the Chitpavan Brahmins of Poona, prominent under Mahratta rule, moved into education in English and on into the public service, the professions and eventually politics, especially when these warmed up c.1900. They played a crucial part in Congress and its splits and protests; and Congress had intricate links in Maharashtra that were parochial, provincial and 'national'.

Across India in the United Provinces, by the late 1880s, threads went back from the local Congress to wealthy city notables thoroughly embedded in 'traditional' society, who (contrary to contemporary British views that Congress embodied no more than disaffected *déracinés*) used it to publicize their interests and grievances. These notables were prominent in acts of conspicuous piety, especially the financing of Hindu religious institutions. Hence Congress rhetoric had to be conveyed in Hindu terms and so contributed to the alienation from it of local Muslim leaders.

It was for the Madras Presidency that David Washbrook and Christopher Baker gave a vivid, though not uncontroversial picture of politics at local and provincial levels under the Raj which is well worth presenting as a case study here. The Presidency, far from being the most politically lethargic of the provinces during the nineteenth century, untouched as it was by the rebellion of 1857, was shown to be alive with evolving activity of a kind that foreshadowed a number of features of the south in independent India. In Madras the British had destroyed the old warrior elite of that highly varied territory, and early relied for *raiyatwari* revenue collection and local administration on members of locally dominant castes, 'rural-local bosses'. Politics was very much a matter of the means by which such 'bosses' exerted economic, and thus political power in the villages, though there were regional differences. From the 1870s onwards the provincial government began to interfere much more in local affairs, forcing the 'rural-local bosses' to take it more seriously when planning their political strategies. With the introduction in the 1880s of local boards and committees, and with the improvement of communications, the increased commercialization of agriculture and other economic changes, the 'bosses' began to operate in a wider arena. From the same period dates the proliferation of new horizontal organizations, including caste associations (see Chapter 2) and communal (including Muslim) bodies. By 1920 some of the 'bosses' were dominating new official district-level bodies and had even begun to enter the Legislative Council.

Meanwhile, some of the Tamil Brahmins (and, slowly, other castes) became English-educated, and set themselves up as intermediaries between the provincial government and both 'rural-local bosses' and city magnates. For various reasons the English-educated elite in Madras was less hostile to the Raj than its counterparts in Bengal and Bombay, and this may have something to do with the Presidency's reputation for quietude. Members of this new elite worked, not only through the Legislative Council, but also through the University and the High Court, and were prone to nepotism, factionalism and shifting alliances. In time they appear as members of various nascent political parties, including the Congress (which gave them a link with national politics) and the Justice Party (see p. 38), which links forward through various transmutations and vicissitudes to that important regional party, the DMK (Dravida Munnetra Kazhagam) of more recent politics.

The Justice Party was the only political party willing to work the Montagu–Chelmsford constitution of 1920, and it did so for a decade. But Congress in the 1920s and early 1930s was rebuilt, and became the channel for all kinds of dissidence in the new political climate; in the later 1930s it grew in importance. It came, not without travail, to link locality to province and province to nation: in the 1920s and 1930s it spread markedly into localities.

Ceylon was too small to exhibit all levels of political activity from locality to province and nation. However, historical studies have enlivened the plain tale of constitutional advance to representative government and independence, by relating political change to movements in local societies.[24] Superficially there are parallels with India, especially the south. Thus the colonial government used local notables as middle-level administrators, and indeed threw its weight on their side in their conflict with the parvenus of the coastal castes. And Ceylon developed its own influential English-educated elite which became prominent in many associations and movements, particularly Buddhist revivalism and pressures for more representative government. But this elite was more varied in composition, by caste, community and religion, than that in most parts of India; rather than acting as brokers for local 'bosses' it absorbed many of them, first in the Low Country and Jaffna, later in the Kandyan hills, last of all in the Dry Zone; held a monopoly of politics at the national level; and often scorned, rather than cultivated links with the villages, till Bandaranaike forged his crucial relationship with frustrated vernacular-educated rural leaders.

Ceylon had, on the face of it, a far easier journey to independence, so that the country and students of it hardly noticed the difference on 4 February 1948. But there had been earlier Sinhala–Tamil wrangles over constitutional reform, and the discontents of the Sinhala village leaders lay only just beneath the calm surface to erupt in communal violence in the years after 1956.

Looking back at the subcontinent as a whole, much research has now been done on the whole complex of changing political relationships between Raj and society in British India, within various frameworks of ideas. We must be struck by the variety of responses to colonial rule, itself far from uniformly applied. We also know something of politics in the princely states, to which, as to popular movements in them, Congress tended to show 'inconsistent and ambivalent policies' to quote Ramusack (1988) while generally giving priority to the British-ruled provinces.

MUSLIM SEPARATISM

It is a simplistic distortion of the history of the British period to trace an ever-widening gap between Muslims and other Indians, or a continuously gathering momentum in the desire of Muslims for separate political treatment culminating inevitably in partition. Muslim separatism has a history of more than a century, in the course of which, under such influences as changing British perceptions and policies, and shifting relations between government, Muslim leaders and organizations, and Congress and other political bodies, the issue appeared in one form or another, then receded for a while, until it reached what many Muslims (and others) would until quite near the end of the story in 1947 have seen as a surprising denouement: partition and the emergence of Pakistan as a separate independent state.[25]

First, however, it is important to ask, in elaboration of what was said in Chapter 2, 'Who were these Indian Muslims?' Throughout the British period they were highly diverse in origin and sectarian allegiance, and also in terms of social and economic status. At one extreme was the old elite of UP, stripped of the power that they or their ancestors had held under the Moguls and their successors; but in many cases retaining land and influence in the villages, and, in some cases, subordinate offices under the Raj. At the other extreme, and most notably in Bengal, they were poor tenant cultivators, usually holding land from Hindus. In between came a wide range of Muslims, varying from area to area, but including cultivators, traders, and weavers, as well as *ulamas* learned in Islamic religious knowledge, who were at a great intellectual distance from those illiterate Muslims of village and town, whom some have seen as practising a 'folk' Islam with accretions from Hinduism. The British came by the last decades of the nineteenth century, however, to see these highly-varied Indian Muslims as a 'community', as an entity contrasting strongly and simply with Hindus because of such factors as their monotheism; their supposed social equality under Islam; and their presumed memory of their days as rulers of all (or most) of India, which was apt to make the British anxious. It was to a considerable extent this British perception of a monolithic Muslim bloc that helped to make Indian Muslims feel that they *were* an entity. The self-image of at least the new, small group of western-educated Muslims came to match that perception. And it was the felt need of the Raj to 'divide and rule' (as some see it) or at any rate to 'balance and rule' (as others, including Peter Hardy see it) that further strengthened a Muslim sense of identity.

But the Muslim self-image was complicated, and Muslim aspirations and actions confused because of controversy about the nature of an Islamic polity, especially when the *ulama* came to be involved in politics. Was India under the Raj *dar-ul-Islam*, 'the abode of Islam', where Islamic law (the *sharia*) was in force? Or was it *dar-ul-harb*, 'the abode of war', not under Islamic law and government based thereon, and to be made so, if necessary by force? If the former, where did the Raj fit into the classical scheme of things, which envisaged *dar-ul-Islam* under a pious Muslim ruler: if not the universal *khalifa* (caliph) of early times, then a sultan acting as his deputy in a specific territory? And at a later stage there was the confusing effect on the Muslim conception of an Islamic polity of essentially western ideas of nationhood. Controversy over the Islamic polity, not least about the nature of an Islamic republic, still continues in Pakistan and in writings about it.

Now when the 1857 rebellion and its aftermath were over and done with, there eventually came about something of a Muslim–British reconciliation, partly, no doubt, because of 'balance and rule' policies, partly because of the ideas and work of Muslims like Sir Syed Ahmed Khan, the founder of what was to become Aligarh Muslim University, for he and his like had no doubts about the legitimacy and benefits of British rule. Muslims, especially the western-educated from Aligarh, grew in community-consciousness, which was recognized and enhanced by the British in the 1880s by the nomination of Muslims to local boards and even more twenty years later by the creation of separate Muslim electorates; and further enhanced by competition for jobs with educated Hindus, and by communal friction and disturbances. Some Muslims joined Congress, but others joined specifically Muslim associations. By this time several different categories of Indian Muslims (with those from UP usually in the lead) had drawn closer together politically: but there was no unanimity about strategy or tactics; the politically active were still largely the English-educated; there was suspicion of 'smart alecs' from Bengal; and the Muslim League was for some years after its foundation in 1906 'a feeble and under-weight suckling', to quote Hardy. M.A. Jinnah, to play such a prominent part later, enrolled in the League in 1913, having already joined Congress. Interestingly, he remained a member of both bodies until 1920.

Violent reaction by some Hindus to Curzon's partition of Bengal (which they saw as favourable to some Muslim claims) further exacerbated communal differences. And educated Muslims began to be affected by the pan-Islamic movement, itself a response to European imperialism and its treatment of Muslims in the Middle East and North Africa. New political linkages were forged when younger Muslims, impatient with the pro-British stance of their seniors, allied with the *ulama*, who had ties with the Muslim masses.

In 1911 Muhammad Iqbal, the notable Urdu poet–philosopher and already a force in the Punjab, proclaimed that the Muslims were a 'nation', albeit one with a peculiar uniting bond. But in 1916 there came the 'Lucknow Pact', under which Congress accepted the idea of separate communal electorates in the provinces. In the next few years Muslims and Congress were further brought together by the assiduous work of Gandhi and by joint agitation over the allied conquest of Turkey and hence of its ruler, seen as the *khalifa*. At this time, though there were many currents of opinion, one prominent view was that of Maulana Kalam Azad (who eventually became Minister of Education in independent India) that Hindus and Muslims should work together against the British, and that free India should be a federation of religious communities: Muslims were 'not to form a separate state'.

Events after the First World War strengthened calls for a combined movement against the British. However, with the collapse of the joint agitation following the abolition of the caliphate by the revolutionary Turkish National Assembly, and given also a number of developments within India, communal antagonisms were once more sharpened, though Gandhi at all times preached communal harmony, and Jinnah wished, it has been said, to cool communal passions down. Jinnah, however, finally parted company with Congress in 1920, ostensibly because of disagreement with Gandhi's policy of non-co-operation with the government. He then endured a period of political isolation.[26] For several years Muslim politics were in a state of division, even confusion. There was some drawing away from separatism in 1927, when Congress agreed to a package deal put forward by Muslim members of legislatures under which, *inter alia*, joint electorates were to be conceded in return for the attainment of other Muslim objectives; and the Muslim League itself split over the attitudes to be taken to the statutory (Simon) commission then in India. In 1929 Jinnah, on behalf of the by then reunited League, proposed his 'Fourteen Points', under which there was to be, *inter alia*, a federal constitution with guaranteed power for Muslims in majority, and safeguards in minority, provinces. These were rejected by Congress. Then came the events leading up to the India Act of 1935, with the British plan for a federation. But Muslim fears of Hindu domination in a new India were not calmed. After 1937 Jinnah set about reviving the Muslim League, capitalizing on a variety of grievances and of Congress activities that might be construed as foreshadowing a Hindu Raj, and endeavouring to overcome opposition among Muslims, particularly in Punjab (still dominated by the Unionist Party) and in Bengal (where, as in other Muslim-majority areas, the League fared badly in the 1937 elections). Jinnah's real base was in the Muslim-minority United Provinces.

The name 'Pakistan' had been invented in 1933 by a Punjabi student in Cambridge, Chaudhuri Rahmat Ali, for a fully independent Muslim territory which he regarded as the home of a separate nation and 'no part of India', to include Punjab, the North-West Frontier Province and Kashmir. It was not until 1937 that he advanced a similar claim for the Muslim majority areas of Bengal. On 23 March 1940, Jinnah having declared that the Muslims of India were a nation needing a homeland, the League passed what became known as 'the Pakistan resolution', declaring, *inter alia*, that '. . . the areas in which the Muslims are numerically in a majority should be grouped to constitute "independent states" . . .'. The wording of the whole resolution was not without vagueness and ambiguity, and has been seen as, in part, an attempt to influence opinion in the Muslim-majority provinces. Congress reactions were not completely hostile, much as its leaders subscribed to the one-nation theory. Gandhi said that, although he would oppose non-violently the partition thought to be implied, he 'could not forcibly resist the proposed partition if the Muslims really insisted upon it'.

Jinnah and the League went on to gain in strength (though still not dominant in Punjab till 1946), forged links with many new groups of Muslims, and did well in elections held in 1946. Congress, however, still sought to inherit an independent and undivided India.

By this time complex negotiations involving the (Labour) Government in London, the Government of India in New Delhi, Congress, and the League were in train. These negotiations were tortuous in the extreme; and cannot be summarized here. It must suffice to say that Jinnah became in effect 'The Sole Spokesman' for the Muslims and won the title Quaid-i-Islam ('The Great Leader') by which he is revered in Pakistan; that his presentation of the Muslim case went through many vicissitudes and apparent, and perhaps tactical, shifts of position and emphasis; and that there were hints that at some points Jinnah would have compromised with a solution short of partition – for example, by means of 'a way of achieving an equal say for Muslims in any all-India arrangement at the Centre'[27] (which, according to Jalal, for Jinnah at least might have been met by a confederation with non-Muslim states, *or* by a sovereign state). Congress opposed such solutions. Further negotiations brought only deadlock.

Mountbatten arrived as Viceroy and, finally but swiftly, and with a deadline to meet, came the plan for the transfer of power to two separate Dominions, India and Pakistan (the latter in two wings, West and East), with conditional provision for the partition of Punjab and Bengal, the actual boundary to be settled by commissions. This did not give Jinnah what he had apparently been playing for; but he, and Congress, agreed to the plan, both with reluctance (though for different reasons).

Thus did independence and partition come on 15 August 1947. To some citizens of Pakistan and pro-Pakistan scholars, partition was the inevitable result of history. To others, it appears as no more than a solution ultimately difficult, if not impossible to avoid. It is clear that to have included the Muslim majority areas in an undivided independent India would have left great tensions to be resolved in the new state. Yet the tensions were far from completely resolved by partition, if only because of the large number of Muslims left as a minority in India. It is particularly ironical that the

Muslims of UP, some of whom had played an important part in the evolution of separatism, were left outside Pakistan, to say nothing of the sizeable communities in West Bengal, old Hyderabad State, Kerala and elsewhere; while parts of Punjab and Bengal, whose Muslim politicians long resisted the League, fell to Pakistan and suffered partition from India.

But the narrative of separatism and partition is not yet quite told. Two days after the inauguration of independence, there came the award of the Boundary Commissions for Punjab and Bengal. Although accepted by the two new states, it increased communal tension and infuriated the Sikhs, who found their historic homeland bisected. Many Hindus and Sikhs attempted to leave West Pakistan for India, and Muslims to move from India to West Pakistan. In the highly-charged communal atmosphere of the time, large numbers of those who tried to move were massacred, Sikhs and Hindus by Muslims, Muslims by Hindus and Sikhs. The Punjab was the worst affected area, but there were parallel movements to and from East Pakistan. The two new countries were thus faced with an extremely difficult situation at the outset of their independence. Some 7.4 million people succeeded in moving from Pakistan to India, and 7.2 million from India to Pakistan.[28] Migrations of Hindus from East Pakistan continued in waves long after partition. The rehabilitation and resettlement of these vast numbers put a severe strain on the newly-independent governments.

The Boundary Commission for Punjab under Sir Cyril (later Lord) Radcliffe were given these terms of reference: 'To demarcate the boundaries of the two parts of the Punjab, on the basis of ascertaining the contiguous majority areas of Muslims and non-Muslims. In doing so it will also take into account other factors'. The Commission for Bengal, also under Sir Cyril, had similar terms of reference. The Commissions in fact drew boundaries that cut across lines of communication, and, in some cases in Punjab, separated the headworks of irrigation canals from the irrigated areas. But the economic and other consequences of partition in general and of the new boundaries in particular: the eruption of the Kashmir dispute and of other problems associated with the accession of princely states to India or to Pakistan; the whole embittered course of relations between India and Pakistan; and the severance of Bangladesh, the former East Pakistan, from the western wing – all of these matters belong properly to ensuing chapters.

4

POLITICAL DEVELOPMENTS WITHIN SOUTH ASIA SINCE INDEPENDENCE

This chapter will be concerned, first, with problems of internal political geography, that is, of the organization of territory within South Asia, beginning with one that was solved with relative ease and with stable results, namely, the absorption of the princely states into India and Pakistan; and moving on to an exception to this generalization – Kashmir, a bone of contention between the two countries to this day; and to a discussion of another dispute between the two neighbours, that regarding the Indus waters. We then turn to the internal territorial problems of Pakistan: tensions between East and West wings, leading to the secession of the former to become Bangladesh, and to other problems of potential secession, or at any rate of separatism or desire for increased local autonomy. (By secession I mean formal withdrawal from a country's political system; by separatism, a movement in favour of separate existence within such a system; by increased local autonomy, a higher degree of self-government within such a system; and by irredentism, the advocacy of political union with groups held to be similar on linguistic or other grounds but presently within a different country.) Corresponding problems will then be taken up for India. Discussion moves on to an examination of the political histories, systems and problems of independent India, Sri Lanka, Pakistan, Bangladesh, and of modern Nepal, Bhutan, and the Maldives.

THE ABSORPTION OF THE PRINCELY STATES

The Indian Empire came to include, in addition to its British-administered provinces, over 600 princely states, covering a quarter of the area and accounting for more than a fifth of the population, and varying from giants like Hyderabad and Mysore, as big as a European country, to tiny principalities covering a few square miles only. Each of them had some kind of treaty relationship with the British, and each recognized British suzerainty. From this suzerainty they were released at independence, leaving them theoretically free to decide their future allegiance. The twelve states falling within the borders of Pakistan (including Bahawalpur, Khairpur and the

47

states of Baluchistan) had Muslim rulers and largely Muslim peoples; they readily joined Pakistan. The situation facing India was a much more difficult one for a number of reasons: the size and tradition of quasi-independence of the larger states; the range of internal economic and social conditions, from relatively progressive and advanced states like Mysore to those with overwhelmingly tribal populations owing allegiance to rulers whom they invested with divine qualities (as in the case of Bastar, north-east of the Godavari in the eastern Deccan); and states where the ruler's religion was different from that of the mass of his subjects.

However, through the vigorous and not particularly kid-gloved activities of the Congressman, Sirdar Vallabhbhai Patel, ably assisted by a remarkable civil servant, V.P. Menon, most of the rulers were persuaded to accede to the Indian Union.[1] In return they were guaranteed their privy purses and personal privileges, later abolished by Mrs Gandhi. Thus ended what many Indians had come to regard as an anachronism and what was certainly the result of the arresting, by the British, of a kaleidoscopic political map made up of very many fragments which had earlier only fallen into a static pattern for relatively short periods, when some great ruler had given a higher degree of internal unity. Certainly too, the simplification of the internal political map in the early months of independence was a great achievement, and provided the base from which further change was to proceed. Some princely territories were simply absorbed into surrounding states (I shall use a capital initial letter for the units that made up, or make up the Indian Union). Some were grouped with neighbouring princely territories to form new units that were to prove no more than transient: for example 'Pepsu' (Punjab and East Punjab States Union), Madhya Bharat (mainly in the Malwa Plateau) and Vindhya Pradesh (in hill areas south of eastern Uttar Pradesh (UP)). Except for Hyderabad, Jammu and Kashmir (to receive special treatment in a moment), only Mysore retained its identity when Patel had completed his activities in 1947 and 1948.

Difficulties arose, however, over Hyderabad, the small state of Junagadh (Junagarh) in the Kathiawar peninsula, and Jammu and Kashmir. The Nizam of Hyderabad was a Muslim supported by a Muslim governing elite and ruling over a mainly Hindu population, and conscious both of his member-ship of an ancient dynasty and of the special relationship he had always had with the British. He understood that, landlocked as his state was, he could not ignore developments in India, but nevertheless he vacillated, hankering after independence. Initial negotiations ended in a standstill agreement to run for a year, during the course of which the Congress organized agitation; some of the Muslims of Hyderabad formed an armed body called the Razakars; and in the mounting disorder the Communists got control of two districts. Before the year was over further negotiations broke down and Indian troops marched in to take over the state in what was officially described as a 'police action'. Pakistan was incensed by this action against a Muslim ruler and his supporters.

One should also recall the annexation by India of Goa and other Portuguese territories after military action in December 1961, contrasting with the cession by France of its Indian territories after peaceful negotiations; and add that the little Himalayan state of Sikkim, which previously had a 'special protected relationship' with India (as earlier with the Indian Empire) became a state of the Indian Union in May 1975.

Junagadh, like Hyderabad, had a Hindu population and a Muslim prince who, though his state was set entirely in Indian territory, acceded to Pakistan. India marched in and held a plebiscite which resulted in a vote for union with India, which then ensued. Pakistan protested without effect. The Kashmir situation was much more complicated and long-lasting.

THE KASHMIR PROBLEM

The state of Jammu and Kashmir covered in 1947 over 80,000 sq. miles of highly varied population and terrain. It included Jammu, peopled mainly by Hindus and Sikhs; Kashmir proper, around Srinagar, with a mainly Muslim population; Ladakh, a high plateau area bordering Tibet, with a sparse, Mahayana Buddhist population; and the Frontier Districts of the north-west, including Baltistan and Gilgit, with mainly Muslim peoples. Before independence both the Muslim League and allies of Nehru and Congress were active in the state; as partition drew near, the former favoured accession to Pakistan, the latter to India. Faced with the same choice as his brother princes, the Maharaja vacillated, and seems to have thought, like the Nizam, of independence. Meanwhile a revolt broke out, first in Gilgit, then in Baltistan; its leaders declared independence from the Maharaja and allegiance to Pakistan. Soon there was rebellion also in south-western Kashmir proper, where Muslims declared 'Azad Kashmir' (Free Kashmir), and established links, which India accused Pakistan of encouraging, with tribesmen in the North-West Frontier areas of Pakistan who proceeded to invade Kashmir proper. At last, by now thoroughly beleaguered and with invaders very near Srinagar, the Maharaja acceded to India. Indian troops were sent in and the tribal incursion halted. The Indian Army was deployed against Azad Kashmir as well as against the tribesmen, and soon Pakistani regular forces were brought in. So, lamentably soon after independence, the two new Commonwealth countries were engaged in hostilities, which in fact continued until, after protracted negotiations, a ceasefire was agreed. The revised ceasefire line or 'line of control' dating from 29 July 1949 but later modified, has become a *de facto* international frontier separating the Indian State of Jammu and Kashmir ('Indian-occupied Kashmir' to Pakistan) from the 'Pakistan-held' territory of Azad Kashmir. To this day neither country recognizes the jurisdiction of the other over the former territories of the Maharaja. A plebiscite, agreed to in principle by India, has never been held. In 1957 the Kashmir Assembly declared the state to be an integral part of

India, without prejudice to India's claim to land beyond the ceasefire line; while the state has a special status, with more than the usual degree of autonomy, under the Indian Constitution.

The Kashmir imbroglio has poisoned relations between India and Pakistan (see Chapter 5) who, in fact fought their second war (that of 1965) largely as a result of tensions in Kashmir, though there had been a separate dispute over boundaries in the Rann of Kutch, involving armed clashes, in 1964–5. There were rumours of wars yet again in 1979–80; and soon increasing and still continuing violence in Kashmir proper on the part of a number of factions pressing, some for an independent state, some for secession to Pakistan. Suppression by Indian troops led inevitably to reactions in Azad Kashmir, Pakistan and the Islamic world more widely. A number of factors have contributed to the more recent turmoil: for example, and not necessarily in order of importance, the increased militancy of Islam generally, largely related to the Iranian revolution and to the growth of fundamentalism; the example, real or supposed, of Mojaheddin ('freedom-fighters') in Afghanistan, some of the more militant of whom were reported active in Kashmir in August 1992; the rise of chauvinistic Hinduism and an increase of Hindu – Muslim tension in India; more troubled relations between the Government of India and that of Jammu and Kashmir; and in that State, as elsewhere in South Asia, the discontents of youth affected by poverty, unemployment and neglect and in turn ready recruits to a culture of violence.

The Kashmir dispute is basically a clash between two principles: that of self-determination, here the right of Muslim majority areas contiguous to Pakistan to accede to it; and that of the right of a recognized ruler, the Maharaja of Jammu and Kashmir, to accede to a territorial union, that of India. In invoking the second principle India has been held to have the law on its side (though it did not recognize that principle in the cases of Hyderabad and Junagadh). Two points remain to be added. First, there has been the strategic importance of Kashmir *vis-à-vis* both the USSR and China (see Chapter 5). And what was serious in the early years of the imbroglio, and might become serious again, is the position of Kashmir in relation to the headwaters of the Indus river system.

THE INDUS WATERS DISPUTE

The construction of major irrigation canals dependent on the tributaries of the Indus (Jhelum, Chenab, Ravi, Satluj (Sutlej) and Beas) and the establishment of colonization schemes in the Punjab, the land of those five rivers, was one of the great achievements of the British period. The Indo–Pakistan frontier was so drawn (with an eye primarily to contiguous Muslim majority districts) as to leave the headworks of certain canals vital to Pakistan in Indian territory: notably the Madhopur works on the Ravi and the Firozpur (Ferozepur) works on the Satluj. The threat to Pakistan became greater with developments in Kashmir, for the Indus, Jhelum and Chenab pass through Indian-held territory there. Following the hostilities in Kashmir, the supply of water from Madhopur and Firozpur was indeed cut off. As a consequence, it is said, cultivation failed on a million acres of land in Pakistan. Nehru intervened to settle this particular incident; but the general question of water-ownership and water-use that lay behind it became a matter of bitter controversy between India and Pakistan. In the event, and after protracted negotiation, the dispute was settled following an initiative taken by the World Bank.[2] The result was the Indus Waters Treaty signed on 19 September 1960, and a permanent Indus Waters Commission. Under the treaty, and in broad terms, Pakistan is assigned the waters of the Indus, Jhelum, and Chenab, and India the remaining three rivers. To make Pakistan's canals independent of these three rivers, massive works were constructed at great expense within Pakistan to take Indus and Jhelum water boldly across country. India, with Ravi, Satluj and Beas water no longer needed in Pakistan, has been able to construct new works designed to irrigate large areas including the colonization schemes in Haryana and Rajasthan.[3] All this is often held up as a positive measure of co-operation between India and Pakistan, who have quarrelled so violently over so much else (and indeed it is): and as a shining example of international helpfulness, for finance for new works came from the World Bank and from a number of western countries, as well as from India and Pakistan. But there is no gainsaying the fact that an economically optimum solution to the utilization of the Indus waters would produce a very different pattern, without the expensive inter-river works (notwithstanding that these were foreshadowed by the British Triple Canals Project (1905–17), with its bold transfer of water from the Jhelum to the Chenab and on to the Ravi to feed the Lower Bari Doab Canal). The simple fact is that a costly solution was forced by the layout of the new political boundaries in relation to the rivers and their dependent canals. Moreover, India's Indira Gandhi (Rajasthan) Canal, made possible by the allocation to it of Satluj and Beas waters, is itself a doubtful proposition in economic terms;[4] though significantly it provides along the border with Pakistan a belt of irrigated and settled country to replace desert and semi-desert that was ideal tank country.

EAST PAKISTAN BECOMES BANGLADESH

Ian Stephens, a great friend of Pakistan, wrote in 1968:

> Regarded simply as land . . . Pakistan seems about the craziest political structure that mankind could have devised. . . . For though she is a unitary national state . . . she nevertheless consists of two entirely separate blocks of territory placed about 1,000 miles apart – and with another, bigger and stronger, and more often than not unfriendly block, India, sandwiched between.[5]

Was, then, the secession of East Pakistan in 1972 merely a matter of strain related to physical separation, in spite of the distance-reducing effects of modern technology? Even if one accepts that the strain was increased by geographical contrast without the complementarity that may go with it (of the sort that classical French geographers emphasized in the case of their country); and was compounded by the cultural and linguistic differences between Bengalis and West Pakistanis: even then one still would have too simple a view of the forces at work.

There has, indeed, been considerable controversy on this matter. Some Pakistanis, and staunch western friends like L.F. Rushbrook Williams, see the separation as basically the result of discontent fostered and fed by an India never reconciled to partition, which armed guerilla bands of Bengalis, and, on 20 November 1971, mounted a full-scale invasion.[6] Rushbrook Williams sees India's hands freed to take military action by the Indo–Soviet Treaty of August 1971; and the USSR, indeed, as lurking only just off-stage. He further sees western liberal opinion, for the most part firmly behind Bangladesh and its 'liberation', as deluded by clever Indian propaganda, particularly about Pakistani atrocities in its eastern wing, and about the magnitude of the refugee problem faced by India.

But the truth involves a number of further factors resulting from insensitivity, incapacity and other failings on the part of successive governments of Pakistan. Some of these are, indeed, admitted by some western writers favourable to Pakistan, though they usually failed, if writing in the 1960s, to see secession as likely. Ian Stephens did, however, say in 1968 that 'Permanent disgruntlement of the East Wing would be Pakistan's death-blow.[7]

And disgruntlement there was a-plenty, and with reason. Because of the relatively low number of Bengali Muslim public servants and military men at partition, many officials and soldiers were brought from West Pakistan: some of these looked down on Bengalis and were insensitive to their feelings. Industrialists and businessmen, too, came in from the West wing, replacing Hindus who went to India on partition, and became dominant. Again, Bengalis are strongly attached to their language, and rightly proud of the very notable literature in it. Jinnah's wish that Urdu should be the national language of the whole of Pakistan was interpreted overzealously, and the language question became a burning issue. A government decision in 1954 to recognize Bengali also as a national language came too late. The original capital was Karachi; and the idea of declaring Dhaka a 'second capital' also came too late: the associated symbolic buildings remained uncompleted at secession. East Pakistanis, too, came to believe, with justification, that it was their wing, rather than the West, that earned foreign exchange and government revenue from which the West wing, with its industrialization, benefited more than they did. Some Dhaka economists proclaimed that their wing was being exploited by the West wing as if it were a colonial possession.

Discontent grew when military rule came to Pakistan in October 1958, and broke out in student unrest and political violence. An underground movement became ever stronger (with what degree of encouragement from India remaining controversial). Matters came to a head when, in November 1970, the relief of distress and loss caused by a devastating cyclone in the Bengal delta was directed with many inadequacies from far away Islamabad; and even more when in the following month a general election at last took place and resulted in a landslide victory for the Awami ('Peoples') League, Sheikh Mujibur Rahman's party, in the East; Z.A. Bhutto's Pakistan People's Party (PPP) won in the West. Thus were politics polarized between the two wings when at last they surfaced from under military rule. The President and Chief Martial Law Administrator, General Yahya Khan, announced on 1 March 1971 that the National Assembly would not meet as previously announced; this precipitated violent demonstrations in East Pakistan. The military regime then harshly clamped down there amid cries of 'Punjabi imperialism', proscribing the Awami League and arresting Sheikh Mujib. Millions of refugees fled to India. A combination of guerilla activity and Indian intervention led eventually to the surrender of the Pakistani forces in the East, the release of Mujib, and early in 1972 the independence of Bangladesh (not recognized by Bhutto, who had taken over the Presidency from Yahya Khan, till 1974).

East Bengal, then, in which the Muslim League had its original home in 1906, became Bangladesh and seceded from Pakistan. It is, perhaps significant, if not prophetic, that East Bengal was excluded from Iqbal's 'Northwestern Muslim State' and from Chaudhuri Rahmat Ali's original delineation of Pakistan (though he envisaged most of Bengal and Assam as a separate Muslim fatherland under the title 'Bang-i-Islam', and Hyderabad as a third, 'Usmanistan').

Now L. Ziring asserted in 1977 that 'To many Pakistanis, the sense of nationalism remains rudimentary', provincialism being a stronger force, and leaders proving incapable of engendering national purpose.[8] Leaders, he says, have provoked 'subnational controversy rather than promoting ideas of national interdependence which might well have avoided the agony of Bangladesh'. To provincialist, secessionist and separatist tensions remaining in Pakistan after the severance of Bangladesh we shall turn shortly. Meanwhile, what of such tensions within Bangladesh itself?

Superficially at any rate, Bangladesh is fortunate in having an overwhelmingly Bengali population with a strong sense of identity; though, in spite of waves of migration to India since partition, there are still Hindu minorities, members of which, especially of the 'clean' castes, tend to be distrusted, while Hindu – Muslim tensions in India may be reflected in Bangladesh, as in 1990; and the so-called 'Biharis', Urdu-speaking Muslims from India, presented a difficult problem because of their language and because, at the time of secession at any rate, they were thought to have pro-Pakistani sympathies (late in 1991 some 250,000 of them were still trapped in camps in Bangladesh). Some strategically-located tribal groups in the Chittagong Hill Tracts east of the delta formed a political movement and broke out in armed insurrection. Tribal grievances sprang from Mujib's abolition of the British protective legal status and later from government-organized Bengali settlement in the Hill Tracts, for which such emollient measures as development schemes have failed to compensate. There have been reports of repression but in 1992 hopes of a solution.

POTENTIAL SECESSION AND SEPARATISM IN PAKISTAN

Secessionist and separatist tendencies in post–1972 Pakistan exist in all three provinces peripheral to the politically and demographically dominant Punjab, that is, in the North-West Frontier Province (NWFP), Baluchistan and Sind.[9]

It will be remembered that Pushtu speakers are to be found mainly along the North-West Frontier, including parts of Baluchistan, and straddle the boundary with Afghanistan. They include turbulent Pathan tribesmen who harassed the Raj as it pushed up into the hills and, in 1893, drew the Durand Line as the frontier with the buffer-state of Afghanistan, dividing the Pushtu-speakers (Pushtuns or Pakhtuns) so that approximately two-thirds were on the British side of the line and one-third on the Afghan. Idiosyncratic political behaviour merging into separatism has long been characteristic of the area. In 1947, however, a referendum in the North-West Frontier Province (NWFP) resulted in an overwhelming vote in favour of joining Pakistan; but Abdul Ghaffar Khan, the 'Frontier Gandhi', boycotted the referendum. He persistently proclaimed that the Pakhtuns formed a nation deserving a territory of its own, Pakhtunistan, and consistently agitated against Pakistan's rule for long years, from exile in Afghanistan. The government of Afghanistan wavered from time to time, but often supported the idea of Pakhtunistan, while, inevitably, some saw the hand of India in the Pakhtunistan movement. More recently dangerous complications have followed events in Afghanistan, from Soviet influence and occupation to conflict following Soviet withdrawal; and from repercussions in the NWFP itself involving floods of refugees, warring Afghan factions, and massive flows of arms. Successive regimes in Pakistan have over the years done something to try to placate their tribesmen, not least by measures of economic and educational development. But sometimes the stick was more evident than the carrot, particularly under Z.A. Bhutto, and tribal reactions were inevitable. It is clear that for the foreseeable future Pakistan will have to deal, not only with the age-old turbulence and lawlessness of the Frontier, but also with the possibility of a secessionist-irredentist movement fomented from outside the boundaries of Pakistan.

Baluchistan has sometimes been included in the claims for a Pakhtunistan.

But Baluchi separatism and secessionism deserve a paragraph to themselves because the Baluchis are a distinct group, to say nothing of the Brahui and other minorities. Like the Pakhtuns, Baluchis also live across the Pakistan frontier, in Iran as well as in Afghanistan. Britain largely ruled Baluchistan through tribal chiefs, most of whom acceded to Pakistan. The post-independence history of Baluchistan has been very turbulent, oscillating for the most part between armed revolt and uneasy peace. Between 1973 and 1977 there was a particularly serious insurgency. Many factions and many complex strands have been involved. But sentiment in favour of greater autonomy or secession have never been far beneath the surface. The more militant elements hanker after a 'Greater Baluchistan' to include Baluchis in Afghanistan and Iran, and appear to have gathered strength with time. It has been claimed that their agitation was encouraged from Iraq, keen to strike a blow at Iran. Events in Afghanistan have clearly done nothing for stability. Pakistan has, as in the NWFP, used both the carrot and the stick.

The ethnic problems of Sind are quite different. Here Sindhi fears of Punjabi domination have been compounded by immigration from other Provinces and, even more, that of large numbers of Mohajirs (refugees), Urdu speakers formerly resident in India, who have come to dominate business in the cities, replacing Hindu Sindhis who fled to India. They formed their own political organization, the Mohajir Quaimi Movement (MQM). Only about 60 per cent of the population of Sind is Sindhi speaking. There is some support for secession, and marked regional separatism; and there have been riots and other disturbances, particularly severe and destructive of life from the mid–1990s (though, as we shall see, by no means all are inter-ethnic or regionalist). These, like other regional troubles, interact with national political events to be recounted later: they contributed to, but did not end with the downfall of Benazir Bhutto, and have intensified more recent conflicts.

Discussion in this section has been in terms of the four provinces: Punjab, Sind, the North-West Frontier Province and Baluchistan, which perpetuate the British pattern but may also be seen as some reflection of linguistic distributions and regional sentiment. It should be noted, however, that from 1955 to 1971 Pakistan was ruled as 'one unit' which clearly did nothing to meet demands for provincial autonomy.

SECESSION, SEPARATISM AND REGIONAL AUTONOMY IN INDIA

Chapter 2 has sufficiently stressed the importance of language in reshaping the political map of India since independence, while we have already emphasized continuing agitation over Kashmir.

However, something must also be said about: (1) recent violent agitation for the secession of, or complete autonomy for Punjab, notwithstanding its separation from Haryana; (2) the forces that revolutionized the map of north-east India and continue to generate tensions and disturbances, especially among tribal people; (3) territorial problems of tribals elsewhere, especially in connection with Jharkhand; (4) wishes to dissect linguistic States on non-linguistic grounds, notably in relation to the Telangana region of Andhra Pradesh; and (5) cases where political feeling in linguistic states has involved a desire for increased autonomy, as in Tamil Nadu.

The violent agitation in Punjab is almost entirely conducted by factions and parties within the Sikh community, seized as it is with a strong sense of identity, yet fearful of absorption by Hinduism; and conscious that it has a bare majority in Punjab as constituted in 1966. The Akali Dal, an exclusively Sikh party, has a long history of seeking greater autonomy for Punjab. But Sikh politics took a more complex and violent turn in the 1980s, some groups working for secession as an independent Khalistan. The Government of India's response to violence and terrorism culminated in June 1984 in an assault on the Golden Temple at Amritsar, the Sikh's holiest shrine. Some five months later there followed, in reaction, the assassination of the Prime Minister, Indira Gandhi by Sikh members of her bodyguard (followed in turn by a deplorable pogrom against Sikhs in Delhi). These violent events were in part related to Mrs Gandhi's practice of intriguing in state affairs, a new twist in Centre-State relations. But violence and secessionism in Punjab did not end with the death of Indira Gandhi, nor with pacifying gestures by her successors. If anything terrorism, especially against Hindus, intensified. In spite of this, an election was held in December 1991 in Punjab, which had been under presidential rule since May 1987. A state government was formed, followed by a government victory in municipal elections, and welfare and development policies announced. But the new chief minister has declared secession 'not negotiable'; and it seems inevitable that violence and political instability will continue, and indeed spread to areas like the UP Tarai where Sikhs are numerous.

The political fragmentation of Assam has been a remarkable feature of post-independence India.[10] Assam at independence consisted of the former British province of the same name, with its princely states and 'excluded districts' in tribal territories, but less Sylhet District, which became part of East Pakistan. But today Assam State proper has become little more than a strip along the Brahmaputra. Around it in a horseshoe run a series of territories small in area and population: Arunachal Pradesh, the former NEFA (North-East Frontier Agency), ruled as a Union Territory until it became a State in 1987; Nagaland, a separate State since 1963, but not without unrest; Manipur and Tripura which graduated from Union Territory to full Statehood in 1972; and Meghalaya, 'the abode of the clouds', in the Khasi, Garo and Jaintia Hills which, after much agitation, became an autonomous State within Assam in 1970 and a full State in 1972. Finally, running south between Manipur and Tripura is Mizoram, first a Union Territory and then a State from 1987 (see Map 1). All of the 'mini-States' are dominated by 'tribal' populations, though there has been substantial Bengali immigration into Manipur and Tripura, as into Assam. Why have such substantial concessions been made to tribal feeling in north-east India? Though there remain irredentist calls for a Greater Nagaland (there are Nagas in Assam State and in Burma) and for autonomy for several tribal peoples left in Assam State (Bodo groups in particular have been restive and violent in pursuit of separatist aims); and though there has been repression as well as appeasement.

First, note the extreme vulnerability, yet strategic importance of north-east India, especially given tensions between India and China. The whole region is joined to the rest of India by an absurdly narrow neck, only some twenty miles wide at one point, running from West Bengal round the north-western extremity of Bangladesh. Not surprisingly, then, India is extremely sensitive to restiveness within its north-eastern region.

Secondly, though some of the hill tribal peoples became Hinduized (particularly in Tripura and Manipur), most of them retained their own religions till western impact: animist in most areas, Mahayana Buddhist in the NEFA. Social distances between plainsmen and hillmen are therefore greater here than in many more Hinduized parts of India.

One of the important effects of British intervention in the hills was the entry and success of Christian missionaries, so that the proportion of Christians is high among many tribal groups (though not in Arunachal): nearly 100 per cent among the Mizos, 50–60 per cent among most Naga groups. With the missions came literacy and an educated middle class with western ideas who spearheaded movements for autonomy and statehood (or even secession) in independent India.

That Indian policy has not altogether succeeded is shown by continuing unrest, complex in detail but fundamentally separatist in essence, among some elements in most States of the north-east; and compounded by border disputes (especially between Nagaland and Assam) and by resentment of settlement by outsiders, particularly Bengalis (who form over 60 per cent of the population of Tripura). Some Bengalis react by showing anti-tribal hostility.

What of the Assamese in their rump of a valley State? Some of them look to India for protection, particularly against Bengali immigration. The plains and hill slopes of Assam were very sparsely peopled in the early nineteenth century;[11] and provided ample scope for tea plantations, which brought in immigrant labourers, some of them Bengali, who stayed to settle as peasant cultivators, and were joined later by numerous Muslims from East Bengal who tended to cultivate more intensively than the easy-going Assamese, to become more wealthy, and to arouse great jealousy. In Assam State, indeed, something of a siege mentality developed. Since 1986 this has been over-shadowed by a renascent secessionist movement, the ULFA (United Liberation

Movement of Asom, as its members wish to call their State after the Thai people who settled in the thirteenth century). The ULFA has conducted violent operations which affected tea plantations as well as Indian military forces, and in November 1990 led to the declaration of President's Rule. The ULFA was later declared illegal. The troubles in this strategically-important State seem set to continue and to be met by a combination or alternation of repression and appeasement.

Of tribal movements in India outside the north-east, as yet unsuccessful in securing autonomy, one of the most notable has been the Jharkhand movement. Founded and sustained by a colourful educated Munda, Jaipal Singh, its objective was the formation of a new State in tribal areas in south Bihar, extending also into West Bengal and Orissa.[12] Various concessions were wrung from the Bihar Government. In April 1992 came a proposal for a Jharkand General Council, but limited to South Bihar and most unlikely to satisfy demands for Statehood in what has become a complex situation. Similar but so far less notable tribal movements and parties, led almost invariably by educated middle-class men, have sprung up in other parts of India, and made even less successful demands for Statehood. And more may arise in future as a new generation of educated tribal leaders is able to capitalize on grievances against intrusive plainsmen in such areas as that known as Dandakaranya, where Madhya Pradesh, Orissa and Andhra Pradesh meet.[13]

Of a quite different character is the Telangana movement. When in 1953 the state of Andhra Pradesh was formed to unite Telugu-speakers in the old Madras Presidency and in Hyderabad State, it was feared by leaders in Telengana, the dry, poor and backward Telugu-speaking part of Hyderabad, that their region would be disadvantaged compared with coastal Andhra, the Krishna-Godavari delta region, with its more sophisticated people.[14] Accordingly, Congress politicians from the two regions reached a 'gentle-man's agreement' to the benefit of the people of Telengana: particularly the use in Telangana of revenues collected there; the reservation of educational facilities, and, above all, of jobs in government service. But later there came a long, tangled dispute, and demands for a separate Telengana State (which had, in fact, been conditionally recommended by the States Reorganization Commission). The dispute provoked a violent reaction from coastal Andhra and from its people resident in Telengana, and to calls for a separate (coastal) Andhra State.

It has been pointed out that there is a fundamental clash here between political regionalism, with its claim for special treatment for local people, and the 'homeland principle', that an Indian has a right to live and work anywhere in India; and that pressure for reserved education and employment is related to the enormous growth since 1960 of educational facilities and, in consequence, of the numbers of those clamouring for jobs, particularly jobs in the government service.[15] The Telengana dispute was in fact settled without the concession of separatism by the Prime Minister, Mrs Gandhi, in 1973, 'one of the few successes of . . . the new pattern of center-state relations' (P.R. Brass).

Not surprisingly, other parts of India have had their regional discontents and separatist movements, notably Vidarbha, in eastern Maharashtra (whose claim was indeed also recognized by the States Reorganization Commission); the Saurashtra (peninsular) area of Gujarat; and the poverty-stricken east of UP.

Again, there is the phenomenon of the pre-existing and stable linguistic State, or of dominant groups within it, working for a much higher degree of autonomy: in particular, that of the DMK (Dravida Munnetra Kazhagam) in Tamil Nadu. This important political party had its historical roots in the anti-Brahmin movement and the Justice Party (see Chapter 3). It fed on the strong emotions generated in Tamil Nadu by the Tamil language and its defence against 'Hindi imperialism', the alleged attempt by the north to impose its language on the south. In the early 1960s the DMK was frankly secessionist. The DMK later split, and now comprises a strong group of parties confined to Tamil Nadu (in spite of the wider 'Dravida' in its title); dedicated to securing the maximum degree of State autonomy within the Union; and with populist programmes having a wide appeal in the State. 1983 saw another regional party (Telugu Desam) returned to power in Andhra Pradesh.

Akali Dal in Punjab is also, of course, a strong party confined to one State which presses for more autonomy (see above). The Communist Party of India (Marxist) in West Bengal, and some groupings in Kerala, are also strong on State autonomy, for ideological reasons.

THE INDIAN POLITICAL SYSTEM

We now turn from these territorial issues, some of which threaten the dismemberment of India and which when overstressed become what Rajni Kothari called 'an almost paranoid concern with stability'.[16] India has always attracted prophets of doom, but also those who have set it on a pedestal as 'the world's greatest (or, at any rate, 'biggest') democracy'.

The Indian political system is simple in its constitutional arrangements; almost overwhelmingly complex and confusing in party politics and political behaviour at its various levels.[17] Morris-Jones has written of the 'diverse and in principle competitive languages of politics': the modern westernized and, one may add, secular language of the constitution, of higher administration and judiciary, of the upper levels of political parties; the 'traditional' language of caste and community 'in a host of tiny worlds'; the 'saintly' language of Gandhi (or some of Gandhi) and of his disciples like Vinoba Bhave and Jayaprakash Narayan.[18]

India, we have seen, has a federal constitution. At the centre, in New

Delhi, are the President, the two houses of Parliament: the Lok Sabha, 'House of the People', directly elected by universal adult suffrage, and the Rajya Sabha, 'Council of the States', which has twelve members nominated by the President and other members elected by elected members of State legislatures; the Prime Minister and Union Cabinet; and the great ministries and departments. In each State capital there is a governor (appointed by the President on the advice of the Prime Minister); an elected assembly and an Upper House; a Chief Minister and a Council of Ministers and the State bureaucracy.

Some subjects are reserved to the Centre, some to the States; some are concurrent, that is, the concern of both, though central laws override State enactments. Central subjects include foreign affairs and defence, communications, banking, and customs. State subjects include agriculture, land revenue, law, order and local government, and education (though there are departments at the Centre for some of these subjects, notably agriculture). The concurrent list includes trade, industry and economic planning. The Centre has a source of financial strength in the fruit of 'growth' taxes like income tax, corporation tax, and customs and excise, though some of these do not grow as much as they might because of widespread evasion. States collect land revenue, sales taxes and a number of other imposts. Land revenue contributes a diminishing proportion of the national budget, taking Centre and States together, while repeated proposals for an agricultural income tax, which would be a State matter, have broken on vested agricultural interests. The Centre, then, tends to be more financially powerful than the States.

The President (who is elected by members of both Union Houses and of State legislatures, sitting together) has considerable powers, including the declaration of a state of emergency under threat of external attack or internal disturbance; and the institution of 'presidential rule', under which a State government can be suspended if the President is satisfied that its rule cannot be maintained in accordance with the constitution; its powers are then exercised by the President, those of the State legislature being 'exercisable by or under the authority' of Parliament in New Delhi. The use of these powers, nearly always exercised on the advice of the Prime Minister, have occasioned considerable controversy. 'Presidential rule' has so far, however, always eventually issued in elections and the restoration of parliamentary government in the States concerned.

A federal constitution is, prima facie, a means of containing regionalism, even separatism, though not secession. But for a federal structure effectively to contain strong separatist tensions demands a certain flexibility and a bargaining capacity. It is certainly possible to maintain that India has shown these qualities, for example, in conceding linguistic States. Problems like those of Kashmir and Punjab are clearly much more intractable.

The constitution provides for an independent higher judiciary which has played an important national role, not least in larger constitutional questions.

General elections to the Lok Sabha must take place every five years, though the House may be dissolved within a shorter period. Elections at the prescribed intervals duly took place until the regular pattern was broken by The Emergency of 1975, of which more in a moment, and by subsequent events. But elections have survived: a situation not unlike that in Sri Lanka up to 1983 at any rate, but very different from that in Pakistan and Bangladesh, to say nothing of the host of 'new' states outside South Asia which have fallen under autocratic rule of one sort or another. Many Indians who speak the language of 'modern' politics take pride in this, even if they stand abashed by The Emergency. Their liberal friends in the West (or some of them) see it as a feather in India's cap. Why has India been able to maintain general elections? At this stage I quote Anthony Low, who invokes such factors as the long history of electoral procedures in India; the dominant role of the Congress Party (shortly to be explored), with its 'modern' ideology, initially at any rate; forces working against military rule (of which more later); and the constitutional means, just outlined, for dealing with 'emergencies' but for which, Low maintains, 'democracy' in India might well have collapsed.[19] His emphasis on the last factor would not win universal approval.

State legislative assemblies (Vidhan Sabha) are directly elected for five-year periods, the constituencies being, of course, much smaller than those for the Lok Sabha. State upper houses are called Legislative Councils (Vidhan Parishad) and filled by a combination of election and nomination. State elections began by taking place when constitutionally due, though later the pattern became distorted by periods of presidential rule and by other factors.

Turning to the main political parties that have contended in the several general and State elections, the scene was not surprisingly dominated for many years by the Congress Party that had grown out of the Indian National Congress and whose history under the Raj was sketched in Chapter 3. In fact, the way through the jungle chosen here is to narrate the story of the Congress Party from independence to the time of writing in 1992, with subsequent paragraphs on other parties not otherwise sufficiently mentioned in passing.

Congress suffered growing pains in developing from a movement into a party. But in the days of Nehru its sway was so generally undisputed that India was often described as a one-party state. Moreover, it could rely on the loyalty of the bureaucracy, the 'steel frame' that the Raj had built (albeit on earlier foundations) and on the armed forces and police; and Nehru is one of those figures in history to whom the overworked word 'charismatic' is aptly attached. In the three elections held in Nehru's lifetime Congress held over 70 per cent of the seats in the Lok Sabha; and a total of over 60 per cent of those in State assemblies.[20] In neither case, however, did Congress ever secure a majority of votes cast. It is thus possible to exaggerate the dominance of Congress, even in the earlier years of independence. But the opposition to it was diverse and fragmented.

As we have seen, Congress before independence was 'not a political party with a single ideology'.[21] In becoming a political party it continued to shelter a wide spectrum of opinion under its spreading umbrella, from Nehru-style socialists, hasty for economic change, to Gandhian idealists, looking back to a supposedly idyllic Indian past that should be a model for the future; from wealthy entrepreneurs and rural 'big men' to ardent champions of the nationalization of the commanding heights of the economy, if not the collectivization of agriculture. But until his death in 1964 the dominating figure of Jawaharlal Nehru held Congress together as a single party; and Nehru saw to it that many, though not all potentially divergent factions were kept under the Congress umbrella. In so far as there was a consensus it was left of centre like Nehru himself.

When Nehru died in 1964 the succession passed smoothly to Lal Bahadur Shastri. But faction and divergence within the party surfaced in the two succession crises that followed Shastri's death in 1966. Towards the end of the Nehru era new leaders, more 'traditional' than 'modern' in political language, had become powerful in the States. A number of these became influential at the Centre. They were known as the syndicate. One of them, Kamaraj, had much to do with the smooth succession of Shastri. But by the time of Shastri's death the position of Kamaraj was weaker, factional division had become evident, and there was a contest between Indira Gandhi (Nehru's daughter) and Morarji Desai, won by the former, rather than a carefully contrived consensus. Dissension, infighting and open defection increased. Mrs Gandhi eventually relieved Morarji Desai of the Finance portfolio, whereupon he resigned as Deputy Prime Minister. Mrs Gandhi then nationalized certain banks: this may be seen as a dramatic vote-catching move, not a lurch to the left. However, it served to isolate the more conservative Morarji and the syndicate. The Congress then split, Morarji and the syndicate heading Congress (O) ('O' for 'organization'), and Mrs Gandhi and her supporters Congress (R) ('R' for 'ruling'). In the 1971 election Congress (O) was routed and reduced to a rump. Mrs Gandhi's great election slogan was *'gharibi hatao'* ('out with poverty'), again more populist rhetoric than ideology or firm intent. Then, on the crest of a wave following the defeat of Pakistan in the Bangladesh war, Mrs Gandhi's 'new' Indira Congress (I) seemed assured in its dominance.

But to a considerable extent this was an illusion; it was certainly not based on the same firm foundations as her father's. R.L. Hardgrave said that Indira Gandhi destroyed the boss-structure of the old Congress, but did not replace it with an effective system linking the Centre with the local party units.[22] By 1974 six chief ministers had been 'eased out of office' and six States were under President's Rule; an exercise of centralized power which grievously weakened the former responsiveness of the Centre to pressures from below.

By 1974, it was clear that Mrs Gandhi's government could not pretend to dispel poverty. While many factors in the situation were well beyond the control of any government, Congress under Mrs Gandhi was still an umbrella organization, with many factions and individuals hostile to radical economic and social change. Inflation, the oil price-crisis and crop failures all fuelled discontent, especially among urban people in low income groups.[23] Then, in 1975, Mrs Gandhi was convicted in the Allahabad High Court of offences in the previous general election. There soon followed, on 26 June 1975, ostensibly because of a gathering threat to internal security, probably more because of the Allahabad judgement, the declaration of The Emergency.

The Emergency warrants a paragraph to itself, novel event that it then was in Indian political life. Under The Emergency many members, major and minor, of opposition parties were imprisoned (including Morarji Desai); civil liberties were suspended and the press muzzled by censorship (though that did not stop people from talking freely to those whom they trusted); and there were many abuses of police powers. It is notorious that a family planning campaign involved enforced sterilizations. And, under the energetic if misguided leadership of Mrs Gandhi's son, Sanjay, slums were cleared in Delhi and elsewhere at a great cost in human suffering. The Emergency alienated many members of the urban elite, particularly intellectuals previously sympathetic to the 'new' Congress but imbued with liberal notions of representative government, and rigidly authoritarian as the Government of India had overnight become. How far alienation spread to other classes was less clear.[24] In January 1977, to the surprise of many observers, a general election was announced, and The Emergency was relaxed; and freedom of speech, publication and assembly were restored.

In the election of March 1977 Mrs Gandhi's party won only 28 per cent of the Lok Sabha seats: Congress was at a low ebb. The new government was in fact formed by the Janata coalition and headed by Morarji Desai. There came a period of recrimination between factions within Congress and a further split in January 1978. Mrs Gandhi and her Congress (I) claimed to be the 'real' Congress, and broke away from an apparently larger group (Congress (S), later (U)). In doing so she once again proclaimed a populist slogan over the heads of the squabbling politicians; this time it was 'forward to socialism'. In August 1979 came the breakup of the Janata coalition and the fall of the government that it had formed. There ensued a general election that resulted in an overwhelming victory for Congress (I) and its allies: a two-thirds majority in the Lok Sabha. In elections for nine State Assemblies held in May 1980, Congress (I) captured power in eight, with absolute majorities in all of these and two-thirds majorities in six. So once more the Congress, or *a* Congress came back to power at the centre and in a significant number of States, confounding commentators who thought that The Emergency had bitten so deeply into popular consciousness that Mrs Gandhi and her Congress, however it was lettered and whatever its rhetoric, were lost for ever. Once again there was controversy over the reasons for Mrs Gandhi's comeback: those frequently cited were the poor performance of the Janata government and the flagrant divisions within it.

But, as we have seen, in June 1984 Mrs Gandhi was assassinated. Her son Sanjay, groomed for political leadership, had already been killed when flying an aircraft. The 'dynastic succession' to the Prime Ministership (as some would have it) passed to her other son, Rajiv, who ironically had worked as an airline pilot. First impressions of him were largely favourable: a 'Mr Clean' who promised reforms in many spheres (not least the economy). But allegations of corruption mounted, as did protest movements over a number of grievances. Instead of linkages to the country he tended to rely on a circle of advisers, while over a number of matters he proved impetuous. In the General Election of November 1989 Congress won only 189 seats in the Lok Sabha: less than a majority but still the biggest party. The National Front won fewer seats but counted (initially at any rate) on the support of other parties, particularly the Bharatiya Janata Party (BJP, a right-wing Hindu chauvinist group) and a Communist-led Left Front. Rajiv, honourably, conceded defeat.

The National Front was itself a coalition whose main architect was Devi Lal, a dominant politician of the 'Hindi Belt'. Its main motivation was the negative one, of defeating Rajiv and Congress, while a prominent component was the (or at least 'a') Janata Party, led by S. Chandra Shekar, a 'moderate socialist', whose origins lay in the ill-fated Janata coalition of 1967. But the leader from the National Front who became Prime Minister was neither Devi Lal nor Chandra Shekhar but Vishwanath Pratap Singh, sometime Rajiv's Finance Minister, who campaigned for clean and incorrupt government; and who duly won a vote of confidence in the Lok Sabha.

V.P. Singh's ramshackle coalition, ranging from the BJP to Communists, had a brief and chequered life. In addition to factional infighting (that with Devi Lal being prominent), and the by-now routine accusations of ministerial corruption, Singh faced wider and more dangerous crises. One of them concerned mounting Hindu–Muslim conflict, centred largely on, but not confined to a disputed mosque in Ayodhya, near Lucknow, whose site was also claimed by Hindus, supported by the BJP. The other was the result of Singh's efforts to increase reservations of jobs for the lower castes (perhaps partly on principle, partly to widen his political constituency) which sparked off widespread and ugly caste riots. Eventually Singh resigned on 9 November 1990.

There followed the appointment of Chandra Shekhar as Prime Minister but this time with the support of Congress and Rajiv Gandhi, who had turned down the invitation to form a government, probably hoping, following an election, to head a Congress with a commanding majority rather than a party, albeit the largest one, in a hopelessly hung parliament.

But this was not to be. The Chandra Shekhar government, beset with much the same problems as V.P. Singh's, and eventually losing Rajiv's support, resigned on 6 March 1991. A general election was called for May 1991. Then Rajiv was assassinated while campaigning near Madras by a woman who blew herself up in the act: she was probably a supporter of Tamil separatists in Sri Lanka, a number of whom were subsequently accused.

The result of the general election was once again to return Congress as the largest party in the Lok Sabha but without an overall majority. The new government was headed by P.V. Narasimha Rao, who had been elected Congress President after Rajiv's widow had declined to take on the office. The new Prime Minister was a septuagenarian politician with a record of solid and unspectacular service. His position in Parliament was strengthened after a number of by-elections in November 1991. He has, however, and to the surprise of some observers, a number of positive achievements to his credit, including those in foreign and economic affairs to be reported in later chapters; but he has also been seen as weak and indecisive in handling the Ayodhya dispute and its bloody aftermath. His future is uncertain. And the future of the Congress Party itself, now perhaps more riven by faction than ever, must also remain uncertain: it is not easy to see how it can regain its former dominance.

As for principal parties other than Congress, enough has been said of parties with an exclusively regional base, though more may yet arise.

There are parties to which the label 'right-wing' has been applied. Thus the Swatantra Party was founded in 1959 as a party of 'free enterprise' just after Congress had taken one of its apparent lurches to the left and declared itself in favour of co-operative joint farming.[25] Swatantra has contained some strange bedfellows: from former princes, landlords and urban businessmen to distinguished liberals. In the 1967 elections it was, with 44 seats, the largest party in the Lok Sabha but has since suffered eclipse. It merged in the Lok Dal in 1974.

Swatantra has never deserved the label of 'Hindu communalist party', but this is not true of the Jan Sangh, in spite of its protestations to the contrary, nor of its parent, the RSS (Rashtriya Swayamsevak Sangh). Jan Sangh has, for example, stood for cow protection and hostility to Pakistan. Its fortunes and alliances have varied over the years. It was a component of the Janata coalition from 1977 to 1979, of various state coalition governments and of Delhi city administrations. Its descendant is the Bharatiya Janata Party (BJP) of the 1989 coalition and later (including the formation of State governments

Rajasthan, in UP, Himachal Pradesh and Madhya Pradesh): of this party, with its disturbing and anti-secular Hindu chauvinism, we have assuredly not heard the last.

The Lok Dal, formed in 1974 by Charan Singh (later caretaker Prime Minister between the fall of the Janata government in 1979 and the formation of Mrs Gandhi's new administration in 1980), embodied, in addition to Swatantra and a number of regional parties, the Samyukta Socialist Party. Charan Singh's own power base lay among UP middle peasants of the so-called 'backward classes' (pp. 10–11). In 1980 the Lok Dal was the second strongest party in the Lok Sabha, with 41 seats, under George Fernandes, labour leader and socialist. It was associated with the National Front, a main element in the government following the 1989 general election. The Lok Dal is very doubtfully dubbed either a right-wing or a left-wing party. Earlier, the Janata Party was an even broader and, as it proved, unstable coalition of the Jan Sangh, Lok Dal, Congress (O) and Fernandes' Socialist Party, joined also by the Harijan leader Jagjivan Ram and his Congress for Democracy. In a different guise, it played a prominent part in the National Front of 1989. Clearly we are here in a world of shifting alliances rather than of stable parties with firm ideological alignments. This is also true of other 'socialist' groups.

Ideological ascriptions have a truer ring when applied to the Communist Parties, of which the chief are the Communist Party of India (CPI), the Communist Party (Marxist) (CPI(M) or CPM) and the Communist Party (Marxist–Leninist) (CPI(ML)). The CPI was generally seen as pro-Moscow (now a difficult stance following the breakup of the Soviet Union), and willing to co-operate with the 'national bourgeoisie' to 'complete the anti-imperialist, anti-feudal, democratic revolution'. It formed that rare species, an elected Communist government, in Kerala in 1958. Its strength lies in that state and in West Bengal. CPI(M) split from the CPI in 1964, holding an ideological position farther to the left. It also is strong in Kerala and West Bengal. The two Communist parties came together in coalition governments in these States in 1967, but more usually have engaged in bitter dissent. The CPI(M) has been the dominant party in coalition in West Bengal since 1977. The CPI(ML) was formed in 1969 to be openly Maoist and revolutionary, supporting terrorist and guerilla movements of the sort that have come to be called 'Naxalite' after an uprising in the Naxalbari area of West Bengal.

Of parties that included 'socialist' in their title, the Samyukta Socialist Party suffered factional conflict and later merged with the Praja Socialist Party. One faction then entered the Lok Dal, which in turn joined the Janata coalition. Another, Fernandes' Socialist Party, entered Janata direct. The story has thus been, and remains, one of faction, divisions, recombinations and coalitions.

This simplified catalogue of political parties serves to establish that the Indian party political system is clearly very different from that of most western democracies: from the phenomenon of single-party near-dominance in the heyday of Congress to the shifting patterns of coalitions and of factional splits and recombinations. (One politician in Haryana is said to have crossed the floor four times in a single day, a form of athleticism that would today be curbed by legislation.)

Faction in Indian politics has for many years attracted the attention of western researchers, sometimes to the annoyance of Indians.[26] Faction is indeed a characteristic of, though assuredly not unique to, Indian politics at all levels, central, State and regional; and extends down to the highly local factions, often cutting across caste strata, that are a characteristic of the Indian village. Are shifting political factions, at higher levels, then, but an upward reflection of an age-old village phenomenon, a translation into the language of 'modern' politics of 'traditional' modes? Some factional splitting is ostensibly ideological and completely 'modern': for example, the schisms to which the Marxist Left the world over is prone, though some communists and socialists, clearly, have entered into apparently unholy combinations to secure an advantage. But faction often seems to be a matter of a leader carrying 'his men' with him from one party into another for perceived short-term advantage. Of course, this is not a practice exclusively Indian, but it does seem in India to be a matter of a 'traditional' mode being used in a 'modern' constitutional frame.

Traditional modes have generally grown more prevalent as vernacular-speaking politicians became of greater importance to those operating in central politics because of the following they command lower down the political system. Indeed 'traditional' politicians like Kamaraj and Devi Lal themselves came to operate at the Centre, learning 'modern' tricks like electoral populism; and are able to bargain for support with lower level politicians because they can offer them the fruits of office (power, influence and affluence) and the patronage that goes with office (jobs for relatives, contracts, preferential access to credit or fertilizer). In this game the bureaucrat holds an uneasy position, tending, at the lower levels at any rate, to find himself in the pocket of the local political 'big man'.

To what extent can the rhetoric of national leaders appeal over the heads of such a man to the actual voter – or how far can there be a wave of spontaneous repugnance amongst the actual electors at, say, The Emergency? And there are related questions: to what extent are Harijans, or Muslims, or other disadvantaged groups, able freely to exercise a protest vote? And to what extent is there substance in claims that India is 'developing' politically, that genuine participation has spread to an even wider populace, particularly with the institution of Panchayati Raj (the system of elected local government at district and subdistrict ('block') level)? Here there is still a dearth of sufficient objective information. It is not enough to write about Indian elections from a desk in the big city. It is somewhat better to canvass voters on their expectations from elections (whether Panchayat, or

State, or national) and on the way they voted, as has indeed been done,[27] but still unsatisfactory because the method may not elicit how voters have in fact behaved, especially if they were subject to intimidation. The truth is only likely to emerge from dispassionate participant observation as understood by anthropologists. Yet in the nature of things it is a rare observer who is able to report freely on actual election behaviour in villages, or in most towns for that matter; if he does so report, there is the vexing question of the honest anthropologist, 'How typical is my village'? It was long the established orthodoxy that in many places 'vote banks' were an established feature: caste leaders or leaders of factions might be able to deliver a block of votes to a candidate. In such cases the genuine wishes of, say, Harijans were unlikely to be met. Trapped in the cellular structure of caste and village, the frustrations of the really disadvantaged Indians tended not to find expression at national, or even state level (except, perhaps, through social workers and sympathetic newspapers). For, in spite of (or even because of) Panchayati Raj, the dominant castes still dominated, by and large. Hence there were severe limitations on the extent to which national leaders could mount a populist appeal over the heads of politicians and 'big men', particularly to disadvantaged rural groups. And doubt had to be cast on claims that this party or that attracts 'the Harijan' or 'the Muslim' vote. But more recently there has been evidence that in some areas, especially in the south, populist measures by State governments have eclipsed vote banks and to some extent liberated the poor from fear of those who ran them. And there is also the fact that there have been waves like that of November 1989 which seem genuinely to reflect public opinion.

But there have been many reports of electoral malpractices, particularly in UP and Bihar, that effectively disenfranchise some, at any rate, of the village poor, and also react adversely on the role of women in elections.[28] These are reported to include the falsification of electoral rolls; the suborning of officials; the location of polling booths in places to which Harijans would fear to come; the 'capturing' of booths; the stuffing of ballot boxes with false papers, genuine voters being excluded; false counting; and various forms of intimidation and violence, including murder. It is clear that in some areas at any rate violence and sudden death have increased at election time (scores of murders were reported from Bihar during the State Assembly elections of February 1990), and that, in a society with massive unemployment and underemployment, there are all too many men eager to be hired as members of a mob or of a gang of intimidators. The late Sanjay Gandhi and his Youth Congress were by no means innocent in this respect. It may further be maintained that, as in other polities past and present, powerful people are all for elections because they know how to manipulate them to their advantage by devices including populism; while election malpractices, including violence, are by no means an exclusively Indian phenomenon.

Now some have seen the Indian political system, particularly as it developed under dominant Congress rule, in terms of bargaining between factions whose power and patronage flowed down through the linkages with lower levels (whence pressures and information flowed upward), as a means by which the country, with its diversity, its cellular structure, its tendency to separatism, its local and regional 'loyalties' was held together as a functioning political system. Blair referred to this as 'the pluralist paradigm', and has cited Hardgrave, Kothari, Morris-Jones and others as political scientists who in their several ways subscribed to it.[29] In Kothari's hands the paradigm became almost teleological: here was an instrument, wielded by Congress, *designed* to keep India together in a way that eluded less fortunate lands, and yet not by autocracy but by democracy, ever flowing down through 'political development' to remote places and lowly strata of society. Some pluralists failed to appreciate that vote-banks and electoral malpractice are hardly politically developmental; others changed their tune because of The Emergency. In favour of the pluralist view, it is indeed remarkable that India up to the 1970s had contained separatist pressures so successfully, most if not all of the potential separatists showing willingness to play the game according to the all-India rules, constitutional, neo-Congressional or whatever, while the one-time separatist reappeared later as a loyal ally of the central government, bargaining, patronage and claims of legitimacy having done their work. But whether the poor and the landless, the urban Muslims and the tribals would be better or worse off if India had not hung together is another matter.

The fact that India has so far contained separatism does not of course mean that it will always do so. The 1980s clearly witnessed both increased separatist and secessionist strains and a diminishing ability on the part of Union governments to contain them while, writing in 1992, Punjab. Kashmir, and the widespread triumph of ethnicity over ideology throw heavy shadows of doubt over the future. Nor does the fact (surprising to many who ask why the poor do not revolt against their evident disabilities) that India so far has not undergone a revolution, agrarian, or urban, or both, mean that it will never do so. But (as was the case in the remote past) caste and its acceptance, cellular structure, and patterns of dominance may well see to it that revolts are local and extinguishable rather than widespread and all-consuming.

Equally (or almost equally), the fact that India (like Sri Lanka but unlike Pakistan and Bangladesh) has so far not come under a military autocracy does not mean that it will never do so. But a number of factors work against a military coup: the vast size of the country; the fact that officers in a number of different command areas would have to concur if military rule was to be more than local (and local rule would carry the risk of armed forces elsewhere moving in to suppress it); the relatively small size of the forces compared with the populations and the fact that in some sense the central government has a legitimacy, or has been able to claim a legitimacy, never so widely accorded to governments in Pakistan.

THE POLITICS OF SRI LANKA

When the Crown Colony of Ceylon slipped quietly into independence on 4 February 1948 its constitution echoed Westminster. King George VI remained King of Ceylon; there was a bicameral legislature; and a Cabinet under a Prime Minister, initially D.S. Senanayake.[30] In 1972 Ceylon became the Republic of Sri Lanka, with a single chamber. A more drastic change came in 1977: a constitution giving the President wide executive powers. Up to 1977 Sri Lanka held general elections at the proper intervals. But in 1983 President J.R. Jayawardene, who had been re-elected for a second term, held a referendum as a result of which the life of Parliament and of his United National Party (UNP) government was prolonged for six years. This, with other acts, such as the proscription of certain political parties following riots in 1983, led to charges of authoritarianism and fears for the future of democracy and of civil rights. In December 1988 an election was held to decide a successor to Jayawardene. The successful candidate was Ranasinghe Premadasa, previously Prime Minister. Mrs Bandaranaike, widow and successor to S.W.R.D. Bandaranaike after his assassination, came second. In February 1989 the UNP was successful in parliamentary elections accompanied by lamentable violence.

It was the UNP under D.S. Senanayake, at first in alliance with Bandaranaike and his Sinhala Maha Sabha, that had carried Sri Lanka into independence. Both groups consisted almost entirely of the upper and middle classes educated in English; and, though dominated by Goyigama, also contained members of the three coastal castes (see Chapter 2) and of the 'Ceylon Tamil' community. From 1948 to 1956 the UNP remained in office. On the death of D.S. Senanayake his son Dudley had become Prime Minister, to be succeeded by his nephew, Sir John Kotelawala. (The initials UNP were held to stand for 'Uncle and Nephew Party'.)

But in 1956 there was a traumatic general election. The UNP was reduced to a rump. The incoming government was formed by an alliance, the Mahajana Eksath Peramuna (MEP), the dominant party in which was Bandaranaike's Sri Lanka Freedom Party (SLFP). Another component was the Viplavakari Lanka Sama Samaja Party (VLSSP), a Trotskyite group. Bandaranaike had also negotiated a no-contest pact with the LSSP, also Trotskyite, and with the Communist Party. Leaving for a moment parties depending mainly on the votes of 'Sri Lankan' Tamils, the Ceylon Workers' Congress (CWC) is both a trade union and a political party representing Indian Tamil estate labourers who have become Sri Lankan citizens (see p. 88). Since 1977 its sole representative in parliament, S. Thondaman, has been an ally of the UNP and a minister. For some years there was a tendency for the UNP and SLFP to alternate in office, so that some authors thought in terms of the firm establishment of a two-party system.[31] But this view is no longer tenable if only because of the UNP's grip on office since 1977: not that Premadasa's position is as secure as his predecessor's: for example, in August 1991 an effort was made to impeach him, with allegations of corruption and other abuses – though the move failed.

Early on the UNP was seen as manifesting conservative, non-ideological, pragmatic attitudes. SLFP governments, on the other hand, were generally seen as well to the left of centre; though it is simplistic to think of the SLFP as an ideology-based left-wing party. Ideology is not surprisingly more clearly defined in the case of the Communist Party and of the Trotskyite parties).[32]

Violence at election times is nothing new in Sri Lanka, though it has increased and become more murderous, as have other forms of violence. In 1971 there was an armed insurrection during the time of an SLFP government. Groups, mainly of unemployed Sinhala youth, joined in the Jatika Vimukti Peramuna (JVP) (People's Liberation Front), which at first professed a somewhat muddled Marxist ideology and scorned the existing leftist parties.[33] The JVP caused much violence and damage, and has survived the killing of some members by government forces. It has adopted a Sinhalese-chauvinist, anti-Tamil and anti-Indian stance in response to the worsening ethnic conflict.

The ethnic conflict has been a dominant theme from the 1980s and is a primary source of violence and death. Much has been written on the history of the Sinhala–Tamil tensions that form the main element in the conflict.[34] It will suffice here to start in 1956, when Bandaranaike fought the election largely on the language issue, promising to make Sinhala the national language and to support Buddhism. He found ready sympathizers, ripe for politicization, in Sinhala rural areas, among groups frustrated by the advantages in increasingly scarce employment held by English speakers, including many 'Sri Lankan Tamils'. Bandaranaike benefited too from a wave of Buddhist revivalism, for language, religion and 'nation' have long been inextricably intertwined in Sinhalese eyes. Tension culminated in the communal troubles of 1958. There were further violent disturbances with varying proximate causes, in 1977 and 1983, the last involving organized attacks on Tamils and much damage to the economy.

Tamil reactions to 'Sinhala only' and to other measures seen as anti-Tamil were at first non-violent, though there was a trend in Tamil parties to move from alliance with the UNP (Tamil Congress) to advocacy of a federal solution (Federal Party) to secessionism (Tamil United Liberation Front, TULF). But from 1972 there arose armed movements among Tamil youth, notably the Liberation Tigers of Tamil Eelam (LTTE), fighting for the independence of the 'Tamil homeland' in the Northern and Eastern Provinces (NP and EP) (though provincial boundaries are a colonial construct). One Tamil claim is that successive governments have planted Sinhalese colonists in the 'homeland', parts of which Sinhalese are apt to claim are their traditional territory. There are also many Muslims in EP who have been drawn into the troubles. Claims and counter-claims have surrounded killings by the LTTE and its factions on the one hand and the security forces on the other, with the JVP also involved. The truth is hard to find.

The ethnic troubles have international dimensions. On the one hand, the Sinhalese, 'a majority (within Sri Lanka) with a minority complex' (*vis-à-vis* the large Tamil population in South India), are ever fearful that Sri Lanka Tamils will enlist help from across the water (where, indeed, terrorists have trained; though they are less likely to do so following the assassination of Rajiv Gandhi). Moreover, the Government of India has a concern with political repercussions in Tamil Nadu as well as with Indian Ocean strategy in general and Trincomalee's magnificent harbour in particular (see Chapter 5). In July 1987 Jayawardene and Rajiv Gandhi signed a comprehensive accord intended to bring peace to the troubled areas of Sri Lanka. NP and EP were to be granted autonomy under a single provincial council. An Indian Peacekeeping Force (IPKF) was sent; but became heavily involved in fighting with the LTTE. The accord was opposed by many Sinhalese, including Premadasa, and (with violence) by the JVP. The IPKF, at first welcomed in NP, became unpopular there too. Eventually the last IPKF troops left in March 1990.

Efforts to resolve the ethnic conflict peacefully (which go right back to the Bandaranaike-Chelvanayagam Pact of 1957 on the language issue) have so far failed, as have all-out military solutions. Killings, revenge killings and disappearances of individuals continue, and the plight of the populations affected, and in particular of refugees, in and from NP, is pitiful. Many fled to Tamil Nadu. Those of us who knew Sri Lanka in the first years of independence and earlier and who conceived a great affection for this beautiful country and its people, cannot but feel a great sadness. And there is no sign of a peaceful end to the civil war or of its wider repercussions.

I conclude by referring to two conceptual matters applicable in a much wider context than that of Sri Lanka in this age, when so many ethnic issues are to the fore. First, the Sinhalese and the Sri Lanka Tamils should be seen as those who, in the present generation, identify themselves as such. It is an unwarranted assumption that all of these Sinhalese (or Tamils) are descended exclusively from people who, in past years, centuries or even millennia similarly identified themselves. Secondly, with this unwarranted assumption about Sinhalese or Tamils over time goes another about the two communities in space: namely, that their respective 'homelands' have always been such. For place-name and other evidence suggests that over the centuries Sinhalese and Tamil settlement has ebbed and flowed over at least parts of northern and eastern Sri Lanka.

THE POLITICS OF PAKISTAN

If independent India has maintained parliamentary government, albeit seasoned with emergencies and violent events, it has been very different with

Pakistan, in which periods of uneasy democracy have alternated with long spells of military rule (from October 1958 to April 1971 and from July 1977 to the elections of 1988).[35] Pakistan started with many handicaps. India inherited far more of the British administrative machine; Pakistan had in many respects to start from scratch. True, it possessed at the outset a remarkable leader, Mohammed Ali Jinnah, the first Governor-General and President of the Constituent Assembly and of the principal political party, the Muslim League. But Jinnah died in September 1948; and Liaquat Ali Khan, the first Prime Minister, was assassinated three years later. India adopted its constitution (which, with amendments, has survived ever since) in 1950. Pakistan did not adopt a constitution until 1956: new constitutions followed in 1967 and 1973. In October 1958, following turmoil, came the first period of military rule under General Ayub Khan, who assumed the office of President and Chief Martial Law Administrator (CMLA). In 1959 Ayub promulgated the Basic Democracies Order, under which electorates of 400 or so voters formed a 'primary constituency'. Eight to ten of these elected a Union Council or Town Committee, termed a 'Basic Democracy'. Above this was a hierarchy of councils, to each of which members were elected by the level next below. There was also at all levels provision for nominated members. The scheme did not outlive the Ayub regime.

Ayub was succeeded in March 1969 by General Yahya Khan, under whom were held the critical elections of December 1970 which led (p. 53) to the victory of Mujibur Rahman in East Pakistan and of Z.A. Bhutto's Pakistan People's Party (PPP) in the West; and so to the events that culminated in the secession of Bangladesh. In December 1971 Yahya Khan handed over the Presidency of Pakistan to Bhutto, who also became CMLA; four months later martial law ended. Under the 1973 constitution Bhutto became Prime Minister. The March 1977 elections were won by the PPP: there were allegations of widespread rigging. In July 1979 a new martial law regime assumed power under General Zia-ul-Haq. Bhutto was later executed for alleged involvement in a political assassination. In February 1985 a general election was held, but political parties were banned. Martial law, however, ended the following December. In May 1988 Zia was killed in a 'plane crash' never officially explained.

The President, Ghulam Ishaq Khan, ordered a general election to be held in November: it resulted in a narrow victory for the PPP under Bhutto's daughter, Benazir, who became the first woman Prime Minister in an Islamic country. But in provincial elections the PPP only won an assured position in Sind, and that in an alliance (which soon collapsed, and was indeed reversed) with the Mojahir Quaim Movement (MQM). Punjab fell to the Islamic Democratic Alliance (IDA), a group of nine parties, the two largest being the Muslim League and the Sunni fundamentalist Jamaat Islam. Benazir faced the severe regional problems discussed above, to say nothing of the parlous state of the economy, the Kashmir imbroglio, and the need to take heed of the strength both of the military and of various shades of Islamic opinion. But she and her government survived until 6 August 1990, when they were dismissed by the President amid cries of ineptitude, inaction, nepotism and corruption. A crucial factor appeared to be her refusal to give the army the powers they demanded in Sind. A caretaker government took the reins during a highly fraught period. The elections of October 1990 gave the IDA a majority in parliament over the PPP though, as often happens, the turnover in seats was greater than that in votes. There were claims and counter-claims of electoral malpractices. Nawaz Sharif, a Punjabi industrialist, became Prime Minister, and survives in office at the time of writing (September 1992), though beset with many severe problems: in particular, the worsened situation in Sind, compounded *inter alia* of violence, banditry, corruption, and conflict with and within the MQM (MPs from which resigned from his alliance in August 1992; as did the Jamaat Islami over changes in policy towards Afghanistan: see Chapter 5). There is also dissatisfaction with government handling of the crisis caused by the terrible floods of September 1992. Benazir Bhutto, it has been reported, is pressing for new elections and seeking an accommodation with the army, which is in turn discontented with the Nawaz Sharif government, an unstable and eroding coalition indeed. In a kaleidoscopic scene yet another military coup cannot be ruled out.

So much for the narrative. By way of further analysis reference will be made to politicians and parties, even though they were not countenanced under Zia; to questions involving the concept of an 'Islamic State'; and to the position of the armed forces. We must also bear in mind the secessionist and separatist forces discussed earlier in this chapter.

Turning to political parties in Pakistan, the Muslim League was, of course, the embodiment of the movement that, under the leadership of Jinnah, carried the Muslim majority provinces of British India into partition and independence. It invites comparison with the Indian National Congress. But such a comparison would be very superficial, for all the long history of the League (from 1906). Congress had its roots in all of the regions of what was to become the Republic of India; and a particular claim to legitimacy. The League had its strongest roots in UP, and either left them there to wither after partition, or tore them up and transplanted them to Pakistan. It was the Unionist Party, not the League, that had been strong in Punjab; while the 'Frontier Gandhi' favoured Congress. The loss of Jinnah and Liaquat in quick succession bore hard on the League. From 1954 or so onwards, in fact, the Muslim League in Pakistan went into rapid decline, though factions of it joined the IDA and fought subsequent elections, including that of 1990.

Not much need be said of most other parties. After the death of Liaquat Ali Khan, and until the coup of 1958, party politics were mainly a matter of shifting alliances (of which the IDA may be seen as one). There was, of course, the Awami League, with its roots in East Pakistan and role, under

Mujib, in the secession of Bangladesh. More must be said about the PPP and its founder, Zulfikar Ali Bhutto, who first sprang to prominence in 1958, when he joined Ayub Khan's Cabinet as 'a young man new to politics'.[36] He resigned over the Tashkent agreement with India and was for a time imprisoned by Ayub. Having rejected the possibility of establishing a 'forward bloc' within the Muslim League, he founded the PPP in 1967. In the 1970 elections the PPP won 60 per cent of seats in West Pakistan; but all save two represented either Punjab or Bhutto's native Sind. His later career and execution have already been described. His memory lives on, kept green by his widow and daughter, Benazir.

Bhutto may be described as charismatic, and his appeal as populist. His democratic credentials may be suspect, given his rise to power under an authoritarian regime and his attempt to eliminate all opposition, within and without the PPP. His policy statements, it has been said, 'represent a blend of Islamic, socialistic, and liberal democratic values and vocabulary'.[37] To some extent, his success came from nailing many different planks to his election platform like Bandaranaike in Sri Lanka. When in power, however, Bhutto did initiate programmes of land reform and economic development (see Chapter 6).

And what of Benazir Bhutto? She inherited her father's charisma, party and populism, and showed considerable courage. Her relative liberalism had wide appeal outside Pakistan, partly because of her opposition to some aspects of fundamentalism. But she is not above wheeling and dealing in the current complex and unstable situation.

As for the Islamic dimension in the politics of Pakistan, Chapter 3 has shown that it was specifically Muslim separatism that led to the birth of Pakistan as an independent country and introduced the controversy about the nature of an Islamic polity. In all the troubled post-independence history of Pakistan, rulers and politicians have proclaimed that Pakistan is an 'Islamic State' or 'Islamic Republic'.[38] And there has been acute controversy and a spate of writings, basically because of the difficulty of reconciling, on the one hand, 'modern' notions like democracy or socialism and of divided loyalties between ethnicity and religion, to say nothing of the needs of a twentieth-century economy, with, on the other hand, Islamic concepts of the state and of divine law in all their variety (variety, that is, given the many schools of thought within Islam, Sunni and Shi'iah, modernist, traditionalist and fundamentalist). Almost all politicians, not least Bhutto, equally with military rulers, have, with greater or lesser sincerity, vied with each other in proclaiming their devotion to Islam, often in a desire to legitimize themselves. However, Benazir Bhutto proclaimed her intention to remove the legal disabilities of women, and inevitably aroused hostility. The devout Zia-ul-Haq went further than most leaders in proposing or enacting legislation in tune with conservative Islamic thought. But even under Zia it would be a false emphasis to read into Pakistan's situation the Shi'ite fundamentalist revivalism that has played such a spectacular part in the Iranian Revolution, and elsewhere in the Muslim world.[39] The majority of Pakistanis are, of course, Sunnis. In the spiralling interaction of religion and politics Sunni–Shi'iah tensions have increased.

During the 1980s powerful military organizations within Pakistan favoured fundamentalist factions within the Afghan guerillas; but by March 1992, in a context of government support for UN peace efforts, this appeared to be no longer so.

The politics of Pakistan cannot be understood without reference to the special position of the military. The British Raj included, under the head of 'martial races', many groups in what is now Pakistan. There is still a strong pride in military service in many parts of the country, and numerous ex-servicemen in such areas as the Punjab Canal Colonies. The Pakistan army has always represented a higher proportion of the population and taken a larger slice of the budget than has India's. Moreover, the establishment of military rule in Pakistan does not face such formidable obstacles as it would in India (cf. p. 69), and is aided by the landlord-dominated social structure with its authoritarian ethos. As in India, however, the higher judiciary has often shown a commendable independence and resilience.

POLITICS AND GOVERNMENT IN BANGLADESH

Bangladesh, as we have seen, started its independent existence under the leadership of Sheikh Mujibur Rahman, whose Awami League had swept the polls in the 1970 elections in East Pakistan.[40] It did so again in a general election under a new constitution that declared its foundation to be 'high ideals of nationalism, socialism, democracy and secularism'. But behind the brave words lay a country devastated by war and riven by faction. Law and order held but a tenuous grip and corruption was rife. The economy was in a poor shape, and some new measures of nationalization were ill-judged. The morale of the public service was low.

A period of great instability and uncertainty began in 1975. In August came a military coup in which Mujib and most of his family were killed. Soon there was a counter-coup, hard on the heels of which came another military coup whose impetus was captured by General Ziaur Rahman. In June 1978 he was endorsed in a nation-wide plebiscite as executive President, under a constitution providing for a single-chamber national assembly. In the elections to that assembly in February 1979 Zia's Bangladesh Nationalist Party (BNP) won a massive victory. But in May 1981, after a score of unsuccessful coup attempts, Zia was assassinated. Abdus Sattar, a judge, was constitutionally elected President, only to be overthrown by yet another military coup in March 1982, as a result of which Lt Gen. Hossain Mohammed Ershad became Chief Martial Law Administrator, and suspended the constitution. He assumed the Presidency in November 1983; was declared victor in presidential elections in May 1986 and March 1988; and held office until his resignation in December 1990.

Why did Ershad survive so long (by Bangladesh standards)? One of the most important reasons was undoubtedly his handling of the army, within whose many factions were hotbeds of coups and attempted coups. The main groups were: 'freedom fighters' who had taken part in the 1971 conflict and tended to be pro-Indian; 'repatriates' who were in West Pakistan in 1971, and tended to be anti-Indian; and officers recruited since independence. The first group, itself varying in ideology and in other ways, had by 1982 been greatly reduced in numbers, partly through executions after failed coups against Zia. Ershad sought to win over the army by increasing pay, by giving it a share in government, administration, and the police, and in other ways. Not surprisingly, rumours of consequent corruption gathered thick and fast. Ershad had, further, tried to widen his power base by gestures to Islamic sentiment (declaring Islam the state religion in 1988) and to linguistic nationalism; while his creation of rural councils gave him linkages with the villages. His own political party, Jatiya, dominated Parliament. To this catalogue of military populism may be added a declared aim of 'democratization', though few members of the politically conscious Bangladeshi elite were impressed by the various elections, reliably reported as manipulated and marred by intimidation.

Ershad's rule led to recurrent protest on a large and often violent scale, particularly in Dhaka: for example, by riots, demonstrations, strikes and boycotts of Parliament by opposition members. There was mounting resentment of Ershad and of the army more generally, though this protest was long ineffective, at least partly as a result of the divided state of the opposition parties. The two principal opposition parties were the Awami League, led by Mujib's daughter, Sheikh Hasina; and the BNP, led with its allies by Zia's widow, Begum Khaleda Zia (some will scent dynasty again, and all will note Muslim women in politics). Minor parties included the splintered Left.

Ultimately the level of protest reached such a pitch, with bloodshed, that Ershad declared a state of emergency, and on 4 December 1990 he resigned. An interim government was set up under the Chief Justice. Subsequently Ershad was convicted of corruption and arms offences, and imprisoned.

After an election in February 1991 the BNP emerged as the largest party in the Assembly, with the Awami League in second place and Ershad's Jatiya Party third. The BNP formed a government with support from the fundamentalist Jamaat Islami. By mid–1992 there was mounting criticism of the government, whose future was by no means assured.

Indeed, given the turbulent and bloody history of Bangladesh and its horrendous problems, one clearly cannot conclude that the future of democracy itself is assured and that there will not be yet more violence and yet another coup.

POLITICS AND GOVERNMENT IN NEPAL, BHUTAN AND THE MALDIVES

Nepal remains a monarchy. But the royal power and its relationship to other political forces have varied, especially since 1951, and even more since 1990.[41] In 1951 the Ranas, originally hereditary 'prime ministers' who had come to hold a monopoly of power, were toppled by a palace revolt (a revolt by, not in, the palace) in which the king (Tribhuvan) was aided by India. In 1959, a constitution, with a constitutional monarchy, was proclaimed, and multiparty elections held in which the Nepali Congress emerged as the dominant party. But in 1960 the king (Mahendra) suspended the constitution and jailed many politicians: he then established a party-less, five-tier 'panchayati' democracy reminiscent of Ayub's scheme in Pakistan. A referendum in 1980, attended by student riots, barely confirmed the choice of party-less panchayats as opposed to party pluralism. Elections to panchayats were held in 1986. But there followed, particularly in 1990, many demonstrations in support of parliamentary democracy, the Nepali Congress and Left parties playing a prominent part. The king (Birendra, who had reigned from 1972) removed the ban on political parties and appointed a new 'Cabinet' from among their members. In November 1990 the king renounced absolute power to become a constitutional monarch in a plural democracy. Elections were held (quietly, it was reported) on 12 May 1991. The Nepali Congress won 110 of the 205 seats. Calm seemed to prevail, but by April 1992 there were once again demonstrations in Kathmandu, expressing discontent with the Nepali Congress. Uncertainty has returned.

Bhutan also remains a monarchy. Since the 1950s a number of political reforms have been made. There is a national assembly, elected, but on a very limited franchise, with the king in effect acting as prime minister. In 1990 there were demonstrations in support of 'political freedom'. There have been reports of the abuse of the human rights of Nepali immigrants, who are numerous. Bhutan, whose foreign relations are subject to the advice of India, is a member of the United Nations.[42]

The Maldive Islands, formerly a sultanate under British protection, became a republic briefly in 1953 and a monarchy again until republican government returned in 1968. In 1965 severance from Britain was declared but the Commonwealth was rejoined in 1982.[43] The Maldives have had their share of troubles: a rebellion in the southern atolls; and in 1988 an inept attempt at a coup by Tamil mercenaries swiftly ended by Indian forces.

5

SOUTH ASIA: INTERNATIONAL RELATIONS

This chapter will be concerned, first, with relations between the several states of South Asia; and then with their relations with the wider world outside the subcontinent. In the pages that follow, 'India' will, except when the context requires otherwise, mean the Government of India at the time in question; and similarly with other countries. This usage must not be taken to imply unanimity of opinion within a country (see p. 82).

INTERNATIONAL RELATIONS WITHIN SOUTH ASIA: INDIA AND PAKISTAN

The unhappy, indeed tragic, animosity between India and Pakistan has overshadowed international relations within South Asia since independence; and has powerfully affected, and in turn been affected by, the relations of both with countries outside South Asia, notably China, the United States and the Soviet Union.[1] Chapter 4 has shown that a series of crises and disputes has bedevilled Indo–Pakistan relations: in particular, Indian action in Hyderabad and Junagadh; the Kashmir imbroglio; the prolonged Indus waters dispute; and the secession of Bangladesh and attendant complications. It has also shown that on no less than four occasions the neighbours have taken up arms against each other. True, there have been *rapprochements*, as at Tashkent in 1966, through Soviet mediation; and at Simla in July 1972, when Mrs Gandhi and Bhutto conferred, agreed on a line of control in Kashmir (while reserving their respective irreconcilable positions on that territory) and reached a more general accord. There have also been other notable and welcome agreements, as eventually in the case of the Indus waters. But after every hesitant *rapprochement*, after every agreement, ill-will has broken out again, as have poisoned suspicion and loud recrimination, often after some incident that, to the outside world, has seemed trivial.

Why this mutual suspicion and ill-will, obsessive and ineradicable as they often seemed to be, when to many uncommitted observers and, indeed, to many intelligent citizens of the two countries there is every advantage in friendship and co-operation, not least in the interests of economic development and the attainment of national security? Why, when both countries are so desperately poor, have such enormous resources been spent on armaments for use by the one against the other, with resultant loss of life and of material assets?

There is, first, the obvious point that Pakistan is very much smaller than India, both in area and population. This was true before it lost Bangladesh and was even more true afterwards. Howard Wriggins, in contrast to authors who stress the uniqueness of Pakistan's position *vis-à-vis* India, developed a general model to explain Pakistan's foreign policy in terms of the anxiety to be expected when a smaller, weaker state borders a larger, stronger one.[2] He quoted Thucydides' tenet that fear is a central driving force behind statesmen to emphasize the special vulnerability of a small Pakistan consisting of two even smaller wings separated by Indian territory; and to claim that India's army was never less than twice the size of Pakistan's. The last point may need some qualification. Onkar Marwah stated in 1979 that after arms began to flow from the US to Pakistan in 1954 its army grew almost to the size of India's, and gained a superiority in armoured divisions that caused anxiety among Indian military planners faced with 'the spectre (historic) of an invasion from the northwest, with Pakistan Patton tanks clanking down the Grand Trunk road to Delhi'.[3] It must not be forgotten that India's north-west frontier is much less defensible than that of the British Raj. On the other hand, India's nuclear explosion in the Rajasthan desert in 1974 not surprisingly raised fear and concern in Pakistan. Anxiety, then, was not altogether on one side. And a certain ambivalence was abroad in Pakistan because of the traditional contempt of Muslim for Hindu soldiers: a certain braggadocio, too (I remember school-children in Pakistani Punjab in 1956 singing about marching on Delhi). Moreover, in various ways Pakistan early on set itself ambitious goals and struck hostile postures before it had the strength to match words with deeds. Nevertheless, Wriggins develops his point convincingly in terms of 'the balancing process' practised by small states throughout the ages who are led to seek alliances with powerful outsiders for fear of a bigger neighbour. Ziring, indeed, goes further and, writing after the loss of Bangladesh, sees Bhutto's foreign policy as 'predicated on maximizing fear of India in order to keep his detractors from further fractioning the state' by exploiting separatist tendencies.[4] However, Wriggins admits that the applicability of his model to Indo–Pakistani relations is limited; and draws attention to a number of particularities in these relations. To these we now turn, and begin by asking the question 'How far has special hostility sprung from unhappy relations between Hindus and Muslims before, during and after partition'?

Doubts may have been sown by the discussion in Chapter 3 of the extent to which Indian Muslims under the British Raj formed 'a community' with uniform ideology and attitudes to their Hindu fellow-countrymen and to the two-nation theory; and there were, and are, many instances of peaceful coexistence of Hindus and Muslims in a number of parts of the subcontinent, especially in the south. But it is certainly possible to speak, albeit with reservations, of the 'traditional hostility' between Hindus and Muslims if one bears in mind the refusal of Islam to go the way of other religions and to be absorbed into the ever-open-door of Hinduism, and the related contempt of its adherents for infidels; and remembers, too, the all-too-frequent, and unhappily continuing, outbursts of communal rioting and carnage. The fact that they were particularly violent just before partition, and even more so as millions of refugees crossed from Pakistan to India and vice versa did nothing to improve relations between Muslim-majority Pakistan and Hindu-majority India; and, indeed, saw to it that, quite apart from other considerations, those relations got off to a lamentably bad start. This was the more so because refugees rose to prominence in politics, especially in Pakistan. The situation was, of course, greatly exacerbated by the Kashmir crisis and the inclusion in India of a Muslim majority state. (The recent activities of the Bharatiya Janata Party (BJP) (see pp. 64–6) have renewed hostilities.)

But the Muslims of Kashmir were not the only Muslims who found themselves in the new India. Pakistan soon set itself up as the guardian, perforce absentee, of all Indian Muslims from the large communities of Uttar Pradesh (UP) to the smaller, but still important ones of Hyderabad and the south generally. Intercommunal incidents and allegations of discrimination against Muslims were duly reported, and often exaggerated, in the Pakistan press, and the notion of independent India as a Hindu Raj faithfully maintained, while Indian Muslim groups, anxious to show that they were good citizens of the Republic, were ignored. India, for its part, sided with Hindus left behind in Pakistan, mostly in the East. India's concern for Hindu refugees thence, while laudable on humanitarian grounds, was not untainted by political calculation, while, on the other hand, reaction in Assam to Bengali Muslim immigration has hardly been friendly.

Again, there was squabbling over such matters as the distribution of assets; the transfer of official records; and the division of the armed forces, made all the more difficult because the British had been careful to ensure that there were no all-Muslim units in the Indian Army. It is indeed very remarkable, and a tribute to the tenacity of its founding fathers, that Pakistan was able to set up a civil administration and an army of its own as quickly as it did.

Further, there was the suspicion, burgeoning into certainty in some Pakistani minds, that the new rulers of India were not reconciled to partition. It is, of course, true that it was with the greatest reluctance that Nehru and his colleagues accepted partition as a means of moving swiftly to independence; and true, too, that some Indian political parties and bodies of opinion have never accepted it. This is especially the case with those, like the BJP, with strong roots in Hindu chauvinism. And many Sikhs do not forget that some of their holiest places lie in Pakistani Punjab. The events of 1971, particularly the part that India played in the secession of Bangladesh, strengthened the conviction that India was bent on annexation. But India did, as we have seen, withdraw and leave an independent Muslim-majority Bangladesh. Perhaps one motive in this (which in its wry way ought to reassure Pakistanis) is encapsulated in William J. Barnds's assertion that most Indians 'want no more Muslims or Bengalis'.[5] Moreover, in the war of 1971 India did not press its advantage on the western front, and withdrew to its former frontiers. But Pakistan has not been reassured by such Indian actions, any more than it was by statements by Indian leaders that they have no territorial designs on Pakistan (for example, that by Nehru, who, in refuting the allegation that a main aim of Indian foreign policy was to weaken and isolate Pakistan and eventually to undo partition, said 'Anything more unrealistic and devoid of fact I cannot imagine').[6]

If such an atmosphere of suspicion has lingered long in the smaller country, India for her part has had some grounds, based on statements by Pakistani leaders and the slant given to press reports, for believing that Pakistan rejoiced in every report of disunity in the enormous and highly-variegated India body politic. Pakistan, of course, suspected that India fomented such divisive activities as those of the Pakhtunistan movement (see pp. 54–5).

It is implicit in some of these points that it is wrong to talk of India and Pakistan in all the tragic history of their mutual suspicion and conflict as though each was a person with a consistent, single view of the other. There have been many people in India who have harboured no ill-will to the people of Pakistan (though few have departed from their government's line on Kashmir). And equally, though the evidence here is harder to come by, there have been Pakistanis who have felt no constant and generalized hostility towards all things Indian. I can testify to the fact that throughout all the troubles, even in the depths of the 1971 war, Indians, Pakistanis (and Bangladeshis when their state emerged) have talked to each other without hostility and, indeed, with friendliness in such academic institutions as the School of Oriental and African Studies in the University of London and the Centre of South Asian Studies in the University of Cambridge. But there have been groups in both countries, whether interest groups, or communally-minded politicians and religious leaders, who did nothing to reduce hostility and in some cases actively fomented it. Wriggins asked[7]

> What were the bureaucratic, professional or economic interest groups within Pakistan that have been most important in shaping the concept of 'national interest' and the making of foreign policy in Pakistan? Did domestic political support at any one time depend as heavily upon a high degree of hostility towards India as many Indians argue?

These questions are almost impossible to answer adequately from the information that has come out of Pakistan or from the secondary literature, largely because of the prevalence of authoritarian regimes (which do not take kindly to enquiry into their decision-making processes). Questions like Wriggins's ought also, of course, to be asked about India. There some answers emerge: for example, about the role of Hindu communalist groups and certain political parties. Others must remain at present unanswered. But one does caution against accepting sweeping statements that 'Pakistanis have this attitude to India' and 'Indians have that attitude to Pakistan'; and that both sets of attitudes are unshakeable whatever the changes in circumstance, whatever the shifts in the internal power and influence structure in the two states, and notwithstanding the passage of time.

Both governments have wrapped themselves in cloaks (rather different cloaks) of moral self-righteousness. But, equally, it is vital that the outside observer does not himself become self-righteously critical: he should remember the wise words of William J. Barnds:[8]

it would have required the foresight of genius and the selflessness of sainthood for the leaders of either country to have acted differently . . . in the midst of one of the major upheavals of the twentieth century.

The atmosphere between India and Pakistan showed improvement in the late 1980s, some tentative moves having been made earlier in the decade, as when Mrs Gandhi and Zia met in November 1982 and, among other matters, agreed to the consideration of a treaty of peace, friendship and co-operation.[9] In 1985 it was agreed to co-operate in agricultural research and development. In 1989 an agreement was reached over the disputed Siachen glacier; and a number of other moves made towards *détente*. A friendly personal relationship in fact grew up between Rajiv Gandhi and Benazir Bhutto and, after a visit to Islamabad, Rajiv actually sponsored Pakistan's readmission to the Commonwealth. By 1990, however, the situation in Kashmir (see pp. 49–51) generated serious tensions, augmented by fundamentalisms on both sides of the ceasefire line. By February 1992, and while Indian and Pakistani forces continue to confront each other across that line, there was the bizarre prospect that each of them would simultaneously face in the opposite direction to head off 'marches' by the Jammu and Kashmir Liberation Front (JKLF) dedicated to a united and independent state. Clearly no end to the Kashmir imbroglio is in sight. There is, perhaps, a case for effective intervention by the wider international community. But admirable though the South Asian Association for Regional Co-operation (SAARC) is, to tackle the Kashmir problem is well beyond its scope (see p. 94).

INTERNATIONAL RELATIONS WITHIN SOUTH ASIA: INDIA AND PAKISTAN AND THEIR RELATIONS WITH BANGLADESH

To begin with relations immediately after the events of December 1971, at meetings between Mrs Gandhi and Bhutto at Simla in 1972, affairs in

Bangladesh were high on the agenda. There was much haggling about the 93,000 prisoners taken in the war (some 15,000 of these were civilians).[10] India was slow to resolve the issue of their release because it did not wish to impair its relations with Sheikh Mujib and with a Bangladesh then dominated by a pro-Indian mood. Mujib's stance was that prisoners could not be released till Pakistan recognized his country; and he also wished to try the 1500 or so prisoners said to have been involved in war crimes. Bhutto would not accept the need for trials (hinting that if they took place he could not be responsible for the safety of the estimated 400,000 Bengalis held in Pakistan); stalled on the issue of recognition; and expressed unwillingness to receive the Biharis in a distressed condition in Bangladesh (see pp. 53–4). Further, Pakistan, with Chinese support, succeeded for some time in keeping Bangladesh out of the United Nations. However, after further haggling an agreement was signed by India and Pakistan, with the concurrence of Bangladesh, in August 1973. All Pakistani prisoners save a mere 195 still charged with war crimes were to be repatriated, as were all Bengalis in Pakistan. An unspecified number of Biharis who wished to settle in Pakistan were to be allowed to go there. Eventually Pakistan recognized Bangladesh in 1974; and at a meeting of the foreign ministers of India, Pakistan and Bangladesh a little later the idea of war crimes trials was dropped altogether and the migration of further Biharis to Pakistan was approved (though the problem still remains). Bangladesh became a member of the United Nations in September 1974, and joined the Security Council in 1978.

Up to a point, then, a satisfactory conclusion was reached on issues arising out of the events of 1971 in Bangladesh. But since 1974 the triangular relationship between India, Pakistan and Bangladesh has been far from a smooth one, for reasons arising basically from disputes between India and Bangladesh, some of which go back in time before the independence of the latter; from changing stances of successive regimes in Bangladesh towards the other two states; and from what India has seen as attempts by Pakistan to reach across to Bangladesh in order to embarrass India.

One of the principal disputes between India and Bangladesh, with important economic implications for both countries, has been that over the Farakka Barrage.[11] This, as Burke says, 'first appeared as a small cloud on the horizon in 1951, and progressively assumed major proportions in the nineteen-sixties'. It thus became one of the many bones of contention between India and Pakistan. The dispute rumbled on into the period of Bangladeshi independence. The physiographic basis of the problem lies in the contrast between the old and new deltas in Bengal (see Chapter 2): the new delta in the east, and covering much of Bangladesh, still subject to actively flooding rivers and to seaward growth; the former, lying mainly in West Bengal and so in India, moribund and not under active construction by its rivers which tend to clog with silt. One such river is the Bhagirathi, which becomes the Hugli (Hooghly) and passes through Calcutta. As long ago as the 1850s British engineers recommended a barrage at Farakka, upstream of the take-off of the Bhagirathi from the Ganga (Ganges), and a canal to the Bhagirathi to increase the flow through it and the Hugli and so to wash out silt from the port of Calcutta. Plans were only finalized in the 1950s, by which time it was anticipated that to benefits in terms of navigation at Calcutta had been added improved drainage, sanitation and water supply to domestic and industrial consumers. Construction began in 1962 and was completed in 1971. Water began to be withdrawn from the Ganga and diverted to the Bhagirathi in 1975.

Why did Pakistan, and later Bangladesh, object to the Farakka barrage, given that it would help to moderate massive floods in the eastern delta? The answer lies partly in the general tetchiness of relations between India on the one hand and Pakistan (and at times Bangladesh) on the other. It also lies partly in a dispute over international law, Pakistan (and later Bangladesh) contending that the Ganga is an international river, so that the lower riparian state has a legitimate interest in its waters, India contending that the Ganga is not an international river, but overwhelmingly an Indian river, given the high proportion of its course in Indian territory. But part of the grounds of the dispute lie in seasonality. Flooded much of East Bengal may be in the south-west monsoon, but water derived from the Ganga is of great importance to agriculture, fisheries and irrigation, actual and potential, in the dry season. It was maintained successively by Pakistan and Bangladesh that the volume India proposed to abstract at Farakka would be ruinous to cultivation and fisheries in the latter; would lead to siltation there and so to increased flooding in the monsoon; and would make land at the seaward margin of the delta uncultivable through the upstream penetration of saltwater. Such consequences were probably painted in too black a colour.

Negotiations dragged on while Bangladesh was still East Pakistan, edging towards some measures of agreement, and narrowing the disputed issues down to the maximum volume India could abstract during the dry season, particularly in its most critical months. Argument broke out *de novo* following Bangladeshi independence, in spite of India's initial patronage of the new state. In November 1975 an agreement was reached on the sharing of the waters for a five-year period and on a joint study on ways to increase the flow of the Ganga. New interim agreements were reached in 1982 and 1985. But arguments continue on means of augmenting the flow of the Ganga, Bangladesh preferring a regional solution involving, for example, storage in Nepal as well as India. Meanwhile, hostility towards India broke out in Dhaka in September 1988: India was blamed for severe flooding in that month (a Ministry of Irrigation report had attributed a rising trend in the Ganga within Bangladesh to Farakka on the grounds that while a fixed flow is sent down the Bhagirathi, the barrage passes excess flood flow down river).

Another source of disagreement between India and Bangladesh, already in evidence before 1971, concerns minor boundary disputes, often due to changing river courses and the appearance of new areas of fluvial deposition known as *chars*. In 1974 a border agreement was reached, but this did not prevent a further dispute in 1979. More serious are cross-border incursions and movements: for example, of dissident Nagas and Mizos 'harboured' in Bangladesh (as they were in East Pakistan before it) and re-entering hill areas of north-east India where, as we have seen, tribal separatism is prominent; or a two-way movement between Mizoram and the Chittagong Hill Tracts of Bangladesh; or the passage of Bengali Muslims into Assam, contributing to the tense situation in that state; or raids from India on Bangladeshi paddy-fields. On the one hand, it may be argued that movements of people are inseparable from such a long, artificial boundary. On the other hand, the seriousness with which these movements are taken clearly depends on their connexion, if any, with internal dissidence or separatism, and on the state of relations between the two countries.

In more general terms, relations between India and Bangladesh immediately after the war of 1971 were friendly, and those between Pakistan and Bangladesh, so far as they existed at all, distant and hostile. In March 1973, India and Bangladesh signed a 25-year Treaty of Friendship, Co-operation and Peace, which included a defence pact; and India was one of the countries supplying aid to restore the war-shattered Bangladeshi economy. Not surprisingly, Pakistan was at that time execrated in many quarters in Bangladesh, memories of atrocities during the period of repression in 1971 still being all too fresh. Few people whom I met in Dhaka in August 1973 admitted to a knowledge of Urdu, because of its Pakistani connotations, in spite of the fact that it had previously been the mother tongue of the old city elite and a lingua franca for others. Bhutto in Pakistan, for his part, spoke slightingly of 'Muslim Bengal' and, as we have seen, dragged his feet, nimble though they were in diplomatic matters, over recognition. But anti-Indian sentiments were still present: slogans like 'quit, Indians' appeared on walls; and some Bangladeshis hankered after better relations with their fellow Muslims in Pakistan, and expressed anti-Hindu feelings. And even Mujib, the proclaimer of a secular state, attended an Islamic Summit.

Relations with Pakistan improved with recognition in 1974. Bhutto visited Dhaka; and ambassadors were exchanged at the end of 1975. By this time Mujib and the coup which removed him had, as we have seen, been followed by a counter-coup, said to have been engineered by pro-Indian elements, only to be followed by yet another coup which brought Ziaur Rahman to power. Pakistan clearly did not regret either the passing of the man they saw as the begetter of secession or the failure of the second coup; and welcomed the possibility of an 'Islamic State' with the arrival of Zia. India, by the same token, viewed these developments with unease. Tension with India rose dramatically when there was an attempt on the life of the Indian High Commissioner in November 1975. However, an Indian delegation renewed offers of friendship, and the short-term Farakka agreement was soon signed. Relations deteriorated again in 1976 with renewed haggling over Farakka and raids on northern Bangladesh by allegedly 'pro-Mujib' forces which, Zia claimed, had received Indian assistance.

During more recent years it has remained broadly true that friendly relations between Pakistan and Bangladesh have been maintained, there being no outstanding major issues between the countries. (Significantly, many more people admitted to a spoken knowledge of Urdu in Dhaka in 1976.) By the same token, relations with India have been less happy, and mistrust has been fuelled by the issues already mentioned. In 1989, however, Ershad was reported as calling for 'the consolidation of ties' with India; while in the same year Benazir Bhutto, in a gesture of reconciliation, paid a visit to Dhaka. The fluctuating relations of India and Pakistan with Bangladesh seem set to continue. The Hindu chauvinism now so evident in India does not endear itself to Bangladeshis; while a strengthening of Muslim fundamentalism in Pakistan has also had its own impact in Bangladesh and on its relationship with India.

INTERNATIONAL RELATIONS WITHIN SOUTH ASIA: SRI LANKA'S RELATIONS WITH OTHER SOUTH ASIAN COUNTRIES

This section will be mainly concerned with Sri Lanka's relations with India, its giant neighbour, with close on fifty times its population and at the nearest point only twenty-odd miles away.[12] Chapter 4 has shown that in the early decades of independence Sri Lanka saw an alternation of governments dominated on the one hand by the United National Party (UNP) and on the other by the Sri Lanka Freedom Party (SLFP). Policy towards India tended to alternate in sympathy, SLFP governments showing more friendliness, and in certain important respects following the Indian line in international affairs more closely, than UNP governments. Indian attitudes towards Sri Lanka were generally more consistent than Sri Lankan attitudes towards India.

In the earliest years of independence D.S. Senanayake and his advisers were in process of formulating a policy towards foreign affairs and defence, which had not been necessary while their country was still a Crown Colony. One strong motive in this process was undoubtedly a fear of India. One reason for this was, of course, a matter of size: if, on the Wriggins model small Pakistan feared huge India, so, *a fortiori*, should even smaller Sri Lanka. Moreover, Sri Lankans were able to quote influential Indian authors who drew attention to the importance of the Indian Ocean, and of Sri Lanka as a strategically-placed island with a superb natural harbour at Trincomalee, to an India no longer able to rely on British sea power for maritime defence. There was, for example, the view of K.M. Panikkar that the Indian Ocean must remain truly Indian; and his dictum 'It is the oceanic space that dominates the strategy of India's defence'.[13] It is not surprising that the intelligentsia of an island that possessed Trincomalee and that had played a great part in the late war should be highly conscious of the sea and of sea power (and, for that matter, of air power too). Some of them were aware, too, of remarks like that made by Nehru who, in 1945 highlighted the cultural unity of India and Ceylon and forecast that the latter would be drawn into political union 'presumably as an autonomous unit of the Indian Federation'.[14] And there were Indian visitors I met who made no secret of their sense of superiority over the Sinhalese. Nehru later repudiated the remark just quoted. But India did not forget that there was an oceanic dimension to its defence, and has built up a sizeable navy.

It was largely anxiety about India that led Senanayake at the time of independence into a defence agreement with Britain, under which a British base remained in Trincomalee. A related fact of his foreign policy was its decidedly pro-western and anti-Communist stance. This did not, however, prevent protestations of anti-colonialism or the refusal of transit facilities to the Dutch when they were clashing with Indonesian nationalists. Nor did it prevent the forging of bonds with Asian and African countries, as at the Bandung Conference in 1955. All this might have made India less irritated by its small and, some said, neo-colonialist neighbour. But it was at Bandung that Sir John Kotelawala, by then Prime Minister, and a much less tactful man than Senanayake, came out with some extremely strong anti-Communist statements and caused friction with Nehru, the high priest of non-alignment and neutralism.

But there has been a further long-standing cause of acerbity in Indo–Sri Lanka relations. This is the problem of persons who had come from India to work on the coffee, tea and rubber plantations established in British days, or to work in Colombo; and of their descendants. Even before independence the Government of India had been concerned over these 'Indian Tamils', whose presence had aroused hostility among some of the Sinhalese, especially the Kandyans. This ethnic reaction exemplifies yet again the Sinhalese 'majority with a minority complex' (see above, pp. 71–2).[15]

One of the first deeds of the parliament of Sri Lanka after independence was to pass the Ceylon Citizenship Act of 1948 and the Indian and Pakistani Residents (Citizenship) Act of 1949. The result of these enactments was effectively to deny citizenship and enfranchisement to the vast majority of Indian Tamils, except where they were able to become 'citizens by registration' under conditions that few of them could readily satisfy. Indian reaction, both official and unofficial, was to denounce the Acts. The Government of India found them completely unacceptable, while *The Hindu* called the Bill that issued in the second Act 'The Indian Ejectment Bill'. The Government of India did persuade the Government of Sri Lanka to amend the 1949 Act, but continued to be dissatisfied with the legislation as a whole and with the very slow progress of applications for citizenship by registration. Behind all the controversy and a whole series of meetings lay a fundamental conflict of principle. As Kodikara put it:[16]

> The Government of India and Indian opinion generally have contended that the majority of the Indian population in Ceylon are permanently settled in the island. The Government of Ceylon, on the other hand, has regarded most Indians as 'birds of passage' without a permanent interest in Ceylon, whose sojourn on the island generally coincides with the duration of their employment.

The Government of India's policy was, in fact, to discourage all overseas Indians from applying for Indian citizenship. The Government of Sri Lanka's attitude was not favourable to the registration as citizens of more than a small proportion of persons of Indian descent resident in the island. The spectre of statelessness thus hung over a large part of the Indian Tamil community.

A change in Sri Lankan government attitudes to India came when Bandaranaike led his SLFP to power in 1956. Generalized fear of India seemed to recede into the background. Instead came official admiration for Nehru's policies of non-alignment and neutralism. The British defence agreement was terminated (amicably), and diplomatic relations were established with Communist countries. These policies did much to promote good relations with India. After Bandaranaike's assassination similar policies were pursued by his widow in her dealings with Shastri and Mrs Gandhi. Some related progress was made, too, in dealing with the problem of the Indian Tamils. In October 1964 an agreement, the Sirima–Shastri Pact, was reached in New Delhi between Mrs Sirimavo Bandaranaike and Lal Bahadur Shastri. The agreement provided *inter alia* that, of the estimated 975,000 non-citizens of Indian origin in Sri Lanka, 525,000 would be granted Indian citizenship and repatriated over a fifteen-year period; 300,000 would become Sri Lankan citizens; and the remaining 150,000 were to be the subject of a separate and future agreement. Fifteen years were allowed for the implementation of the agreement (that is, to 1979). The Sirima–Shastri Pact did not produce a wholly favourable reaction in India, notably among members of opposition parties and particularly in the Dravida Munnetra Kazhagan (DMK) of Tamil Nadu (see p. 59); while *The Hindu* thought that concessions had mainly been on the Indian side, and viewed with apprehension the number to be repatriated.

The UNP government of 1965 announced that it would honour the pact. To summarize the complex and confusing story of subsequent developments, the terms of the pact were modified on a number of occasions as a result largely of consultations between the two governments; and complicated by controversy (for example, about repatriation: was it to be voluntary or compulsory?). By 1984, however, some 400,000 Indian Tamils had been granted Sri Lankan citizenship, while in November 1988 the Parliament of Sri Lanka agreed to give that status to 'all stateless persons of Indian origin', estimated to number 260,000. But in May 1990 a minister was reported to have announced that Indian passport-holders were to return to India as soon as the international ferry service, suspended because of the fighting in the north of Sri Lanka, was resumed. Repatriation created great problems in India, especially in Tamil Nadu, which also had to cope with refugees from the fighting. In fact, the Indian Tamil problem seems set to complicate Indo–Sri Lankan relations in the future as it has in the past. Meanwhile, the Indian Tamils remaining in Sri Lanka have improved their economic and political status, with help from leaders like Thondaman (see p. 70).

But by the 1980s the issue of the citizenship status of Indian Tamils had been completely overshadowed by, and had interacted with, the ethnic tensions and violence discussed in Chapter 4. True, the citizenship laws were from the outset a result of Sinhalese ethnic feeling, not to say prejudice; while the Jatika Vimukti Peramuna (JVP) insurrection of 1971 was, amongst other things, anti-Indian (and indeed anti-plantations). But the ethnic violence of 1981 and 1983 was of a different nature and scale, that in the latter year being an integral part of the widespread communal conflict that justifies the name of 'civil war', while the JVP made damaging attacks on tea plantations in 1987. To the interaction of these troubles with Indo–Sri Lankan relations we now return, continuing the discussion in Chapter 4.

First, what R.W. Bradnock has justifiably called the massacre of Tamils in 1983 understandably brought a low point in Indian relations with Sri Lanka.[17] Then, as the civil war mounted in intensity, there developed a 'war of words'; and Indian concern for the fate of Tamils in northern Sri Lanka led to the delivery of supplies, eventually by means of an air-drop. The Sri Lankan response, and not only the Sri Lankan, was to shout loudly about a breach of sovereignty. But fortunately the war of words did not pass into armed conflict, as some had feared it would, perhaps because of mediation by Commonwealth countries; and not long afterwards, in July 1987, came the Jayawardene-Gandhi Accord already mentioned in connexion with the Indian Peacekeeping Force (IPKF) (see Chapter 4). The Accord contained clauses in addition to those designed to end ethnic violence. For example, a declaration on the preservation of the sovereignty and territorial integrity of Sri Lanka; and, in an exchange of letters, an agreement by Sri Lanka not to make Trincomalee and other Sri Lankan ports available for military use by any country in a manner prejudicial to India's interests.

But the Accord in general was bitterly opposed by Sinhala chauvinists; and by Premadasa, President from December 1989: and so, eventually, led to the withdrawal of the IPKF amid much acrimony. In fact, relations between the two neighbours fell back into an unhappy state once again. Further, the circumstances of the assassination of Rajiv Gandhi in Tamil Nadu in May 1991 led to a reduction in sympathy and support in that state for the many thousands of refugees from Sri Lanka; and to an Indian ban on the Liberation Tigers of Tamil Eelam (LTTE), with support from the Government of Tamil Nadu. It was reported that Delhi was hinting that Colombo should not legitimize the LTTE by negotiating with it. In this context the outlook for Indo–Sri Lankan relations remains unsettled.

But we must look briefly at Indo–Sri Lankan relations in a wider context and with a longer historical perspective. Up to a point, non-alignment survived changes of government in Sri Lanka, UNP governments not attempting to reintroduce British bases; and this, *a priori*, should have made for good relations with India. But UNP governments tended to favour links with the west, SLFP governments to cultivate good relations with China: neither posture was altogether pleasing to India. Moreover, rather incompletely formulated concepts saw Pakistan and China before 1971 as a counterpoise to India. But the events of 1971 clearly altered the balance of power in South Asia; and Sri Lanka noted that China did not leap to Pakistan's defence.

What of Sri Lankan relations with Pakistan, before and after the independence of Bangladesh, and with Bangladesh? The vague view of Pakistan as a counterpoise became a little less nebulous in 1987 at the time of tension with India, with talk of seeking assistance from Pakistan, which was already supplying arms. It was also reported that Pakistan, with Britain, was trying to mediate at the same tense time.

One facet of Bandaranaike's 'Switzerland of the East' concept is worth a mention here. He, and his widow after him, saw their neutrality as a good basis on which they could mediate. One of the conflicts in which Mrs Bandaranaike offered to mediate, having declared her strict neutrality, was that between India and Pakistan over Bangladesh in 1971.

As for Sri Lanka's relations with Bangladesh and Nepal, nothing need be added here.

INTERNATIONAL RELATIONS WITHIN SOUTH ASIA: RELATIONS OF NEPAL, BHUTAN AND THE MALDIVES WITH OTHER SOUTH ASIAN COUNTRIES; MULTILATERAL RELATIONS IN SOUTH ASIA

In the early years of India's independence its relations with Nepal were close.[18] Nehru made it clear that, while recognizing the independence of Nepal, India would not brook foreign interference in that country, stretching as it did for 500 miles along India's northern frontier. He seemed blind, however, to the geography and history of a mountain state that, for all its cultural dominance by Hinduism, had maintained long-standing relations with Tibet and so with China, for he said 'One cannot go to Nepal without passing through India'.[19] Perhaps he was here, as in a wider context, misled by the weakness and passivity of Tibet (and of China) during the British period, and by illusions of lasting Chinese friendship. But this is to anticipate.

India's special relationship with Nepal, embodied in a treaty in 1950, dominated the Himalayan kingdom's foreign contacts during the period up to 1955. Nepal, indeed, relied on Indian help in a number of internal crises: notably, India gave asylum to King Tribhuvan when he fled his country during his conflict with the Ranas (see p. 78), and aided his successful return. The two countries signed a mutual assistance pact, and India sent troops to Nepal to help to quell an uprising. It continued to recruit Gurkhas from Nepal as the Raj had done (and as Britain continued to do). Indian economic aid steadily increased in amount and scope. Such Indian dominance was not without its critics in Nepal and outside. Some argued that India's treatment of Nepal was inconsistent with recognition of its independence and with a posture of anti-colonialism. And the relationship between the two countries was punctuated by unpleasantness; thus when Nehru visited Kathmandu in 1951 there was a hostile demonstration.

In 1950 Communist China established its control over Tibet, on which its immediate predecessors had had so loose a grip. It is ironic that it was India that encouraged Nepal both to 'regularize' relations with Tibet and to establish diplomatic relations with China if it so desired. In 1955 Nepal did in fact establish such relations, the two governments declaring that their basis was Panch Shila (see p. 95).

This new relationship between Beijing and Kathmandu marks a turning point in Indo–Nepali relations and in Nepali foreign policy. This was by 1957 directly in the hands of King Mahendra, a more formidable figure than his predecessor, though a monarch who could not but be aware of his weakness. There is something of a parallel with Pakistan's efforts to balance one power against another. But there was much less consistency in Mahendra's quest for a counterbalance to India; for, notwithstanding anti-Indian feeling among some of his subjects, he and most of his elite lacked the special reasons for fear and hatred of India that so unfortunately operated in Pakistan.

True, the establishment of diplomatic relations with Beijing were followed thence by offers of aid to Nepal from China which touched off alarm bells in New Delhi (the USSR also offered aid at about the same time). But a professedly pro-Indian and anti-Chinese Prime Minister was appointed in Nepal in 1957 and Nepalese policy veered back towards India. Meanwhile, India's honeymoon period with China was at an end and Panch Shila had gone sour, with Indian realization that China had established itself in territory that India claimed. The Himalayan frontier, dormant in British days, came alive and grew intensely dangerous. India looked once again at its relations with Nepal (and with Bhutan and Sikkim); and in 1959 Nehru affirmed that any attack on Nepal would be construed as an attack on India. Indian troops were, in fact, sent at the request of the Nepal government to man a number of posts on its northern frontier. Indian economic aid increased. But anti-Indian feeling surfaced once again, in spite of joint declarations on the preservation of Nepal's independence and integrity.

Nepali policy was, by 1960, shifting towards neutrality in the Indo–Chinese dispute, and deliberate efforts were made to establish closer relations with China and Pakistan, both eager to embarrass India. Nepal and China came to a frontier agreement (though there were border clashes too); and China also agreed to build a road north from Kathmandu through the Kuti Pass in the Himalayas to Kodari (much to India's chagrin, though it continued aid, which also included roadbuilding). So it was that, in the Chinese incursion into India in 1962, Nepal went unscathed but, equally, did not come to India's assistance. One Indian author sees the period 1960–3 as one of a 'widening gulf in Indo–Nepali relations'.[20]

The same author sees 1963–72 as a period of improving relations between the two, and credits India with a more realistic and sympathetic policy towards its neighbour. It is, however, better to see this period as one in which Nepal continued to veer now towards India, now away from it, constantly seeking to maintain some sort of balance amid the shifting sands of international relations; and taking aid from a wide range of donors, from India (usually the largest single source) to China, from America to the Soviet Union, from Britain to Switzerland. And disputes with India were not absent in the period.

Since 1972, a new factor in Nepal's calculation is the strengthening of India's dominance within the subcontinent following the Bangladesh war. No longer is there much to be gained by playing off Pakistan against India. It is arguably more important for this land-locked state to seek good relations with Bangladesh, whose northernmost point is only some 20 miles from Nepali territory and whose port of Chittagong presents Nepal with a potential alternative to Calcutta (though still not accessible by land except by crossing Indian soil).

Since 1973 the swings to and from India have continued. Thus in 1973 a peace and friendship treaty with India was revived. But in the following years relations were described as 'estranged' because of Nepali hostility to what was seen as the Indian 'annexation' of Sikkim; while efforts were made to please China by taking a firm line on refugees from Tibet. In 1979 it was Pakistan's turn to excite a demonstration in Kathmandu, because of the execution of Bhutto. In 1984 a Report to the Government of Nepal made recommendations, alarmingly reminiscent of the citizenship laws of Sri Lanka, and partly in response to large-scale migration into the Tarai (see p. 88), that persons 'of Indian origin' but not Indian nationals should lose citizenship rights in Nepal. Some years later, relations between the two governments reached new levels of acrimony, originally over terms for the renewal of the trade and transit treaty that lapsed in March 1989. India refused transit to and from Nepal at all but two border crossing points, causing severe hardship, not only to the 'modern' sector, but also to poor people who, for example, needed paraffin for cooking stoves; and also increased government financial problems. It is also clear that the Government of India was piqued by the citizenship issue and by such Nepali actions as the purchase of arms from China. Nepal, for its part, could once again raise cries of 'Indian imperialism'. However, relations improved, and the prospects for a new trade and transit agreement brightened, with the more conciliatory attitude of V.P. Singh's government. But the ensuing and continuing uncertainty in Indian domestic politics is no environment for the thoughtful solution of Indo–Nepali problems.

Nepal, then, has adopted varying postures in its search for survival, particularly given the dominance of its enormous neighbour to the south and the power of China to the north, and is likely to maintain its own version of non-alignment between these two neighbours (the first of them, ironically, the arch-exponent of that posture). An official visit by Birendra to Sri Lanka may be seen in 1980 as an attempt to strengthen his ties with a South Asian country other than India.

As we have seen in Chapter 4, Bhutan's foreign relations are subject to the advice of India.[21] Consequently, Bhutan has so far had a more constant and exclusive relationship with India than has Nepal. But it is always possible that the incipient internal politics mentioned briefly in Chapter 4 will lead to a less settled state of affairs, especially in view of the Nepali element in Bhutan's population.

The Maldive Islands present a different case again. The historical facts about the relationship with Britain and the Commonwealth were sufficiently narrated in Chapter 4, as was the role of India in suppressing a coup attempt. This episode, however, illustrates the importance of its navy in establishing and maintaining India's regional dominance.

It is appropriate to mention, and to give two cheers for, an example of multilateral relations between states, namely, the South Asian Association for Regional Co-operation (SAARC). Suggested by Bangladesh in 1979, it was at first greeted with some suspicion by India (for fear of other states combining against it) and by the others (for fear of Indian domination). But in 1987 its headquarters were set up in Kathmandu. Under its auspices are held, amongst other things, annual meetings of the heads of all South Asian states. But SAARC only deserves two cheers because its charter specifically rules out contentious bilateral issues, and hence it lacks political punch. Behind it, too, lies the relatively low level of economic relations between its members.

SOUTH ASIA'S RELATIONS WITH EXTERNAL COUNTRIES: CHINA, AFGHANISTAN, BURMA AND SOUTH-EAST ASIA

We now turn to relations between South Asian countries and China, Afghanistan and Burma (Iran also has a border with Pakistan: see p. 55). It has been impossible to omit earlier reference to these states, since the affairs of South Asia are not conducted in subcontinental isolation. To some extent, then, the sections that follow involve the pulling out and tying together of threads.

China has come to play a major role in the international politics of South Asia, as we have already seen in discussing the foreign relations of Pakistan and Nepal. Now while the Indian Empire and Ceylon were moving towards independence after the Second World War, the Chinese Communists were successfully establishing themselves in their own country (they were firmly in control in Beijing by October 1949); and were winning the sympathy of Nehru and other South Asian leaders, who perceived in the Chinese Revolution a parallel with their own struggle against imperialism. True, 'China proper' never had its whole territory occupied by European coloniz-ing powers. But it did suffer the indignity of the Treaty Port system;[22] and much of its territory had been overrun by the Japanese in the years before and during the war. Communist China occupied Tibet in 1950, putting an end to its near-independence and to the theocratic rule of the Dalai Lama (who submitted to Chinese sovereignty in return for provisions purporting 'to guarantee Tibetan autonomy and religious freedom' in an agreement signed in Beijing in May 1951).[23]

The Chinese action in Tibet aroused some anxiety in India. But this was the era of 'Hindi–Chini bhai-bhai', the proclaimed brotherhood of Indians and Chinese in their common struggle against imperialism. So it was that in 1952 India implicitly recognized Chinese sovereignty in Tibet and was allowed to open a Consulate-General in Lhasa (China reciprocating in Bombay). In 1954 a more comprehensive agreement was signed. India had already announced its intention to give up the extra-territorial rights in Tibet inherited from the Raj. The treaty was largely concerned with facilities for merchants and pilgrims. In the preamble Panch Shila, or five principles of peaceful coexistence, were declared to be the basis of Sino–Indian relations. These were: 'mutual respect for each other's territorial integrity and sovereignty; mutual non-aggression; mutual non interference in each other's internal affairs; equality and mutual benefit; and peaceful coexistence'. The treaty was greeted in India and more widely as a great achievement and a victory for Nehru and his policy of non-alignment.

But hopes of eternal friendship with China and, for that matter, of an autonomous status for the Tibetans, were soon dashed. Alarming reports began to reach Nehru (though not the educated Indian public, or that articulate and irrepressible body might have reacted sooner) of intense Chinese military activity and roadbuilding in Tibet. The People's Republic, Marxist though it might be, was losing no time in reoccupying the marchlands of the Chinese imperial order. And it was not long before India was locked in a border dispute whose roots go back to British days and indeed earlier.[24] Indian patrols discovered Chinese incursions into territory that was believed in New Delhi to be Indian. In 1958 the Chinese were found to have built a strategic road linking Tibet with western Xinjiang across Aksai Chin, which India claimed as heir to the territories of the Maharaja of Kashmir.

In 1959 the Dalai Lama fled to India. By that time the Sino–Indian border dispute was in full swing, and relations had worsened, to the great perturbation of the Communist Party of India.[25] The dispute concerned not only Aksai Chin and other western areas but also the then North-East Frontier Agency, now Arunachal Pradesh, where India claimed a boundary along the McMahon Line following broadly the Himalayan crest-cum-watershed, which had been accepted by Tibet in 1914, but never ratified by China; whereas the Chinese claimed a line on the edge of the plains of Assam. India increased its military forces in the border areas, and allowed the treaty of 1954 to lapse without asking for renewal, thus greatly offending China.

In 1962, the Chinese swept in force across the McMahon Line (which, as India correctly pointed out, was the *de facto* boundary) and were soon poised to threaten the plains of Assam. Indian defence degenerated into a notorious débâcle. Then, when India and the world were wondering what was to happen next, the Chinese announced a unilateral ceasefire. But India did not capitulate to China's demands on the location of the ceasefire line; and the border dispute remained unsettled. An attempt at mediation in December 1962, on Sri Lankan initiative, ran into the sand: Nehru was apparently willing to 'forgive and forget', though not at the expense of what he conceived as India's territorial integrity; but China's attitude was equivocal.

Now Nehru was an idealist who, as Dorothy Woodman put it, 'romantic-ised policy towards China';[26] whereas Chou En-lai and other Chinese leaders saw him as a bourgeois nationalist, if not a lackey of the imperialists, who had kept his country in the Commonwealth. The actions of the Chinese in Tibet and on the border, and finally the war of 1962, more than disillusioned Nehru and perhaps hastened his end (he died in 1964). By then many sections of public opinion in India saw in Communist China no more than the old Chinese Empire wrapped in a red flag.

Why did the Chinese invade in 1962 and so quickly declare a ceasefire? One motive for the attack was perhaps to deal a severe blow to a 'bourgeois' government that aspired to leadership of the non-aligned and anti-colonial world. But a more specific motive was possibly to bring pressure on India in order to achieve a compromise on the border issue that would concede Aksai Chin to China (which had good reason, given the mounting hostility of the Soviet Union, to hold its strategic road) in return for the acceptance of the McMahon Line in the north-east. But even though Nehru apparently began to think of a compromise along these lines, no such solution emerged.

After 1962 relations between India and China remained bad. Neither country suspended diplomatic representation in the other, but it remained at chargé d'affaires level. There was a long series of border incidents and protest notes; and claims that China was training Naga and Mizo dissidents. In 1968 China exploded a nuclear device, to India's great alarm, and perhaps stimulated India's own explosion in the Rajasthan Desert in 1974, declared to be for peaceful purposes. In the years 1969–72, however, India made cautious hints to China on a possible *rapprochement*, fortified at the end of that period by its success in the Bangladesh war. In 1976 relations were 'normalized' and ambassadors were exchanged. From 1977 onwards the Janata government gradually improved relations with Beijing; and in 1979 its Minister of External Affairs was in China discussing a wide range of issues, including the border dispute, when the news came of the Chinese invasion of Vietnam, by then in the Soviet orbit. The minister immediately returned to New Delhi, and his government heavily criticized Beijing. However, between 1981 and 1988 there were no fewer than eight rounds of inconclusive talks, punctuated by reports of border clashes and of Chinese military build-up in Tibet; and in 1987 by Chinese annoyance at India's elevation to statehood of disputed Arunachal Pradesh. In December 1988 Rajiv Gandhi visited Beijing. There emerged proposals for a joint working party on the border issue and talk of expanded ties. The Chinese Prime Minister visited Delhi in December 1991 and agreement was reached on a number of matters; while the President of India went to Beijing in June 1992. In the same month there took place at Rio de Janeiro the UN conference on Environment and Development, for the purposes of which China and India had found common cause in making the Beijing Declaration of the previous year and encouraging the formation of the G77 group of developing countries to confront the G7 group of the world's most industrialized states. (But already by the time of the conference G77 was in disarray and seems unlikely to survive as an effective and unified body.)

Some measures of contact between India and China there have, then, been. But at the time of writing (summer 1992) the border dispute remains unresolved. It is possible that a solution may emerge from further *rapprochement* given that both India and China are concerned about world dominance by the United States (US) following the collapse of the Soviet Union.

For it was the presence of a powerful Soviet Union that greatly complicated relations between South Asia and China for much of the period just reviewed. The rift between the Soviet Union and China was already wide by 1960 and due, it would seem, to a combination of ideology and power politics, or perhaps the second masquerading as the first. Khruschev in that year was already denouncing China for its attitude to India; though (with the Cuban missiles crisis hanging over it) the Soviet Union appeared to lean towards China when the latter made its ceasefire proposals after the 1962 incursion. But thereafter the USSR and China drifted farther apart and India and the USSR nearer. It thus became possible for Pakistan to look to China as part of its balancing act (see p. 80) and, amongst other things, to build jointly with China a strategic road over the Karakoram, completed in 1978, linking Islamabad with the Chinese Tibet-Xinjiang communications system.[27] And China settled its boundary with Pakistan in 1963, to India's annoyance: for the area concerned lay in Azad Kashmir. But China did not come to Pakistan's assistance in the war with India in 1965 or in the Bangladesh war of 1972, though it did twice veto the admission of Bangladesh to the United Nations.

Sri Lanka sought closer relations with China when the SLFP was in power: it was China that donated and constructed a large international conference centre in Colombo.

We have seen how Nepal has used China as a counterpoise to India and to some extent to the USSR. China settled its boundary with Nepal without much difficulty, though there was a temporary setback when China claimed the whole of Mount Everest (the international boundary, it was later agreed, runs through the highest point in the world).

Turning to South Asian relations with Afghanistan, Pakistan is the country most involved for obvious geopolitical reasons. The problems of the Pakhtunistan and Baluchistan agitation have already been discussed in Chapter 4. Pakistan has suffered the effects of disturbed conditions in Afghanistan during and after the Soviet incursion, in terms of floods of refugees and Mojaheddin ('freedom-fighters') and vast inflows of arms, mainly supplied by the US to aid the Mojaheddin against the Soviet-installed government of Najibullah in Kabul. The Mojaheddin were and are split into many factions: some ethnic, Pushtu, Tajik and Uzbek; some sectarian, Sunni, Shiah and Wahabis supported by Saudi Arabia; some more fundamentalist than others. From Zia's day onwards Pakistan tended to back the Hezbe Islami of Hekmatyar, a fundamentalist 'Pushtun chauvinist'; but later established relations first with a UN mission seeking a settlement in Afghanistan and then with the Council of diverse elements set up in Kabul. (In consequence the Jamaat Islami withdrew from the ruling IDA in Islamabad: see Chapter 4.) Further, Pakistan holds the nearest oceanic port (Karachi) to the Central Asian Republics of the former USSR but the potential connecting route, albeit short, lies through Afghan territory, which thus acquires added significance to Islamabad in a complex and unstable situation.

India too has a geopolitical interest in Afghanistan. With its long-standing Soviet links it displayed some sympathy with Najibullah.

In the early years of independence India, identifying what it saw as yet another victim of colonialism, was supportive of Burma; though not without strain, as when in 1964 there was an exodus of Indians from Burma following the nationalization of various enterprises. But in 1967 agreement was reached for the delimitation and demarcation of the Indo–Burmese boundary.

Relations between Bangladesh and Burma were adversely affected in 1991–2 by an incursion of Muslim refugees (Rohingyas) fleeing from the latter's obnoxious regime.

Apprehension about China as a threat to India via the peninsulas, islands and seaways has been a prominent motif in the policies of New Delhi towards South-east Asia, particularly from 1980 onwards.[28] Another and familiar motif has been sympathy towards nations newly-emerging from colonial rule and professing non-alignment. This has been especially so with Indonesia (though not without periods of tension). Indian relations with Vietnam and Cambodia have been much more complicated, while, broadly speaking, Thailand, Singapore and the Philippines have been seen from New Delhi as too US-oriented, though this may change. India did, however, support Malaysia during its period of confrontation with Soekarno's Indonesia. All of these Indian perceptions of South-east Asia, and indeed the mention (necessarily brief) here given to them, need to be seen against the background of India's self-image as the now-dominant regional power. Not far away, of course, looms Japan, a superpower in the making if ever there was one, and one that shows an increasing interest in Asia.

SOUTH ASIA'S RELATIONS WITH EXTERNAL COUNTRIES: THE SUPERPOWERS

I shall be concerned here primarily with relations between India and Pakistan on the one hand and the US and USSR on the other.

If one of the tragedies of international relations in South Asia has been the animosity between India and Pakistan, another was that a subcontinent, one of whose national leaders was a leading exponent of non-alignment, should have become so heavily involved in the tensions between the United States and the Soviet Union.[29] An optimist of liberal disposition might have thought in 1947 that the auguries were good for the preservation of the region from these tensions, especially if he underestimated the poison from the Indo–Pakistan estrangement, and was lulled by 'Hindi–Chini bhai-bhai'. Certainly neither the United States nor the Soviet Union played more than a minor role in South Asia for the first few years after independence.

But by 1950 the US was shaken by the Korean War and by other involvements with the Soviets and Chinese into the belief that the Communist powers were bent on aggressive expansionism; and that the protection of the 'free world' demanded a network of strategic alliances backed by superior force. The Cold War had arrived. Nehru was convinced that such a policy would, far from containing aggression, merely serve to provoke it. His sermons on this theme often annoyed the Americans. Pakistan, starting from a not dissimilar neutralist position, preached less, and differed less from the United States, while dissenting over various issues, particularly support for Israel. (Sri Lanka under early UNP rule, especially under Kotelawala, took a staunch pro-western stance till Bandaranaike led his country into neutralism.)

Soon came the American notion that Pakistan might be a useful military ally, strategically placed in relation to the Soviet Union; Pakistan's search for both arms and allies; an arms and mutual security agreement between the US and Pakistan in 1954; and, eventually, Pakistan's adhesion to two of the networks of alliances built up by the US: the Central Treaty Organization (CENTO) linking the arc of countries from Turkey to Pakistan; and the South East Asia Treaty Organization (SEATO).

Nehru was impressed by the model of industrialization in the USSR: he saw it as consistent with non-alignment to wish for friendship with it, but moved with some caution. The USSR, after an initial period of heavy-handed criticism of India's 'bourgeois nationalism', reappraised its South Asian policy and perceived, amongst other things, the benefit of cultivating India and so embarrassing and opposing Pakistan and thus its western ally. It had also come to appreciate the geopolitical importance of India to it, notably *vis-à-vis* China. India, reacting to Pakistan's arms deal with the US, then responded to Moscow's overtures and offers of economic aid, very desirable given the ambitious industrial content of its Second Five Year Plan (1956–61). Before long, the Sino–Soviet rift having appeared, Pakistan was able to establish links with China, as a counterbalance to India; while following a visit by President Nixon to Beijing, there came a *rapprochement* between the US and China. So, it might be thought, all the principal players had chosen their partners. But it is simplistic to see the international relations of India and Pakistan with the superpowers and with China in terms of complete polarization, with India and the USSR on one side, and Pakistan and the US on the other.

True, India's relations with the US frequently reached a point of shrill annoyance. If Nehru's neutralism and sermonizing irritated Americans, Indians (and their friends) were offended by American politicians and 'experts' who were tactlessly and shamefully ignorant of India's justifiable pride in its history, civilizations and modern achievements. But the US has had some staunch friends of India among its ambassadors, notably J.K. Galbraith. It did not crow over India's débâcle in 1962: in fact this brought rapid shipments of arms from America and Britain, but none from Moscow. American economic aid was sometimes crucial in terms of food supplies. President Kennedy sought more friendly relations with India, though his success was limited, partly because of his continued support for Pakistan. And by 1965 (when, in another blow to simplistic perceptions, the USSR mediated between India and Pakistan at Tashkent) the US was more doubtful about the utility of cultivating good relations with India, perhaps now perceiving South Asia as a whole as marginal to US strategic interests (though central to a view of geopolitics from Moscow).

In August 1971 India and the Soviet Union signed a twenty-year treaty of friendship and co-operation (not a military alliance, it is important to stress). Indo–American relations became more distant; and strained when later that year the US extended some support to Pakistan as it strove to suppress the Bangladeshi revolt, sending a naval task force into the Indian Ocean. The USSR helped India in various ways, including the supply of arms, during this period. The US and USSR did, however, both join other countries in helping Bangladesh in the daunting task of post-war reconstruction.

With India's military success and rise to dominance in the subcontinent in 1971, the US and India once again reappraised each other; and there ensued a new round of oscillations in their relationship. Indeed, Nixon spoke of India as a major country with 'new stature and responsibilities'. But some observers saw a contradiction between this recognition and what they perceived to be America's self-characterization as regional security manager, using the Indian Ocean base at Diego Garcia (a far cry from neutralist notions of that ocean as a zone of peace). And India's explosion of a nuclear device in 1974 was not calculated to please the US. However, in 1977, following the inauguration of President Carter in the US and of the Janata government in India, cordiality once again entered Indo–American relations and some coolness into Indo–Soviet relations. In 1979, when the USSR invaded Afghanistan, India demanded the withdrawal of Soviet forces but fell short of outright condemnation. In the 1980s both Mrs Gandhi and Rajiv were interested in improving India's relations with the US and the west; and in remaining rather less friendly with the USSR. The latter, for its part, employed a number of means (including visits by President Gorbachev) to express the hope of maintaining traditional ties and, indeed, of strengthening them by new forms of economic co-operation; all this suggested the continuing value of India to the USSR. Rajiv was striving at the same time to revive the flagging non-aligned movement (NAM).

Turning to variations in Pakistan's relations with the superpowers, as is only to be expected whenever the US looked with favour on India suspicion was aroused in Pakistan. Thus arms aid to India in 1962 caused a reappraisal of foreign policy in its neighbour. A little later the US reconsidered the value of its alliance with Pakistan, given such matters as the strengthening bond between Pakistan and China, and some of the pronouncements of Bhutto. And, whatever Nixon's view of events in Bangladesh in 1971, a section of American public opinion was hostile to what it saw as Pakistani oppression. But then came the *rapprochement* between the US and China, reducing the former's worries about Pakistan's ties with the latter. However, the containing belt of alliances collapsed: CENTO faded in the late 1970s, and the Iranian revolution (with its anti-American dimension) broke in 1979. A higher value was then placed by the US both on the Indian Ocean and on Pakistan. But in the 1970s there was some hostility to the US in Pakistan for reasons that included the failure of America to support Pakistan more effectively in the Bangladesh war; and stronger links between Pakistan and the Islamic world, which saw the US as a friend of Israel. In 1979, in fact, a mob burnt down the US Embassy in Islamabad. The Afghan crisis of 1979 brought offers of US arms and economic aid to Pakistan. But Pakistan did not neglect to listen to the Soviet Union on the Afghan situation, and remained a member of NAM. US aid was suspended from November 1990 because of suspicions (later confirmed) that Pakistan possessed nuclear capability. But following the outbreak of the Gulf War Pakistan sent a contingent to Saudi Arabia (in response there was anti-American and anti-western agitation at home). Bangladesh also sent troops. India, for its part, tried to exert a neutral influence through the NAM.

Clearly, then the relations between India and Pakistan on the one hand and the US and USSR on the other have not been constant, but have ebbed and flowed with a variety of factors: for example, domestic politics, links with other countries and preoccupations of the superpowers elsewhere.

But by February 1992 a completely new situation, clouded with many elements of unpredictability, had been precipitated by the collapse of the Soviet Union and the economic chaos within its former republics; and by the association of many of these within the Commonwealth of Independent States (CIS), itself facing an uncertain future. Of the countries of South Asia it was understandably India that was the most disturbed by these dramatic developments, given the past importance of the USSR to it in trade, arms supply and general support. One reaction by New Delhi has been to confirm ties with the CIS and the Russian Republic. (In May 1992 it signed trade and economic co-operation agreements with the latter.) Another has been to mend bridges with Washington, though it must constantly show awareness that the US is not universally beloved by Indian opinion, nor India by Americans. Still another reaction may be to hasten *rapprochement* with China along lines already mentioned. Meanwhile Pakistan also has bridges to mend with the US, not least over the nuclear issue. It has indeed already proposed a five-nation conference on the curbing of nuclear proliferation in South Asia, a move not admired by India.

SOUTH ASIA'S RELATIONS WITH EXTERNAL COUNTRIES: BRITAIN AND THE COMMONWEALTH

Since conceding independence to its former territories in South Asia, Britain has played a far smaller part in the external relations of the successor states than have China, the USSR and the US. Indeed, its role has declined in importance over the years; but this is not to say that it has been negligible. For instance, Britain, a permanent member of the Security Council of the United Nations, has been far from inactive in utilizing its experience both of diplomacy and of South Asia in advising on issues affecting the subcontinent.

A significant link between Britain and the successor states of South Asia has been that through the Commonwealth of Nations, of which the Queen is Head. Before independence it had been supposed that India at any rate would reject Commonwealth membership, which was then on offer in the form of Dominion Status, unacceptable to many Indian nationalists. After independence, with Britain's continued alliance with the US and membership of the North Atlantic Treaty Organization, it seemed to some that Commonwealth membership would imply taking sides in the Cold War. But it became clear to Nehru and his colleagues that this was no necessary implication, and that there were many advantages in continuing links, given *inter alia* the ties of many kinds with Britain and the information and consultative services that the Commonwealth provided. And, when it was agreed that India could remain a republic, Commonwealth membership was assured, and has been maintained.

This is not to say that relations with Britain have not from time to time been strained, as, for example, during the Suez crisis of 1956, and when it became clear that the British South Atlantic island of Diego Garcia was to be an American base. But on the whole Indian relations with Britain have been a good deal more harmonious than those with the US. And India has played a notable and constructive part in Commonwealth matters: such was the role of Rajiv Gandhi during a crisis over sanctions on South Africa in 1985. Indeed, its membership has made it much easier for other territories to remain in the Commonwealth as they gained independence.

Although many of the arguments for continued Commonwealth membership applied with equal force to Pakistan at independence, the fact that India was to be a member caused heart-searching there. In the event, however, Pakistan became a member, and stayed until it resigned following British recognition of Bangladesh. It rejoined in 1989. Bangladesh, of course, became a member of the Commonwealth.

Sri Lanka joined the Commonwealth at independence, as a kingdom: the Queen was Queen of Ceylon until a republican constitution was instituted in 1972; but Sri Lanka retained its membership.

The Commonwealth is less of a force in international affairs today than it was forty years ago. Certainly it plays a declining part in the calculations of South Asian countries, for whom the alliances, balancing acts and neutralism discussed in this chapter are far more of the stuff of everyday diplomacy and of strategic planning. But the Commonwealth could yet play a part in solving the Kashmir problem; and relations with Britain, and with other Commonwealth countries, are still important in terms of economic aid and of cultural links. Many able South Asian scholars and research students still wish to read British books and to come to British universities, where they are welcome. But the relationship between South Asia and the United Kingdom, which many of us, South Asian and British, cherish, has been eroded, as Michael Lipton and J. Firn have emphasized; and conscious efforts must continue to be made if they are not to decline further, to mutual disadvantage.[30]

SOUTH ASIA'S RELATIONS WITH EXTERNAL COUNTRIES: THE MIDDLE EAST

Pakistan has consistently professed to have more in common with the countries of the Middle East than with those of South Asia. It has striven to establish good relations with those countries and to proclaim its solidarity with them. In the last years of the Shah's rule Iran provided useful aid to Pakistan; and later, following the conclusion of the Iran–Iraq war has, sought to repair severed economic relations. In 1985 it revived an Economic Co-operation Organization, of which Pakistan is a member. But elsewhere in the Middle East many of Pakistan's efforts proved less fruitful, largely because of the disunity of the Islamic world, and of the Arabs within it – except in their hostility to Israel and its supporters, in which Pakistan has usually joined.[31] Egypt and Syria often seemed closer to India and to its policies of non-alignment than to Pakistan; while Rajiv made cautious overtures to Saudi Arabia. Some Middle East states, however, in due course provided aid to Pakistan, which in its turn helped with their military training; while the oil-producing countries have provided large numbers of jobs, contracts for contractors and remittances to benefit the home economy. In this benefit Bangladesh also has joined: but so have India, especially Kerala, and Sri Lanka. But in 1990 came the Iraqi invasion of Kuwait and the Gulf War. Large numbers of South Asian workers suffered great hardship in fleeing from the hostilities and attempting to reach their home countries. Some of the economic effects of the Gulf bonanza and of its sudden disappearance will be taken up in Chapter 6.

India did not send a contingent to join the US-led multinational force confronting Iraq. Pakistan and Bangladesh did do so. In response to a situation that could be perceived as an American attempt to dominate and to attack Islam there were many demonstrations and riots in India as well as in Pakistan and Bangladesh, and that not only among Muslims. However, January 1992 brought India to a new retreat from non-alignment and a further move towards the US when it announced that it was establishing diplomatic relations with Israel.

Clearly uncertainty over the future shape of the Middle East makes it very difficult to discern likely trends in South Asian relations with it and with external powers involved there.

CONCLUSION

A similar conclusion on the discernment of trends applies in a much broader context.[32] True, India is likely to remain dominant in the subcontinent but to retreat from non-alignment, though the summit of the NAM held in Djakarta in September 1992 may give a new fillip to the movement and renew the involvement of India and of South Asia more generally.

This chapter and its predecessor have shown the dangers of an internal instability which must be reflected in uncertain international relations in India as in other South Asian countries. Looking briefly at the wider context, another and even greater area of uncertainty has been opened up by the collapse of the Soviet Union, though it seems clear that its successors will place much less value on South Asia and be able to exert less influence there, leading to a stronger impact of the US and to changing reactions by South Asian states and interactions between them.

6

ECONOMIC DEVELOPMENTS IN SOUTH ASIA SINCE INDEPENDENCE

This chapter outlines the changes in the economies of the South Asian countries since independence. It will begin with sketches of those economies at that time, and of the immediate consequences of partition in India and Pakistan. There will follow an indication of the context for economic affairs in South Asia. This will partly be a matter of reminders of certain points already made in preceding chapters, but it will also be appropriate to dwell on a very important part of the context of economic change, that related to population, as it stood at independence and as it has grown in the ensuing years. There will then follow a country-by-country survey of economic policies, achievements and problems.

ECONOMIES AT INDEPENDENCE: INDIA AND PAKISTAN

The economy that India and Pakistan inherited from the British Indian Empire at independence was, of course, overwhelmingly agricultural. Over 80 per cent of the Indian population lived in villages, nearer 90 per cent in Pakistan; and some 65 per cent of the population was engaged in agriculture. Most cultivators were concerned with food crops for themselves and their families or for sale within the Empire. Rice was by far and away the dominant food crop, grown in *kharif* in the Indo–Gangetic plains, and in other seasons as well, especially under irrigation, in the Bengal delta and in the plains and deltas of both coasts of the peninsula.[1] Wheat was a crop of the *rabi* season in the northern parts of the plains, while the various grains commonly lumped together as millets were the main food crop of the drier, unirrigated parts of the peninsula. In many areas pulses, and in some groundnuts, were subsidiary food crops. A comparatively small proportion of the cultivated area was in what were officially but misleadingly (given sales of foodgrains) known as cash crops. These included jute, cotton, tea and sugar. Locally, however, one of these was important if not dominant: for example, tea in parts of Assam, and what was to become Kerala; jute in Bengal; sugar in parts of Uttar Pradesh (UP) and of the hinterland of

Bombay. In addition to the massive construction during the British period of new irrigation canals in the Punjab, in western UP, and to a lesser extent elsewhere, village tanks had grown in numbers, especially in the south, and were beginning to strain water resources; and wells had been sunk in many areas, above all in the plains, water being lifted from them almost everywhere by human or animal power.

In many parts of the Indian Empire by 1947 growth of population had led to severe pressure of people on land. This was especially the case in northern Punjab, outside the canal colonies; in eastern UP, Bihar and Bengal; and in the south. With this pressure had come subdivision of holdings till many of them were too small to support a family at subsistence level; and, increasingly, severe poverty, undernourishment, indebtedness, and landlessness, and, less certainly, declining soil fertility. It will be remembered, however, that landlessness was no new phenomenon in Indian society (see pp. 30–1); and recognized that the plight of the small cultivator and the landless labourer cannot be understood merely in terms of population pressure, but also involves other factors, especially land tenure.

Chapter 3 showed that Indian systems of land tenure have long been very complex and that whatever else the British contributed it was not simplification. At independence, landlordism of one sort or another, often capping a pyramid of rights to land, was characteristic of much of the Indian Empire, whether under *zamindari* or *raiyatwari* tenure; and that there were gross inequalities in landholding, income and power, particularly where landlords had large holdings, as in parts of what was to become West Pakistan. Not even there, however, were there many absentee landlords holding vast areas. Most landlords were village-based (indeed, legislation enacted in British days was designed to prevent land passing to 'non-agricultural classes'): a 'big man' in such areas as Bengal or Madras Presidency was one who owned a score or so of acres (while the small farmer held a fraction of an acre).

In terms of their agriculture and agrarian structure, then, India and Pakistan inherited a situation with parallels in many other parts of the Third World: particularly a high degree of dependence on agriculture; food production mainly for internal consumption; population pressure; inequalities of income; intense poverty afflicting a major part of the rural population; and an ever-growing landless class. But the Indian Empire on the eve of independence differed from many of its contemporaries in a number of important respects. First, it possessed a respectable infrastructure: not only irrigation works but also railways, roads, and commercial and other institutions; and an administrative and legal system almost without equal in the colonial world, at least so far as British India and the more progressive princely states were concerned.[2] Secondly, it was producing considerable quantities of minerals, notably coal (some 30 million tons per annum), and iron and manganese ore (though it produced but little oil). Thirdly, although much of the mineral production was exported, part (especially of the coal and the iron óre) was used at home, notably in the giant Tata steelworks at Jamshedpur in Bihar, claimed to be the largest in the Commonwealth at independence, when India was making about three-quarters of its requirement of steel.[3] Tata, it should be noted, was an entirely indigenous enterprise. Fourthly, and in addition to the surviving, and in some cases reviving handicraft industries, there were modern textile mills in Calcutta (notably for jute), Bombay, Nagpur and Ahmedabad (cotton), and also in Kanpur, Madras and Coimbatore (also cotton). At independence installed capacity in these mills was second only to that in the United States. Fifthly, there were also many sugar factories, a number of cement and railway works, and the beginning of the factory manufacture of consumer goods. Indeed, at independence 50 per cent of exports by value were of manufactures.

But considerable though these industrial developments were, Chapter 3 has shown that their impact on the Indian Empire must assuredly not be exaggerated. India was still highly dependent on imported manufactures, especially of consumer goods, and on the United Kingdom market. Factory industry only employed some 2 per cent of the labour force, and was highly localized geographically: virtually confined, in fact to Calcutta and Hugliside, with an outlier in Jamshedpur; to Bombay and axes running thence north to Ahmedabad and east to Nagpur; to Kanpur in UP; and to Madras and Coimbatore in the south. In such areas modern urbanization was most rapid. But over vast areas of the plains and over most of what was to become Pakistan, little sign of modern industry or mining was to be seen: everywhere, there was nothing but the endless fields of innumerable villages, with the occasional ancient city or town (sometimes sheltering craft industries). The same was true of much of the Deccan, except where fields gave way to jungle. Clearly, then, the new states were to face highly-uneven regional development, not surprising given such a huge and varied subcontinent. But that is not to say that such spatial inequalities were more important than interclass and intercaste inequalities.

Bhagwati and Desai drew attention to other attributes of manufacturing industry at independence, such as the tendency for industrial enterprises to congeal into large groups related to the origins of the entrepreneurs in tightly-knit merchant caste and kin networks; and the lack of research and development.[4]

The overall poverty of the Indian Empire and the limited impact of modern industry is further demonstrated by relevant indices of development quoted in Norton Ginsburg's *Atlas of Economic Development* which, though published in 1961, is based on data from the early 1950s.[5] (A warning must be issued on the reliability of some of the data for India and Pakistan, as for most developing countries.) These show a Gross National Product per capita of US $84 for India and of US $56 for Pakistan, placing them respectively 84th and 91st (equal) of the 96 countries ranked by Ginsburg. The calories per capita per day are cited as 2125 for Pakistan and 2000 for

India, respectively 66th and 78th out of 93 countries. Gross energy consumption is given as 2.7 megawatt hours for India and 2.4 for Pakistan, respectively 86th and 87th (equal) in a list of 124 cases. And these aggregated national indices tell us nothing about interregional disparities, or about inequalities of income and consumption in this region of fabulously rich Maharajas and unbelievably poor rural Harijans and city slum-dwellers. The claim that manufactures composed 40 per cent of the Indian Empire's exports at independence is placed in perspective by Ginsburg's citation of India's annual trade per capita as US $0.7 and Pakistan's US $0.9, both very near the bottom of his list (though it must be remembered that other things being equal a large country registers a much lower index than a small because of the possibilities of internal trade).

THE IMMEDIATE CONSEQUENCES OF PARTITION FOR THE ECONOMIES OF INDIA AND PAKISTAN[6]

Chapter 3 has shown that, in the partition of 1947, Pakistan secured almost all of the land irrigated by the Punjab canals, often a food surplus area, but cut off by the new frontier from its previous markets. The raw cotton of West Pakistan and the jute of East Pakistan were similarly severed from the mills that had processed them; for there were very few cotton or jute factories in either West or East Pakistan at partition. West Pakistan retained its natural port in Karachi, but East Pakistan and its intricate and well-developed network of waterways were cut off from Calcutta. The same was true of Assam; as late as 1968 I saw many barges laid up, idle, at Gauhati in that state, which suffered also because of its roundabout land link with the rest of India. It will be appreciated, too, that the economy of newly independent Pakistan, divided as it was by a thousand miles of India, was fundamentally difficult to manage. The consequences of partition would, of course, have been less severe if the two successor states had not been such bad friends, so that economically logical measures like a customs union or rights in each other's ports were out of the question.

Partition, with its dislocation and vast exchange of populations also spelt severe short-term consequences in terms of the resettlement and rehabilitation of refugees[7]); not so short-term in the case of continued migration from East Pakistan to India. Altogether, these consequences spelt a great strain on resources, administrative and financial. But there were, of course, wide areas of both countries that were not affected directly by migration, devastation and resettlement.

THE ECONOMY OF CEYLON AT INDEPENDENCE

In some ways the economy of Ceylon at independence was similar to that of the Indian Empire across the water. Over 80 per cent of the population was rural and over 50 per cent of the work-force engaged in agriculture (somewhat differently defined, however). The principal food crop was rice. Pressure of population on cultivated land was evident in the Wet Zone and in the hills. And the economy was beyond dispute that of a less-developed country.

But that economy was essentially an export economy.[8] Trade per capita was cited by Ginsburg as US $8.3, placing Ceylon about half-way up the rank order for this index. Ceylon in fact exported tea, rubber and coconut products, largely to Britain; and imported foodstuffs (especially rice and manufactures). The sector producing, processing and handling these export crops was often called 'the plantation sector', but this was to ignore the substantial contribution of small-holdings, especially of rubber and coconuts. The 'traditional' sector was seen as that producing rice and other foodstuffs, and long neglected (though the colonial government had begun the restoration of ancient Dry Zone irrigation works). Writers like D.R. Snodgrass saw the two sectors as the separate parts of a dual economy. But many links between them had developed by independence, for example, through the employment of local capital and labour, not only in commerce associated with the export crops, but also in plantation ownership, and through the cultivation by 'peasants' of both paddyfields and holdings of rubber or coconut. But Ceylon at independence had its problems of regional disparities, if only because of the generally sparse population of its malarial Dry Zone.

Also in contrast to the Indian Empire, Ceylon had few modern manufacturing industries (though some handicrafts survived): but there was a fair amount of repairing and, indeed, making of machinery for the plantations. And it had a higher proportion of its workers in transport and commerce – with a good road network in the Wet Zone and in up-country plantation areas. Its GNP per capita as cited by Ginsburg was US $122, almost twice that of India and more than twice that of Pakistan round about the time of independence. Ceylon's higher figure was mainly due to the export sector. But, as in the case of India and Pakistan, an aggregate national figure conceals gross disparities between groups of people, notably in Ceylon those between affluent Colombo citizens, grown fat on the export economy, and Tamil labour on the plantations or the poor Sinhalese peasant.

THE ECONOMY OF NEPAL, BHUTAN AND THE MALDIVE ISLANDS IN 1947

Nepal was, of course, never formally part of the British Empire, but was protected and fossilized, creating conditions in which population grew and pressed on land resources. But in 1947 Nepal was still an almost entirely agricultural and pastoral country, approximating closely to the stereotype of a peasant 'subsistence economy'. There was very little industry, just a few miles of railway running into the country from India, and hardly any metalled roads. Quantitative data for the period are either lacking or of doubtful authenticity. Ginsburg, however, puts it at the bottom of his table of GNP per capita, at US $40; and quotes a very low adult literacy figure (1–5 per cent).[9]

The economy of Bhutan in 1947 was even more divorced from the modern industrial and commercial world and its villages even more remote. As for the Maldive Islands at the same period, they certainly were anything but remote: their seafarers were renowned, as were their shipbuilders. There was, however, a great need for imports, especially of food; and there were few commodities to export in exchange apart from coconut products and dried fish. Neither Bhutan nor the Maldives appear in Ginsburg's tabulations.

THE CONTEXT OF ECONOMIC DEVELOPMENT

The context of economic development in South Asia since independence consists not only of the demographic situation in the next section, but also of a number of features touched on in earlier chapters and now recapitulated.

The earlier part of Chapter 2 dealt with the resources and limitations of the natural and man-modified environment, especially its soils and climates in their enormous and insufficiently-recognized variety. Discussion ran on to the vital theme of conservation, particularly to anxieties about the earth's future as a human habitat and to the need for sustainable development in a situation of rapid population growth. Awareness of these matters should have been heightened by the United Nations Conference on Environment and Development held in Rio de Janeiro in June 1992 and by publications cited in connexion with it in Chapter 2. One hopes that such awareness will form an essential part of the context in which economic development in South Asia is considered and executed in the years ahead.

The second part of the same chapter introduced the South Asian social environment. Here I highlight the built-in inequality of society. 'Tribals' as well as Harijans are notoriously disadvantaged, while certain castes tend to be dominant in landholding, wealth and power in many villages. Further, 'village republics' are of doubtful utility as a basis for rural development, while urban elites are detached from their rural roots, which they tend to despise. On another plane the force of linguistic regionalism is such, in India at any rate, that States formed under its impact have been the only effective units at the immediately subnational level, whether in politics or in planning, unstable though some of the States and their boundaries are.

From Chapter 3 I propose only to draw two threads. First, given the existence of change in these supposedly changeless oriental societies, even though it was not at the pace predicted by nineteenth-century observers, it is unrealistic to see most South Asian economies and societies in 1947 as a static tableau, awaiting the magic wand of independence before it could spring into life. Secondly, the relatively high levels of education and of literacy in the Indian Empire and Ceylon provided the successor states with a very different base from that of many less-developed countries.

The latter part of Chapter 4 discussed politics in South Asia. It will be evident that government intervention in economic affairs in India has operated in a federal system in which both the Centre and the States are constitutionally concerned with economic planning, the central Planning Commission being, however, extraconstitutional. The chapter also showed that the Congress Party, so long dominant, covered with its umbrella a diversity of interest groups. So, in a different way, did the Janata coalition briefly in office from 1977 to 1979, and non-Congress governments in precarious power more recently. Other political parties, notably those of the left, have had a clearer economic ideology, which they have been able to deploy in some State governments. Behind all this has lain the factional fighting and other complexities of the Indian political scene, not least the instability of recent years: all not without influence on the actuality of economic change.

In Sri Lanka the early alternation of parties in power meant some oscillations in economic policy, though at times, particularly those of armed conflict like the unhappy present, official thinking on economic policy has taken a back place. Meanwhile, as we shall see, the economy as a whole has been in decline, and the ever-growing army of unemployed have been the worst sufferers.

Pakistan's long periods of military rule interspersed with bouts of uneasy politics and its development of concepts of an 'Islamic State' have sent it on an economic course generally very different from that of India, though with some superficial convergence of declared policies (some would say rhetoric) in the Bhutto era.

Bangladesh has suffered long spells of instability and military government which have provided much of the political context for the country's struggle to survive. Nepal has precariously remained a monarchy, though with recent concessions to democracy after much unrest.

So much then for a reminder of some of the strands in the 'political economy' of South Asia.[10] Finally, the international relations of the several South Asian countries have affected economic change, not least through foreign aid policies and programmes. But there remains a part of the context of economic change, population, which deserves a separate section that will deal, not only with the situation at independence, but with change since that time. And, since population, particularly in its interaction with society and the economy is a not uncontroversial subject, something will have to be said on differing viewpoints and conclusions.

POPULATION IN MODERN SOUTH ASIA

First I make some points on the availability and reliability of data. Definitive reports tend to appear long after a census. But the Indian Census

Commissioner and his opposite number in Bangladesh are to be commended on issuing provisional results within a few months of the 1991 Census. The major countries of the subcontinent have relatively sophisticated census organizations:[11] they have, indeed, increased in sophistication since independence. More reliance may, *a priori*, be placed on census data, especially for total population and its distribution, than in most Third World countries. But such reliance is relative. Censuses have sometimes taken place under disturbed conditions that have affected their accuracy: for example, in West Bengal in 1971, while no enumeration at all was possible in Assam in 1981, nor in 1991 did one take place at the proper time in Pakistan or in Jammu and Kashmir (India) or in any part of Sri Lanka. In any case, the census is conducted by a vast army of enumerators of varying skill and conscientiousness who are supposed to visit every house and question the occupants. But houses may be missed (as my host's was in Colombo in March 1981), and questions misunderstood. When a sample post-enumeration check was conducted in Bangladesh in 1991, a 3.08 per cent undercount was revealed. Not all tabulations take account of underenumeration: this may be a reason for differences between figures cited in different secondary publications. Not all of these, for example, agree that the population of Bangladesh declined from 1941 to 1951 (by 65,000 according to official sources), though 3 million are estimated to have died in the Bengal famine of 1943. For such reasons as these, data for Bangladesh, India, Pakistan and Sri Lanka must be treated with some reserve. Data for Nepal are dubious, those for Bhutan and the Maldives even more so. To quote populations other than in millions and tenths (as in Table 6.1) or growth rates other than to the nearest 0.1 per cent (as in Table 6.2) gives a spurious appearance of accuracy.

Censuses are usually taken at ten-year intervals. But the notes to Table 6.1 indicate some variations from this pattern. Since, however, Table 6.2 has been calculated in terms of average *annual* compound (or exponential) growth rates, sound comparisons may be made (subject always, of course, to reliability of underlying data).

Demographers rely for analysis, and for projections, on data additional to census population figures, in particular, data on the age and sex composition of the people. In South Asia these are even less reliable than population totals. Many people do not know their age; while in a male-dominated society data on females tend to be less accurate than those on males. Again, through incomplete registration, published birth and death rates tend to be inaccurate, so that estimates of population in intercensal years may go wildly astray. Thus in India in 1961 the census registered a population 8 million higher than had been projected only two years earlier.[12]

Unquantified migrations are another source of error.

Tables 6.1 and 6.2 taken together give a perspective on populations in South Asia and on rates of growth. Thus in South Asia as a whole in 1990

Table 6.1 Population of South Asian countries (in millions)

	1941	1951	1961	1971	1981	1990	1991
Bangladesh	42.0	41.9	50.8	71.5[a]	89.9[b]	–	108.0[b]
Bhutan	–	–	–	–	–	–	0.6[b]
India	318.7	361.1	439.2	547.8	683.3	–	843.9[b]
Maldives	–	–	–	–	–	0.2	–
Nepal	6.3[c]	8.7[d]	9.8	11.5	14.2	19.0[c]	–
Pakistan	28.3	33.8	46.1	65.3[e]	83.8[b]	112.0[c]	–
Sri Lanka	6.7[f]	8.1[g]	10.6[h]	12.7	14.6[b]	17.0[c]	–

Sources:
Reports on national censuses – World Bank (1992) *World Development Report*, for 1990 estimates, used where 1991 data were not available at the time of writing.
India – Cassen, R.H. (1978) *India: Population, Economy, Society*, London; Unwin, P.T.H. (1981), 'The census of India 1981', *Geography* 66: 221–2; Bose, A. (1991) *Demographic Diversity of India: 1991 Census*, Delhi.
Nepal – Karan, P.P. (1960) *Nepal*, Lexington, Kentucky; Macfarlane, A. (1976) *Resources and Population: A Study of the Gurungs of Nepal*, Cambridge, especially p. 204.
Pakistan – Johnson, B.L.C. (1979) *Pakistan: a Geography*, London, p. 14;
Sri Lanka – Balakrishnan, N. and Gunasekara, H.M. (1977) 'A review of demographic trends', in De Silva, K.M. (ed.) *Sri Lanka: A Survey*, London, 109–27.
Notes:
a 1974.
b Provisional figures.
c Estimate.
d 1954.
e End of 1972.
f 1946.
g 1953.
h 1963.

Table 6.2 South Asia: average annual compound rate of population increase

Bangladesh	%	Nepal	%		
1941–51	0.0	1941–54	2.5		
1951–61	2.0	1954–61	1.7		
1961–74	2.7	1961–71	1.6		
1974–81	3.3	1971–81	1.4		
1981–91	1.9	1981–89	3.3		

India	%	Pakistan	%	Sri Lanka	%
1941–51	1.3	1941–51	1.7	1946–53	2.8
1951–61	2.0	1951–61	3.1	1953–63	2.7
1961–71	2.2	1961–72	3.0	1963–71	2.3
1971–81	2.2	1972–81	2.9	1971–81	1.4
1981–91	2.1	1981–90	2.9	1981–90	1.7

Source: Derived by the author from data in Table 6.1.

there were about 1000 million people. Of these some 80 per cent were in India. It will be clear, too, that the population of Pakistan has roughly trebled since independence in 1947, while those of India, Bangladesh and Sri Lanka have more than doubled. This at once gives some measure of the weighty burden that population growth has placed on national economies.

Table 6.2 shows that from 1951 to 1961, and excluding Nepal with its doubtful data, each country experienced an average annual compound population growth rate equal to or greater than 2 per cent. Bangladesh, it would appear, saw its growth rate rise since 1961 to reach, for the Period 1974–81, a frightening annual rate of 3.3 per cent; and this in a country with one of the highest densities of rural population in the world which has been seen as an actual or potential Malthusia.[13] (It is not yet possible to comment on the reasons behind the figure for 1981–91.) India, with a rate for 1981–91 approximately the same as that for 1961–81, gives some indication, to the optimist at any rate, that a plateau has been reached in terms of growth rates. But it cannot be too strongly stressed that there is still a steep upward slope in terms of total population. An annual growth rate of 2.1 per cent means that India enters the decade 1991–2001 with an annual increase of population of nearly 18 million; and this annual increment will itself increase at compound rates unless the growth rate falls sufficiently. However, current growth rates vary considerably within India: from 1.3 per cent in Kerala and 1.4 per cent in Tamil Nadu to 4.1 per cent in the Union Territory of Delhi (now centred on a city of over 9 million that owes much to immigration) and, it is reported, 4.5 per cent in Nagaland.[14]

Pakistan demonstrates the steadiest compound growth rate at around 3.0 per cent. from 1951 to 1990. The Sri Lanka case is, however, different. Here one can with reasonable clarity discern a descent from a plateau at 2.7–2.8 per cent in the periods 1946–53 and 1953–63 to 2.3 per cent in 1963–71 and 1.4 per cent in 1971–81, though perhaps up to 1.7 per cent more recently.

Not surprisingly, then, population growth and its consequences have overshadowed all of the countries of South Asia and most of the States of India in the years since independence; and none of them, with the possible exceptions of Sri Lanka, Kerala and Tamil Nadu, can look forward for the immediate future to a certain and significant decline in their rates of population growth, still less to a stabilization of absolute population levels.

Population increase in a country is, of course, due to an excess of births over deaths, plus net international immigration. Such immigration has not been of great importance in South Asia since independence once the immediate consequences of partition were over and done with, except from Nepal and into Bhutan (though there was an intermittent stream of refugees from East Pakistan, as it then was, accelerating in 1971; and in recent years Sri Lanka has seen an out-migration of persons of Indian origin and of refugees from the troubles). As in many other parts of the Third World, the countries of South Asia have seen a declining death-rate, mainly as a result of the reduced impact of famine, disease and infant mortality. According to official data, crude death-rates per 1000 persons fell in India from 27.4 in 1941–51 to 14.9 in 1971–81 and (provisionally) to 11 in 1989.[15] There were comparable falls in Pakistan (from 23 in 1960 to 12 in 1990) and in Bangladesh (from 23 to 14 between the same two years). In Sri Lanka there was a more spectacular fall from 13 at independence to 6 in 1990. In Nepal the crude death-rate is quoted as having fallen from 29 in 1960 to 14 in 1990. All this is not to say that disaster, malnutrition and disease no longer stalk the countries of South Asia, nor that death rates and infantile and maternal mortality are not still unacceptably high among poorer people and in poorer regions: the national data just cited conceal wide regional variations.

While death-rates were falling in these ways, crude birth-rates have continued to run at a much higher level; but do appear now to be falling, though differentially, and still at a level far above crude death-rates. At independence crude birth-rates in India were running at around 45 per thousand: in 1981 they were of the order of 34 and in 1990 of 30. In Pakistan the birth-rates have fallen from 49 in 1960 to 42 in 1990; in Bangladesh, it is reported, from 47 to 35 over the same period; in Nepal, for what the figures are worth, from 46 to 40 over the same period. In Sri Lanka, again the odd man out, crude birth-rates fell from 39 at independence to 20 in 1989. The decline in recent years has been attributed mainly to an increase in the age of marriage.[16] If this in turn is related to unemployment and financial distress, then an improvement in the economic position may have the perverse consequence of helping to raise the birth-rate.

One important consequence of the 'population explosion' occasioned by the huge surplus of births over deaths has been, for all of the South Asian countries, a very high proportion of children and young people in their populations. Thus in 1989 some 37 per cent of the Indian and 32 per cent of the Sri Lankan population were under the age of 14. Many results flow from such age composition figures: for instance, the large resources that have to be, or ought to be, devoted to education; the vast numbers clamouring for land and employment; and the increasing size of the reproductive age groups as today's juveniles become tomorrow's parents (so that even if the birth-rate stays constant, or falls, but inadequately, the annual number of births will increase).

Future increases of population primarily depend on the balance between births and deaths; there are a great many imponderables in the assumptions that must be made as a prelude to population projections.[17] It seems very likely that death-rates will continue to decline, barring a Malthusian disaster; but at what rate, and when, they will flatten out and at what level, must remain uncertain. Birth-rates seem set to decline slowly. Many authors envisage that the decline will be, or would be helped by increasing urbanization; by economic development and raised income levels; and by improvements in literacy, especially among females; and in the social and economic position of women; and there is some evidence that a declining birth-rate is indeed correlated with these economic and social phenomena, and that they may lead the countries of South Asia slowly towards 'the widespread voluntary adoption of the small family norm'. But these forces are slow-acting at best, and are likely to act differentially on different parts of South Asia's segmented society. For instance, Muslim women are likely to benefit less compared with their Hindu and Buddhist sisters, and the poor less and last. For what they are worth, projections at the national level by the World Bank may be of interest.[18] They cite the 'hypothetical size of stationary population' in millions as 257 for Bangladesh, 1862 for India, 59 for Nepal, 399 for Pakistan, and 28 for Sri Lanka. These are indeed terrifying figures; and will, to many minds, conjure up the Malthusian nightmare.

Not surprisingly, South Asian governments have pursued conscious population policies with more or less vigour and success, and in the face of formidable difficulties.[19] The Indian Third Plan of 1961 set the stabilization of population 'within a reasonable period' as a firm objective; and in the early 1960s an organization was designed to spread methods of family planning. The difficulties were seen not so much as religious or ideological objections as administrative and technical problems; and Cassen in 1978 believed that 'the socio-economic conditions for widespread voluntary acceptance of birth control did not exist'. The excesses of The Emergency (see Chapter 4), which included compulsory sterilization, did nothing to improve the image of the programme. On the other hand, from regionally differential growth rates and declining birth-rates it appears that some family limitation is being practised. In 1989, in fact, Rajiv Gandhi, then Prime Minister, made a powerful plea for recognition of India's demographic diversity and for a family planning programme radically adjusted to take account of it.

Sri Lanka at first lacked a clear population policy, though voluntary agencies were at work and received a government grant. In the 1970s, in spite of fears that its differential impact would alter ethnic balances, a clearer policy emerged; but family planning has probably had less effect on diminishing the birth-rate than delayed marriage. The impact of family planning seems to have been less in other South Asian countries, though voluntary organizations and some official agencies exist.

So far, the discussion has been generally consistent with a neo-Malthusian position: with, that is, a fear of population growing faster than the means of providing for it. Some Marxian analysis plays down 'the so-called population explosion' as a cause of such ills as unemployment, whose origins it sees as structural.[20] Others, and not only Marxians, have argued that poorer rural people firmly believe that a *large* family is an economic advantage, primarily because sons at any rate can earn from a quite tender age;[21] or, alternatively, and sadly, be sold into bonded labour. Those who know the Indian village are apt to see the force of their belief.

It is now time to turn to the broad economic strategies adopted by South

Asian countries since independence, to what has been achieved by way of development, and to what problems have emerged.

INDIA

Strategies and policies since independence

In none of the economies of South Asian countries is there more interest than in that of India.[22] One important reason is that Nehru and his sympathizers in India and abroad saw as a unique contrast, both to the capitalism of the west and to the communism of China, his vision of a democratic socialist India with a mixed economy, central planning and public sectors coexisting with private enterprise, which should improve the condition of the poor without revolutionary upheaval. It has helped economic research that India has generally been accessible to foreign scholars, while it has produced its own economists of world stature. Again, data is plentiful, even if statistics are not always reliable.

In 1938, and in anticipation of independence, Congress created a National Planning Committee, which in turn set up a number of subcommittees. Given what has been said of the all-embracing nature of Congress, it will be no surprise that the Planning Committee included persons of widely diverging interests and ideologies: Gandhians, western-style socialists, communists, industrialists and others, all under Nehru's consensus-seeking chairmanship;[23] or that there were contradictions between the recommendations of different subcommittees, and even within a single report of the same committee.

In many of the reports one can discern the influence of Nehru and his fellow western-style socialists, impressed by the Soviet model and in favour of central planning of the economy, as opposed to the Gandhians who, looking back to their idealized Indian co-operative village, did not favour central planning and the establishment of heavy industries. Bhagwati and Desai[24] put it:

> This basic opposition of rival ideologies and political forces was to continue into the post-independence period. While sentiments continued to be expressed in favour of radical reconstruction of the social and economic order, the actual programmes to be recommended, and even more the attempts at implementing them, were to represent compromises between different ideological positions on these questions.

Many foreign friends of newly-independent India who were not socialists of any hue, and who felt sympathy with Gandhian ideals, nevertheless supported central planning and saw a need for a massive public sector for reasons that varied with the individual, but usually included the value of building on, rather than destroying, the paternalistic colonial legacy, not

118

least in infrastructure; and the prevalence of a development theory that gave government a central role, not least in mobilizing savings and in industrialization. As we shall see, opinion at home and abroad has tended to change in more recent years.

Immediately after independence the attention of the Government of India was mainly directed towards areas and sectors of the economy most affected by partition and the associated migrations (see p. 46). The greatest disruption was felt from Punjab eastward to western UP, and again in West Bengal and Calcutta; the least in the south. Care for and resettlement of refugees was, as we have seen, a major problem. Many agriculturalists were, however, settled on land abandoned by Muslims in Punjab; and numbers were rehabilitated in colonization schemes, particularly in the UP Tarai and in the Dandakaranya area of the eastern Deccan.[25] Delhi and Calcutta bore the brunt of the influx of urban refugees, but other towns and cities also grew rapidly because of their arrival.

Meanwhile the government, under Nehru's leadership, was preparing a number of measures to bring about a 'socialist pattern of society' (adopted as an aim by the Lok Sabha in 1954), albeit with a mixed economy. The Planning Commission in New Delhi was for some time of prime importance in this context, though always an extraconstitutional body. It has been responsible for the formulation of successive Five Year Plans, the first in respect of the years 1950–5, with two basic tasks: to decide on the amount of plan investment in the economy, and to allocate that investment between alternative sectors and uses. The amount to be invested in the public sector has been derived by 'state accumulation' from taxation, government revenues, and foreign aid; and in the private sector from non-government sources. In the allocation of foreign aid the Ministry of Finance has also played a key part, and grew in power after Nehru's death. Increasingly, debates in the Planning Commission came to involve current expenditure (for example, on agricultural extension) as well as capital investment.

The National Development Council (NDC) was set up in 1952 and consisted of the Prime Minister, the Chief Ministers of States, and members of the Planning Commission. The NDC became *inter alia* a sounding-board which could be used to try out on the chief ministers the political feasibility of various proposals and alternative economic policies. It has played a crucial part in Centre–State planning linkages, all the more important as the States came to develop their own planning machinery; to formulate their own Five Year Plans; and to chafe at the power of the Centre.

In Indian development strategy, industrialization, especially the establishment of heavy industries, has taken a central place. There were a number of reasons for this emphasis in the thinking of Nehru and of his associates, who notably included P.C. Mahalanobis, a socialist statistician. Modern medium- and large-scale factory industry were seen as progressive, as essential to a viable state with the power by its own efforts to escape from

119

the shackles of colonialism. Here one hears echoes of the 'nationalist' view that the colonial impact had nipped an endogenous industrial revolution in the bud (pp. 31–2). Moreover, the vision was of an independent India, self-reliant, and able to defend itself and to play a leading role in the affairs of the subcontinent and of the wider world: and this spelt a modern industrial state. Again, rising living standards for the masses meant consumer goods from textiles to bicycles that were seen as inevitably the products of modern Indian industry.

Important manufacturing industries were to be reserved for the public sector. An Industrial Policy Resolution of 1948 designated new iron and steel plants and new production of ships, mineral oil, coal, aircraft and telecommunications equipment for public enterprises. The resolution rejected the nationalization of existing private businesses for a ten-year period. Here one can surmise the influence of the industrialists' lobby within Congress. A second Industrial Policy Resolution of 1956 added to the list of reservations for the public sector.

The emphasis on heavy industry within the public sector was particularly evident in the Second and Third Five Year Plans (1955–60 and 1960–5), when the influence of Nehru and Mahalanobis was at its height. The arguments for this emphasis may be seen as a conflation of ideology, prestige and pragmatism. Both men were impressed by what they perceived as the Soviet achievement in developing a modern socialist society, through the choice of heavy industry as a leading sector, in a country that had been backward and ravaged by war and revolution. Further, heavy industry, and not just manufacturing, seemed necessary to their vision of a modern India. For, if the need for industrialization was accepted, it was thought difficult to expand traditional exports like tea and textiles sufficiently to pay for imports of the capital and intermediate goods necessary to the production of the requisite consumer goods. Capital and intermediate goods had to a large extent, then, to be made in India; and this necessarily entailed heavy industries. Prudence, as well as the attainment of a socialist pattern of society, demanded that these be in the public sector.

But the private sector had also to play its part in the development of modern industry, outside the areas reserved for the public sector. But, partly because of suspicion of 'business' in some Congress quarters, it was to be subject to strict government control, notably under a system of industrial licensing designed to ensure that industrial investments were consistent with plan priorities and targets; that 'small' industries were protected and encouraged; that concentration of ownership was prevented; and that 'balanced regional development' was secured. No new industrial undertaking, and no substantial extension of an existing undertaking, could be made without a licence.[26]

What, amid all this planned development of modern manufactures, of Gandhian notions of decentralized cottage industries? It is clear that, generally speaking, these notions as a broad strategy fell by the wayside as the juggernaut of industrialization, and especially its heavy-industry manifestation, ground on. True, the early Five Year Plans dutifully contain a section on village and small industries. A plethora of bodies such as the Village and Small Scale Industries Committee was established in the early years of planning; and, as we shall see, handloom and small-factory cloth production has increased very substantially (p. 139). Some attention was also given to the establishment of industrial co-operatives, and of industrial estates to help small-scale industries by such means as technical assistance and the provision of power. But only 3.6 per cent of the planned public sector outlay in the Second Plan was allotted to village and small-scale industries, compared with 17.5 per cent to large-scale industrial and mineral development. And not even this relatively small outlay was in line with Gandhian ideals of village handicrafts; for industrial estates and other measures are intended for modern, machine industry, albeit on a small scale, and in the private sector (to government control of that sector, one must therefore add a modicum of government assistance). Very modest provision and encouragement for the small-scale industrial sector, incorporating both village-traditional and modern, has continued through all the ensuing Plans, up to and including the Seventh (1985–90). The sector was also helped by the reservation to it of specified manufactures; while States also included it in their own plans. During the time of the short-lived Janata Government of 1977–9 there was a policy declaration that all that could be made by village industry should be so made; that as much as possible of the remainder should be the preserve of the (modern) small-scale sector; and that only the residuum be allotted to large-scale industry. Here one can see the influence of old-style Gandhians like Morarji Desai. But the policy was soon overtaken by political events. It remains to be seen what emphasis will be given in the Eighth Plan. Meanwhile, a thorough investigation of Indian small manufacturing enterprises has been made from a neo-classical standpoint in a World Bank Report.[27]

Notwithstanding the mentions of 'balanced regional development' and the inclusion of a chapter under this title in the Third Plan, Indian planning has from the outset been overwhelmingly sectoral and based to a great extent on sophisticated models of the economy as a whole. However, as the States grew into more powerful means of dispensing regional patronage; and as some States came to have non-Congress governments unwilling to accept all that New Delhi decreed, the bargaining power of the States grew at the expense of the Centre; and in a sense each State, with its own plan, became effectively a planning region in its own right. Uneasy Centre–State relations had in fact a great deal to do with the so-called 'holiday from planning' from 1966 to 1969, as a result of which the Fourth Plan did not come into force until the latter year. But for a State to press for, let us say, a steelworks to enhance its own prestige, and because of the opportunities for patronage that would arise from such a massive development, is a far cry from 'balanced regional development' aimed at the uplift of backward regions, which anyway rarely coincide with State boundaries. Formulae were, however, devised to weight central plan grants to the states in favour of remote and relatively backward areas like Jammu and Kashmir, and Assam.

Indian planning has been criticized, justifiably, for its relative neglect of agriculture. The Second Plan thus allotted considerably less to agriculture and community development than to (large-scale) industries and minerals. It is also true that, for all the resolutions before and after independence on co-operative and communal organization, and for all the objectives of a socialist pattern of society, government regarded agriculture as essentially in the private sector, the preserve of myriads of cultivators spread throughout the length and breadth of the land. Nevertheless, ever since independence government agencies have continued to build and to maintain major irrigation works and rural roads; to undertake crucial agricultural research; to organize extension; and in many other ways to foster agricultural production.

Finally, it must be emphasized that government has also made itself responsible for very considerable general infrastructural investment, notably in roads and railways and in power; and also for expenditure on education, health services (including family planning), and housing (rural and urban). In the Sixth Plan many of these sectors were seen as contributing to minimum needs programmes.

Now, it may appear from this account that Indian economic policy has, over the years since independence, maintained continuities: notably in its emphasis on central planning and on industrialization in the public sector. But there has not in fact been an unchanging strategy, still in the 1990s running smoothly and reflecting that of Nehru and Mahalanobis. A number of observers date a certain faltering in the strategy as early as the mid-1960s; indeed, it was to some extent presaged by difficulties during the period of the Second Plan (1956–61), particularly a shortfall in public sector investment and in food supply.[28] A number of reasons have been adduced for this faltering and for subsequent changes of strategic emphasis. For example, Nehru's successor, Shastri, insisted that more resources be devoted to agriculture, following severe droughts and the need for food imports and food aid. There ensued a reappraisal of agricultural policy, especially given alarming population growth (which also gave new urgency to family planning). Again, heavy industry ran into recession while Centre–State relations became more strained with the election in 1967 of a number of non-Congress governments. The Planning Commission's macroeconomic models and data had, moreover, been heavily criticized by economists. Morale in the Commission fell and it found its strategic influence reduced; Treasury orthodoxy tended to prevail. In terms of financial resources, too, troubles came thick and fast. The halcyon days of the First Plan, when India still had sterling balances, were over and gone. A yawning gap between planned outlay and available resources surfaced in the Second Plan period and became even more evident in the next, compounded by inflation. Pressure came from chief ministers to reduce the overall size of the plans while increasing State outlay at the expense of the centre; from industrialists to limit taxation and provide incentives; from ever more powerful rural interests to diminish or to abolish land revenue and to resist proposed new taxes like agricultural income tax. The yawning gap, and associated foreign exchange shortages, meant large-scale use of foreign aid, notwithstanding original and constantly proclaimed goals of self-reliance.[29] Now pipers call tunes: for example, in 1965 the United States changed its aid policy and began to require 'adjustments in indigenous rural policy'.[30] Pressure from the World Bank and from the International Monetary Fund (IMF) had much to do with the Indian devaluation of 1966, which had repercussions for the economy and for planning; while stringent conditions attached to IMF assistance in the 1980s. Again, American aid was suspended during the wars with Pakistan in 1965 and 1971.

The central planning process seems to have become increasingly distanced from implementation and from the pressing problems of real life as it is lived, especially in the countryside, and failed sufficiently to redefine objectives and to choose decisively between alternatives (hence some at least of the apparent continuities in planning), though Streeten and Lipton see a shift in aims at the time of the gestation of so-called 'holiday from planning' from self-sustaining growth to rapid growth, from railways and heavy industry to roads, light industry and improved seeds;[31] while Francine Frankel regards post-independence history, especially since 1965, as an accelerating retreat from socialist objectives, leaving only rhetoric like that of *gharibi hatao* (see p. 62).

But, dating from Rajiv Gandhi's period of office in the 1980s, there have been in many ways more fundamental pressures for change in Indian economic policy.[32] Some of these derive from Rajiv's own predilections on 'modernizing' technology and the economy and for playing the part of a 'Mr Clean' who would root out corruption. Some are a response to internal and external forces already mentioned in preceding paragraphs, for example, internal resistances to taxation and external pressure from the IMF. Further, Indian industrialists have never ceased to complain that the system of controls lacked rational criteria and introduced delay and inefficiency. Observers from outside India have variously seen the system, with attendant import licensing and other measures, as a constraint on free capitalist enterprise (and in particular on the attraction of foreign capital), a source of distortion in the Indian economy, and an exemplification of the impossibility of turning a public service, excellent as a 'steel frame', into a dynamic agent of development.

The phrase 'a constraint on free capitalist enterprise' brings us to wider considerations that have been, and are being brought to bear on Indian economic policy. Few now would be impressed, as Nehru and Mahalanobis had been, by the Soviet model, Marxist as its origins were and in full retreat as it is in its former home territory and elsewhere; or by central planning and other aspects of the command economy. 'Liberalization' is the cry of the moment. Further, there has been a perception that a capitalist market economy as practised in countries like Taiwan and Singapore was achieving faster growth than that in India.

Something has been done to liberalize industrial licensing and import restrictions, and to permit investment by foreign capital, not without vigorous opposition from the Left; and the Seventh Plan (1985–90) did to some extent reflect Rajiv's concerns for modernization. The budget presented to the Lok Sabha in March 1992 went farther down the road of liberalization, notably in terms of incentives to foreign capital and some privatization of industry but, with an eye to the needs of the poor, food subsidies were left in place. One hopes that this and other measures sufficiently recognize that poverty and unemployment, those intractable features of Indian society, will not yield to market forces and 'trickling down', a point that the Prime Minister is reported to have made to the National Development Council in June 1992, while advocating a higher priority to employment generation. Again, market mechanisms and conventional national accounting cannot cope with many long-term aspects of environmental concern, as some economists are now stressing. It is, however, time to turn in more detail to what has been accomplished, or not accomplished in India since independence. This will be done under the heads agriculture; agrarian structure; mining and manufacture; regional and 'target group planning' and foreign trade.

Agriculture since independence

In terms of aggregate agricultural production, India can claim notable achievements since independence. As with most South Asian countries, official statistics are neither completely reliable, nor consistent as between different sources, but at least convey orders of magnitude.[33] According to such sources, total food grain production increased from about 60 million metric tons in 1949–50 to nearly 90 million tons in 1964–5, before the great drought and the 'green revolution', and to 118 million tons in 1970–71, an average of 138 millions for the years 1979–81, and, after slower growth in the mid-1980s, to some 180 million tons for 1988–90. Both before and after the great drought, however, there were bad years, but buffer-stocks have been built up in good years. The general trend of aggregate food grain production has kept ahead, even if only just ahead, of population. It must never be forgotten, however, that aggregate figures tell us nothing about distribution, and that great numbers of the poor are still undernourished: indeed, there are groups whose nutrition has deteriorated.

Up to about 1962, it would appear that about half of the increase in food grain production came from increased crop area. After that year increases in yield became progressively more important; indeed, in some regions the area under foodgrains has retreated in the face of 'commercial' crops like sugar-cane.

Not all food grains have participated equally in aggregate growth. Production of milled rice, the most important food grain, stood at about 24 million tons in 1949–50 and climbed to 39 million tons in 1964–5 before plummeting to some 30 million tons in 1965–6. Since then it has risen, with shortfalls in poor years, to something over 50 million tons in the late 1980s: not perhaps a spectacular rise given the expectations of the 'green revolution'.

Wheat production climbed, with oscillations, from some 6.6 million tons in 1949–50 to 12.3 million tons in 1964–5; after the lean years it rose spectacularly to 26.4 million tons in 1971–2 and following a relapse, to an average of some 35 million tons for 1979–81; then on to 40–50 million tons per annum in the late 1980s. The rapid rise is undoubtedly to be associated mainly with the 'green revolution'.

No other food grains are as prominent in India as rice and wheat But the so-called 'coarse grains', which comprise maize, barley, and millets like *jowar* (sorghum), *bajra* (bulrush millet) and *ragi* (finger millet), are very important in dry, unirrigated areas, especially to poor people. Some of these crops are also used as fodder. On the whole, production of 'coarse grains' has registered a relatively slow rate of increase, but climbed from 22 million tons in 1972–3 to over 30 million tons in the late 1980s, notably accounted for by improved varieties of sorghum and maize.

Pulses are of nutritional importance as a source of protein, especially for vegetarians. But production has only increased by about 50 per cent since independence, to some 14 million tons in 1989. In some regions the area under pulses and groundnuts has fallen, to be replaced by high-yielding varieties of cereals. Much the same is true of oilseeds, which totalled 8 million tons in 1978–9, but it was reported that bumper crops took the total to an estimated 15 million tons for 1988–9. Sugar-cane production has nearly trebled since independence, to almost 200 million tons (of cane).

Turning to the production of two important non-food crops, that of cotton (as lint, the fluffy raw commodity) has risen to almost 1.5 million tons, partly at any rate as a result of sowing new varieties, while that of jute and related products climbed rather more slowly to about the same total.

Government agencies, whether responsible to the central or to State governments, claim, and can take some of the credit for, increases in aggregate production, but must also be blamed for certain shortcomings. Official agricultural research in India did not begin with independence, but has been strengthened since and has included some highly-important work. But it has nevertheless been somewhat uneven (thus rice-breeding for some time tended to lag behind wheat-breeding). Feedback from farmers to the research stations has been inadequate, not surprising in such a hierarchical society. Links between research and extension are sometimes tenuous and obstructed by bureaucratic attitudes. (I remember an extension officer who would not profit from the work of a colleague literally over the fence, insisting that the fruits of research could only reach him through the State Department of Agriculture.)

Again, agricultural extension and schemes for rural uplift are not new arrivals on the Indian scene. But in 1952, and with American assistance, fifty-five 'community projects' were started to stimulate agricultural development in areas with good water supply. But Nehru objected to the concentration on already-favoured areas and to an exclusive emphasis on production. So under the Second Plan, Community Development (CD) was born, with the purpose, not only of agricultural improvement, but also of general rural uplift, especially of the poor. The whole of India was then divided into blocks of a number of villages, each under a Block Development Officer (BDO), under whom were generalist village level workers (VLWs or *Gram Sevaks*), and specialists, notably in agricultural extension.

Another parallel development was that of *Panchayati Raj*, seen by Nehru as a means of shifting power in the village towards the poorer classes and to be associated with village-level co-operatives and, originally, co-operative or collective cultivation.[34] In 1958 the control of community development at block level was moved from appointed officials to elected *Panchayat Samitis* (committees), while later a further body, the *Zila Parishad*, was established at district level. All were to be associated, in the minds of Nehru and his planners, with land reform (see pp. 131–5). While one can appreciate the motives behind the rapid spread of community development to the whole country, its impact was thereby necessarily diluted; and, not surprisingly, it proved difficult to find enough able and dedicated officers to fill the ranks of BDOs, VLWs, and associated extension staff. Again, some BDOs were well-motivated and effective, particularly those who avoided exploiting or condescending to the less-privileged classes. Others allowed themselves to be submerged in the mountain of paperwork that all too readily builds up in India, and rarely if ever visited their villages. However, in our survey of North Arcot District of Tamil Nadu, John Harriss reported that 'the effectiveness of some extension activities in information dissemination appeared quite strong', though Robert Chambers and B.W.E. Wickremanayake had critical comments to make.[35] The effectiveness of agricultural extension is very difficult to measure objectively and accurately, not least because information can reach farmers in so many ways, for example, through the vernacular press, through the radio, and through conversations with other farmers. And farmers assuredly do not lack initiative.

What is quite clear, however (and will be no surprise to the reader) is that, whatever the wishes of Nehru and the planners in terms of the uplift of the poor and their growth in political power, there is a very strong tendency for institutions, whether *panchayats* or co-operative societies or other bodies, to be captured and turned to their own use by the dominant groups in the villages (who are, moreover, important to politicians).

Now already in Nehru's day there were portents of a strategy which had profound, if selective and controversial effects, on Indian agriculture.[36] In 1959 a Ford Foundation team advised an approach that involved a reversion to concentration on areas with good water supply, and the intensive advocacy to farmers in them of a 'package of practices' to include fertilizers, improved methods of cultivation, and new crop varieties. So was born the Intensive Agricultural District Programme (IADP), deployed in seven districts in 1960–1 and later extended, but still on a highly-selective basis,[37] while the less-concentrated IAAP (Intensive Agricultural Area Programme) was applied to certain other areas. In the mid–1960s Shastri's concern for agricultural production,[38] advice from the World Bank and the United States Agency for International Development (USAID), and changing US aid policies converged to associate IADP and IAAP with a 'new agricultural strategy' that also involved strengthened research and more reliance on incentives to farmers, though they were still to be assisted by improved credit facilities. Now, while IADP and IAAP recognize interregional differences (as economists and planners rarely do to a sufficient extent), they equally clearly tended to exaggerate spatial differences in average income levels, and to contrast with the (theoretically) uniform spread of CD. Indeed, some saw the new strategy as a triumph of the technocratic and production-oriented over the distributive and socialist policies of early independence. But CD continued, albeit somewhat eroded as the Seventh Plan admitted, and new official measures designed for rural uplift, such as the Integrated Rural Development Programme and the National Rural Employment Programme have been initiated.

The 'new agricultural strategy', by the time that it had been more completely formulated in the mid-1960s, involved yet another programme, the High Yielding Varieties Programme (HYVP or HVP), basic to the so-called 'green revolution',[39] the popular (and to some extent misleading) title for the introduction and spread from the mid-1970s onward of high-yielding varieties (HYVs) of cereals in association with chemical fertilizers, insecticides and pesticides, controlled water-supply (usually irrigation), and improved cultural methods. These together were usually seen, in IADP terms, as a 'package' to be adopted as a whole by the cultivator. The HYVP was originally planned to be applied to the IADP districts in the expectation that improvement would spread outward from them.

We have already seen that Indian wheat production has leapt upward (p. 125), nearly trebling between 1963–4 and 1971–2, and, with oscillations, climbing upward to a level in the late 1980s of 40–50 million tons per annum. Wheat was, indeed, the crop that has benefited most from the new technology, which in terms of varieties has been based on dwarf wheats derived, many of them in India itself, from Mexican progenitors. At first, adoption of these HYVs was mainly a matter of Punjab, Haryana and western UP; but it has spread down the plains to eastern UP and Bihar and even to West Bengal. In these more eastern states (and indeed elsewhere) increased production has been underpinned by a massive increase in tubewells for irrigation. Many of these have been the result of initiative on the part of farmers (in Bihar, where the water-table is near the surface, enterprising cultivators have sunk bamboos in place of the usual, and much more expensive steel tubes). Another crucial factor has been the very extensive use of chemical fertilizers. But the HYVs and the associated technology have so far had much less impact south-west of the plains, in the drought-prone areas of the western Deccan, except locally where well irrigation is feasible.

Rice production has told a very different story. True, there have been success areas – or, rather, success seasons in specific areas. Most of these bear out the old school geography-room dictum that rice flourishes when its feet are in the water (at controlled depth, one should add) and its head in the sun. Thus HYV adoption has reached high and increasing levels, and yields increased markedly, in many areas with irrigation, and with a sunny season to maximize photosynthesis: such areas as Punjab and its plains neighbours under canal and tubewell irrigation in the south-west monsoon season of light rains and much sunshine; West Bengal in the *boro* or winter (north-east monsoon) season, given irrigation; and dry seasons, again given irrigation, in the south.

But HYV adoption has been much lower, and increases in yields much less marked, in two contrasting areas: those characterized by waterlogging or deep flooding; and those prone to drought unalleviated by irrigation. The first of these is quantitatively very important, constituting about three-quarters of Indian rice-growing areas, particularly in the lower Ganga and Brahmaputra plains, in the east coast deltas and in Kerala, where, moreover, no other foodcrop can be grown, but where a wide range of traditional varieties, each suited to a particular environment and length of growing season, have been selected by cultivators through the millennia. A number of factors contribute to this situation. The HYVs are dwarf, so easily overcome by submergence, which they cannot survive, by relatively shallow flooding; they are of short duration and non-photoperiod sensitive or 'date-fixed' (so that if sown early in the monsoon they come to maturity while the rains are still pouring down); they, or many of them early on proved very susceptible to the pests and diseases that proliferate under hot, humid climates; and some of them are vulnerable to the soil toxicity that may build up under anaerobic conditions when fields are flooded or waterlogged. In terms of most of these considerations, the deeper the flooding, the greater the problem; and, while there are traditional deep-water or floating rices that will produce small though acceptable yields in depths of one to six metres, the problem of producing HYVs to boost yields under these conditions is a difficult one, though attempts are being made. An alternative strategy is to reduce reliance on deep-water rice by growing HYVs under irrigation in the dry season (*boro* in Bengal). Less intractable, though still difficult, are the problems of land subject to more shallow flooding and to waterlogging. Here Indian research has made some progress by breeding new medium-tall or semi-dwarf varieties, some with notably greater resistance to pests and diseases. The International Rice Research Institute has also bred some encouraging new varieties, and supplies genetic material to Indian researchers.

As for drought-prone regions without adequate irrigation, research is also in progress to produce water-sparing varieties of rice: this is was a need emphasized in the Sixth Five Year Plan and after. So was the enhancement of the irrigated area.

Now, although HYVs (of wheat as well as rice) are efficient in terms of grain production per unit of nutrient, there is a case on national environmental grounds for breeding even more efficient varieties, to reduce both dependence on non-renewable resources involved in fertilizer manufacture and the dangers of pollution. From the point of view of the poor farmer, who must never be forgotten, such varieties would reduce dependence on a costly input and on what may well be corrupt channels of supply (that is, be more 'rascal-proof' in Sir Joseph Hutchinson's memorable words).

Irrigation is clearly a crucial factor in agricultural improvement in India. According to available official statistics, since independence India has approximately doubled its net irrigated area (though there are qualifications to be applied shortly to this achievement).[40] The proportionate increase in area irrigated from wells has been greater than that from canals or tanks (small reservoirs). Much of this astonishing growth was accounted for by tubewells, many of which are now pumped by electric motors or diesel engines, and which have had a greater impact on Indian agriculture than many of the spectacular post-independence dam-and-canal schemes like Bhakra–Nangal, the Rajasthan Canal and Kosi.[41]

But the irrigated proportion of the net sown area (officially defined as 'the net area sown with crops and orchards, areas sown more than once being only counted once') varied widely: for example, from very low in Kerala, Madhya Pradesh, Maharashtra and Karnataka through 40–50 per cent in Tamil Nadu, Uttar Pradesh and Haryana, to over 75 per cent in Punjab. In some states, of course, a low proportion results largely from a lack of need – for instance, in well-watered Kerala and the eastern parts of Madhya Pradesh. But it is clear that the need is great, and to a considerable extent unmet, in many of the dry Deccan districts of Karnataka, western Madhya Pradesh and Maharashtra. And there is a limit to the renewable water resources, whether surface or underground, of such drought-prone regions – and, for that matter, elsewhere. There are areas, like interior Tamil

Nadu, where underground water is held in a shallow aquifer (and therefore accessible by means of open wells) over crystalline rock, and is being pumped out faster than it is recharged by rivers and rainfall, so that the water-table is falling.[42] It cannot be too strongly emphasized that there are hydrological constraints, as well as economic limits, to the extension of irrigation in India. Estimates of a potentially irrigable area in excess of 100 million hectares must be treated with caution.[43] There are also political constraints in the shape of inter-State disputes over the use of river water, for example, between Maharashtra and Andhra Pradesh over Godavari water, between Karnataka and Tamil Nadu over Kaveri water, and between Gujarat and Madhya Pradesh over Narmada water.

It is a gigantic scheme, supported by the World Bank, to harness the Narmada that has more recently aroused a furore in India, partly on grounds of exorbitant cost, but also for environmental and social reasons. The scheme involves some 30 major dams on the Narmada and its tributaries and would, if completed, irrigate some 120,000 hectares in a drought-prone region as well as providing power. But a vast area of agricultural land and forest would be submerged and a large and variously estimated number of people, especially tribals, ousted. Protests have united environmentalists and activists from local communities, and in June 1990 Japan withdrew financial support on environmental grounds.

Even those areas already irrigated have their problems. Irrigation, especially from unlined canals, can, in the absence of adequate drainage works or sufficient pumping from tubewells, lead to a rise in the water-table and eventually to waterlogging and, through capillary action from a near-surface water-table, to saline and alkaline deposits on field surfaces which may put land out of cultivation. Some 6 million hectares have, it is reported, been damaged already.[44]

In some major schemes, it has been found impossible to irrigate the planned area. Thus the original target of 0.6 million hectares for the Kosi canal system in Bihar has had to be reduced to some 360,000 hectares, for reasons that include here, as elsewhere, over-optimistic assumptions about the area irrigable by a unit volume of water, inadequate appreciation of topography and soils, and channel siltation.[45] In major schemes, more generally, there has been concern at the difference between area irrigable in theory, and area actually irrigated; hence the institution in the Fifth and subsequent Plans of the Command Area Development Programme charged with the integrated development of areas in major schemes through such measures as the construction of channels, the levelling of land, and the improvement of cropping patterns and input supply.

A final and important qualification to statements about the growth of irrigation on India concerns inadequacies in the distribution of water to the actual cultivator, especially if his fields lie at the tail end of a system. There are many factors at work: notably defects in official organization and maintenance, the theft of water by farmers higher up the system, and pervasive corruption. As R. Wade has shown, some of these problems are dealt with in certain areas by the farmers themselves, operating their own organizations. But these cannot be imposed from on high, not least because the cultivators using irrigation water, when they can get it, are not automatons, but people set in India's very unequal society and complex polity, on whom many socio-political constraints operate. This brings us to questions of equity in Indian agricultural development and, first, to land reform.

Agrarian structure and related problems

Chapter 3 has shown that the distribution of land in pre-British India was very unequal, the landless already existing, and that one consequence of British rule was an increase in landlessness, while another was a strengthening of the *zamindars*, revenue collectors for the Raj and powerful landlords. There was agitation in the 1890s for the abolition of *zamindari*, which gathered strength with the nationalist movement and broadened into discussion inside and outside Congress on the reform, or even abolition of tenancy, the imposition of ceilings on holdings, and proposals for collective and co-operative cultivation. Some of this discussion was spurred on in 1945 by a notable book, *Poverty and Social Change: a Study in Economic Reorganisation of Indian Rural Society*, by Tarlok Singh, who was later Secretary of the Planning Commission.[46] In 1949 Congress appointed an Agrarian Reforms Committee, 'a major product of socialist–Gandhian collaboration'.[47] Rejecting both a capitalist structure and wholesale collectivization, the Committee chose a third and composite solution: the amalgamation of very small holdings for joint cultivation; the survival in individual tenure of holdings from one to three times the size of an 'economic holding'; and a ceiling pitched at three times an 'economic holding', defined as one which could afford a reasonable (sic) standard of living and provide full employment for a normal family and for at least a pair of bullocks. There was dissent within the Committee, especially over compulsory co-operative farming. But opinion in favour of this was boosted by an Indian delegation which visited China and reported favourably, if naïvely, on agrarian co-operatives there; while in 1959 Congress passed its Nagpur resolution in favour of co-operative joint farming, but such that property rights were maintained and a share of the net produce allotted to workers, whether they owned land or not.[48] (From dissent over this resolution sprang the Swatantra Party (see p. 65).)

What has actually been achieved by way of land reform in India since independence is but a pale shadow of these radical proposals. M.L. Dantwala said many years ago, 'If you ask me what is the most important feature of land reforms I would say non-implementation';[49] and much the same could be said today. True, *zamindari*-abolition was accomplished fairly quickly between 1950 and 1954 by implementing state legislation, in spite of a rearguard action by the *zamindars*. But this was primarily a change in the tax system. Tenants who formerly paid revenue to *zamindars* now paid direct to government. Though in some states the position of tenants was improved, the distribution of landownership was not affected. Indeed, *zamindars* retained land for 'personal cultivation' and received compensation for the loss of their revenue-collecting status, with which could be bought yet more land, while some former tenants of *zamindars* lost their rights and became landless labourers. Altogether, the much-trumpeted reform did not increase equity in landholding, and often tended to decrease it.

The paragraphs that follow, and the literature on land tenure and land reform in India, demand an understanding of the fact that such categories as landholder, tenant and landless labourer are not necessarily mutually exclusive. A landholder may both rent in and rent out land, and so both be a tenant and have tenants (who may or may not be share-croppers). Again, many holders of very small parcels, as well as the landless, may labour on the land of another, and, increasingly in some areas, obtain in addition some non-agricultural employment. Official statistics, and some secondary literature, are replete with ambiguity about these matters (not surprisingly, given the abiding complexities of Indian land tenure) and it is often better not to give a false air of precision by quoting numbers alleged to fall into particular categories.

It is clear, however, that would-be reformers had to deal with a highly-skewed distribution of landholding in the decade or so after independence. About a fifth of Indian agricultural households held little or no land at all.[50] Another quarter held less than an acre. Here lay the great mass of disastrously impoverished villagers who, unless they could find non-agricultural employment, were dependent on tenancy, or agricultural labour, or some combination of the two. Perhaps three-quarters of households held less than five acres, covering about a sixth of agricultural land. At the other end of the scale, India was not, and is not a land of vast *latifundia:* a 'big man' in a South Indian village is a man with, say, 15 or 20 acres;[51] though there, and even more in the north, much depends on the nature and irrigability of the land. The holder of 50 acres of land in Rajasthan with irregular and low rainfall and poor soil would regard three acres of fertile, irrigated and double cropped land in the south as a prince's patrimony. Clearly there cannot in logic be a uniform all-India ceiling.

In turning to the question of ceilings on landholdings and the redistribution of surplus land in excess of ceilings (seen as a way of reducing inequity in the distribution of land ownership) it must be stressed that land reform is constitutionally a State subject. Whatever the recommendations of central government bodies like the Planning Commision or the Ministry of

Agriculture (which, incidentally do not always see eye to eye), the enactment and implementation of relevant legislation is a matter for State governments. In the vast majority of States, ceiling legislation was in fact enacted in the 1950s and 1960s, and in some of them subsequently amended with lower ceilings after prodding in 1969 from Mrs Gandhi, concerned at both agrarian unrest and her populist image. But generally speaking, and over and above foot-dragging in enactment, much legislation was so drafted as to ensure that, as Warriner puts it, 'a ceilings law was enacted in accordance with official (that is, Central) policy, while its intentions were neatly bypassed by other provisions in the Acts':[52] for example, exemptions for particular categories of land such as tea plantations; a raising of ceilings for allegedly dependent relatives; the admissibility of transferring excess land to 'heirs' within a given period *after* enactment. Who has need of a lawyer to find loopholes when the draftsman has built them into the Act? Not surprisingly, land declared surplus (that is, in excess of the appropriate ceiling and available for distribution) was in most States only slowly assembled, and then totalled much less than had been anticipated by the would-be reformers. The Mid-Term Appraisal of the Seventh Plan (1985–90) claimed that some 7.8 million acres (3.2 million hectares) had been declared surplus of which 5.8 million acres (2.3 million hectares) had been resumed to public ownership and 4.5 million acres (1.8 million hectares) redistributed to landless persons, with many complaints of procedural delay.[53] Indeed, ceiling legislation has in most States not had more than a slight impact, if that, on the skewness of landholding. The bold and radical programmes, the assumption that distributive measures could and would be taken and that they would not only promote equity and relieve poverty but also stimulate production (given the 'inverse relationship' that productivity per acre was higher on smaller holdings than on larger): all of this has been lost in a tangled thicket of politics, involving in particular Centre–State relations, the power of rural interests which would lose from thoroughgoing reforms, and caste. Even in West Bengal, where left-inclined governments have pursued tenancy reforms with vigour, ceiling legislation has been ineffective for reasons that include poor land records, bribery and evasion.

The systems of tenancy that were inherited and modified by the British Raj and in turn passed on to independent India were complex and widespread, and varied in incidence and detailed character from region to region. In North Arcot District of Tamil Nadu, for instance, there was relatively little tenancy. The control of tenancy, with the objects of achieving for tenants security of tenure, 'fair rents' and a right of purchase was a main plank in the platform of the would-be reformers at the time of independence. Tenancy legislation was, with the customary foot-dragging, passed in most states by the early 1960s; but there were many loopholes. Landlords were able to resume land for 'personal cultivation', ejecting tenants and reducing some of them to the status of labourers. Even where the law should have protected tenants, enforcement was absent or weak; and many tenants were either ignorant of their rights, or afraid to press them against powerful landlords who were also moneylenders to whom they were indebted. True, in West Bengal governments formed by the Communist Party of India (Marxist) (CPM) and its allies has energetically pursued 'Operation Barga' under which share-croppers (*bargadars*) are registered and given legal protection. Some 1.6 million of them have, it would appear, been registered. But there have been difficulties (for example, evasion because of pre-existing relations between government officers and landholders who, as a class, the government has found it politically important not to alienate). In some other areas tenants have been able to improve their position, for example in Kerala and in Karnataka. In others their position worsened, as in Thanjavur District of Tamil Nadu, notorious for its agrarian unrest. By and large the equity goals of the would-be reformers have not been widely achieved; and positive production effects of tenancy legislation (on the assumption that insecurity is a constraint on the application of inputs) are hard to find.

The land-reform programme as a whole has receded in prominence from the more recent Five Year Plans and other policy statements. Its ceiling and tenancy provisions clearly run counter to the interests of powerful figures in the villages and in politics.

What then of co-operative cultivation, so assiduously pressed by the would-be reformers, some of them with notions of the re-creation of an idyllic village that never was (pp. 118 and 131)? By 1968 there were apparently only 1347 co-operative farming societies in India, of which only 381 were collectives (in which landownership subsists in the society), the rest being joint farming societies (in which ownership was merely pooled, and reflected in the 'dividend' of the cultivator).[54] Of these, some were no doubt bogus, like the one I visited in the Chambal Valley in 1963, where an extended family had formed a co-operative on paper and so secured land and government subsidies, but were in fact operating an estate growing long-staple cotton, many of the 'members' being absentee and employed elsewhere. It is doubtful if there are now more co-operative farming societies than in 1968, probably fewer. The subject is, in fact, virtually dead, for all the zeal of the reformers.

Two further measures are often included as government contributions to land reform. The first of these is land settlement, particularly of landless labourers on wasteland marginal to existing villages, or in entirely new villages (when it qualifies for the title 'agricultural colonization').[55] Some see such settlement as dodging the issue of radical land reform, since it does not affect the hold of dominant groups on land already in cultivation. But, in my experience, the process, especially when land is given to Harijans on the edge of villages, can provoke profound resentment among these groups, since it tends to remove the beneficiaries from a subservient role and to involve land that such groups covet (and may, indeed, forcibly occupy). But probably far more waste than that made available under official schemes has been, and is being, brought into cultivation, licitly or illicitly, by spontaneous action by cultivators who already hold land. And agricultural colonization has not only benefited the landless, but also refugees, those who have lost land through the construction of irrigation works, and even ex-*jagirdars* (essentially *zamindars* with local administrative and judicial functions) in Rajasthan, and has had production as well as equity motives.

The other measure, land consolidation, is designed purely to increase production. Its aim is to rearrange each fragmented and scattered holding in a village into a compact block of equivalent area, due account being taken of land quality, under appropriate legislation (which may involve compulsory powers) and with Central government subsidies. Considerable progress has been made in several states, notably Punjab, Haryana and western Uttar Pradesh (where consolidation is hailed as a factor in the 'green revolution'). Care should, however, be taken in the blanket application of consolidation to paddy-growing areas, where the possession of land in a number of different categories (for example, always irrigable, irrigable only if water is plentiful, liable to or free from flood, and so on) may be a positive advantage to the cultivator, though, I suspect, one of which the holder of a small amount of land in few parcels, or only one, is unable to take advantage.[56]

Turning to the question of the equity effects of the 'green revolution', a question on which much literature has accumulated, there was early on some optimism that the new varieties and the associated technology would usher in an era of universal prosperity (which would, *inter alia*, keep 'red revolution' at bay: this was the period of the cold war and of US involvement in Vietnam). This optimism was soon found to be facile; and the shadows deepened when it was realized (by some, at least) that the spatial impact in India was so uneven, some of the poorest and most densely peopled rice-growing and other areas being but little affected. It also came to be claimed that the effects of the 'green revolution' are very uneven, not only between areas, but also between classes in the same area; that disparities of income and of wealth widen, the poor get poorer, and (in some views at any rate) agrarian unrest leading to revolt would be generated. For, it was argued, it is the larger farmers who can take greater risks, who can procure the inputs and therefore the benefits, who can obtain credit, and who become (if they are not already) rural capitalists. Small farmers and tenants lose out, and in Marxist terms 'the peasantry is differentiated'. Landless labourers are in even worse plight, it was argued, there being decreased employment for them (especially where there is mechanization or electrification); and their numbers are swollen by the impoverishment of the small farmers and tenants.

But, as research and speculation have continued, the range of conclusions has widened. Among the more important reasons are lack or unreliability of data; studies made at different points in the process of adoption, or in years of abnormal weather or prices; the filter of ideology that can intervene between the observer and the agrarian scene and lead, amongst other things, to wishful thinking (at one extreme, that growth in production and income from it are bound universally to trickle down, at the other that a revolutionary situation lies just round the corner); confounding the lack of equity effects of the new technology with those due to deficiencies of land reform; and, of very great importance, over-generalization to an all-India, or at least to state level, of conditions that obtain only in a more restricted area.[57]

Now, careful field studies in some areas show that small farmers do adopt the HYVs and, by hook or by crook, often by incurring increased indebtedness, acquire fertilizer, pumpsets and so on;[58] though they may well adopt later than big farmers. Michael Lipton (1989) in a notable and far-ranging study (with many references to India) concludes that in most areas of HYV adoption 'small farmers' (often with a time-lag) adopted no less widely, intensively and productively than others'.

It has also become clearer with the passage of time that labourers in India may find increased work with HYV adoption (for example, for women in the weeding needed by the HYVs) but lose employment because of whatever mechanization has been introduced. There are many complications. On balance, however, and generalizing rather wildly, landless labourers have often (though not always) gained less than any other class, and may sometimes have lost out in absolute terms. Their plight tends to be compounded where increases in food prices have been greater than increases in wage rates, the old payments in kind having been replaced by payments in cash. But in some areas at any rate, including North Arcot, fears of concentration of ownership and of the differentiation of the peasantry have so far been greatly exaggerated.

But the poor, whether small landholders, tenants, or labourers, tend only to revolt sporadically. I for my part do not think of rural India, for all its sufferings, as in, or entering a 'revolutionary situation', except perhaps locally. But this is not meant as a complacent conclusion. The plight of many of the rural poor should indeed arouse compassion and prompt and determined action: for it is very severe indeed.

It may be argued that, even if land reform has in general failed, other government programmes to assist the small farmer and the labourer have done something to ameliorate their condition. This is indeed to some extent true of Community Development, Integrated Rural Development and the National Rural Employment Programme (see above, p. 126). There has also been credit provision on the one hand, and on the other special schemes like Small Farmer Development Agencies (SFDA) and projects for Marginal Farmers and Agricultural Labourers (MFAL).

Government intervention in the provision of credit goes well back into the days of the Raj.[59] More recently 'official' credit has come to depend on three main agencies: a country-wide network of co-operative societies; the nationalized commercial banks; and the newer regional rural banks. There are areas in which these agencies, and especially the co-operatives, have played a notable part in the provision of credit for agricultural purposes, for example, in the Punjab, Maharashtra, and more recently in Tamil Nadu. But in other areas provision has usually fallen short of targets; and recovery of loans has been lamentable. Many studies show that access to credit for the 'weaker sections' has been far short of need, in spite of pious aspirations voiced in, for example, the Seventh Plan. The 'big men' understand the system, control the co-operatives as they control the *panchayats*, and can manipulate the bureaucracy. The small men still have to rely, for the most part, on traditional village sources – mainly the 'big men' themselves. Thus in our North Arcot study in 1973–4 only 10 per cent of the paddy cultivators with holdings between 0.4 and 1 hectare drew credit from co-operatives, compared with 62 per cent of those with more than three hectares,[60] though the situation has now improved. Dependence on private sources of credit is, of course, another name for indebtedness, and the state of many small farmers in that regard is chronic.

SFDA were instituted in the Fourth Plan in order specifically to assist with credit, services and supply 'farmers' whose economy was potentially viable, but specifically excluding even smaller farmers and agricultural labourers. For them MFAL schemes were set up under the same plan, involving subsidies for improved agricultural practices and auxiliary enterprises. B. Dasgupta, reviewing a number of studies on these programmes in 1977, concluded that both have had a limited impact, and that both have often helped, not those for whom it was intended, but larger farmers who have faked the land records or manipulated the bureaucracy.[61] 'Trickling up', to use Barbara Harriss's telling term, was, and often is, very much in evidence in India.

Now we strike off and look briefly at the Indian 'cattle problem', confining our attention to bovines (including buffaloes) associated with agricultural villages. Now everyone knows, or thinks that he knows, that India has a 'cattle problem': that vast numbers of useless cows wander through town and village alike and pass into a decrepit old age because no Hindu will countenance their slaughter. So runs the received wisdom. To it, some would add that there is no tradition of pasture management: and that this contrasts with the care lavished on paddy and other terraces (though fodder crops are grown, competing with food crops). However, the distinguished Indian economist, K.N. Raj, has concluded, after interesting empirical work, that, under population pressure (bovine and human), cows are underrepresented in the bovine population, most notably in UP and Bihar, strongholds of Hindu orthodoxy: so killing must be taking place, if only by infanticide and deliberate starvation. The conventional wisdom thus stands challenged.[62]

It must be remembered that cattle play a very important part in the village

137

economy. Bullocks, and sometimes bulls, supply power for ploughing and other field operations, and for cart-pulling, as do buffaloes in wet rice areas. There are some splendid breeds for these purposes; for example, the Kangayams of Tamil Nadu. Official schemes cover breeding and the dissemination of improved breeds; but it will occasion no surprise to learn that better-off farmers appear to benefit most.

Cows usually supply milk in pitiful quantities compared with western dairy cattle. Yields are, however, higher in areas like the Punjab and in some towns, where the animals are better fed. She-buffaloes also provide milk. Cattle in some areas supply a useful income for poor people, even some of the landless, because the animals can scrounge a meagre living on roadsides and waste. Some co-operative ventures help small producers to market their milk: those in Gujarat, which produce Amul cheese from buffaloes' milk, are famous. Now, R. Crotty has demonstrated that 'Operation Flood', under which EEC dairy surpluses are transferred to the Third World and which was extended during the Seventh Plan, reduces the cost of milk for urban consumers while increasing the revenue of the Indian Dairy Corporation, which handles the operation in India.[63] This means that the Corporation can in turn pay a higher price for Indian milk and transport it to towns over longer distances, so that it becomes more difficult for the rural poor who have no female cattle to buy milk, their only source of animal protein. Moreover, there is an inducement to those who have such cattle to keep more, thus putting increased pressure on communal pastures and on fodder prices, so making it harder for the poor and landless to keep them. In short, a well-intentioned programme of food aid has perverse effects which bear hardest, like so many other things, on the rural poor.

From the discussion in the above sections it appears to be the case that independent India has more to its credit in increasing agricultural production than in reforming its agrarian structure and achieving a more equitable society to share in the benefits of that production.[64] This is in spite of the sincere motives and principles of Nehru and many of his associates, and in spite of the proponents of 'trickling down' (growth in production is indeed a necessary, but not a sufficient, condition for greater equity). To put it in a nutshell, India's hard-earned and sometimes vaunted buffer-stocks would vanish overnight if everyone had a square meal.

This situation is not surprising if one remembers Indian society as it was in 1947 and as it has evolved since, not least politically; and it is saddened realism, not ill-founded pessimism to conclude that it is not easy to see how the position is to be changed generally for the better.

Now all this is not to say that there are not dedicated Indians in many walks of life, particularly but not exclusively those touched with the Gandhian spirit, who genuinely seek the uplift of India's rural poor. Some of them press hard on government through voluntary bodies. Some are able academics active in field research. Some of them are in the ministries and the Planning Commission of New Delhi. But the problem is to make the goodwill, the noble sentiments, the knowledge, the intentions of the great and good effective at village level, where the needy groups live. One does not have to be a Marxist, or even a Marxian, to be forced to the conclusion that such effectiveness will not take place generally without drastic social and political change and without extraordinary political will.

Mining and manufacturing

Agriculture and agrarian conditions are so vital to India, as to other South Asian countries, that I make no apology for treating them in some detail, compared with other aspects of the economy: first, mining and manufacturing, related, of course, to the industrialization so prominent in policy and planning (see Table 6.3).

Table 6.3 makes it clear that Indian mining and manufacture have made great strides since independence, not least in those industries that lie in the public sector, though some manufactures, particularly cotton-weaving in 'modern' mills, have done less well, and, indeed, have been in decline of recent years. The increasing share of production from handlooms and small-scale industry is remarkable. Products useful to agriculture, such as fertilizers and tractors (of doubtful general utility, however, given the need for rural employment) show increases; as do bicycles, of great importance to dwellers

Table 6.3 India: production of selected products of mining and industry (metric tons)

Item	Unit	1950–1	1979–80	1986–7
Coal	mill.tons	32.8	104.0	182.0[a]
Petroleum				
crude	mill.tons	0.4	11.8	34.5[b]
products	mill.tons	0.3	26.0	42.7[b]
Steel ingots	mill.tons	1.5	10.0	9.1
Cement	mill.tons	2.7	17.7	36.5
Fertilizer				
nitrogenous	thousand tons	11.0	2,226.0	5,410.0
phosphatic	thousand tons	11.0	757.0	1,660.0
Tractors	thousand	0	62.5	80.0
Bicycles	thousand	99.0	3,780.0	6,100.0
Cotton cloth				
mill-made	mill.metres	3,728.0	4,085.0	3,300.0
handloom				
and small-scale	mill.metres	1,008.0	6,350.0	10,033.0
Jute				
manufactures	mill.tons	0.8	1.3	1.4

Sources: Official, not always consistent. For 1986–7 Mid-term Appraisal, Seventh Five Year Plan 1985–90.
Notes: a 1987–88.
b 1989–90.

in town and country alike. A number of items not tabulated, such as railway locomotives, electric pumpsets, and industrial machinery generally, as well as electronic goods, are also now produced. There has been a massive growth in generating capacity, which in 1989–90 was likely to stand at 275 billion Kwh (some 2 per cent due to nuclear power stations). This growth has enabled current to be brought to thousands of villages and energized millions of irrigation pumps. Power shortages have, however, continued to be endemic in various parts of the country.

Foreign aid has contributed to industrial growth: for example, Britain, West Germany and the USSR all helped with new steelworks.[65].

But all has not been well with Indian industry.[66] Production increased by an annual average of about 8 per cent up to 1964, but then tended to flatten off. Many causes have been contributed to this faltering: for example, the passing of the early years of import-substitution industry with a captive market, ensconced behind tariff walls and with little salutary experience of facing competition in overseas markets; and the effects of disastrous droughts, which damaged important agricultural processing industries like rice-milling and sugar-making very directly, and also had far-ranging economic effects.[67] Blame has also been placed on lack of investment and shortage of inputs like coal and power; and, increasingly over the years, on inefficient management, high costs and underused capacity. J.K. Jha stressed problems of management in a broader sense, to include the assumptions, models and methods of the planners, fiscal and taxation policy, and the 'black economy' which by definition avoids the government's resource-gathering net.[68] But he also mentioned the lack of effective demand, on which other observers place great emphasis. The capital goods sectors of industry (nearly all publicly owned) were, to a considerable extent, providing goods for other public sector industries (for example, the steel industry for the railways), so that shortfalls in production are closely related both to planned targets and to inefficiencies on the demand side. The private consumer goods industries produce very largely for the urban middle and upper classes, to whom are sold the superficially impressive and certainly growing array of goods, from cosmetics to television sets, displayed in the shops of New Delhi. The relative prosperity brought to some areas and classes by changes such as those associated with the 'green revolution' in Punjab has drawn some of these products farther afield. (The other side of the rupee appears to be burgeoning consumerism as known in the West and enhanced greed in dowry-seeking: see pp. 21–2). But deeper in the country-side and among the poor of both village and city few of the new consumer goods penetrate, except perhaps for wrapped soap and electric torches. All-too-prevalent poverty cannot but affect aggregate demand for industrial products.

More recently, of course, the inefficiencies and deficiencies of Indian industry have become a focal point for discussions of fundamental change in economic policy, especially liberalization (see above, p. 124), with deregulation and an export-oriented emphasis).

Turning from production in modern factory industry to its welfare implications, it would appear that factory employment, which stood at about 2.5 million at independence, had grown to 6.2 million by 1977–8;[69] but rising less rapidly than output. It was, however, projected to rise at 4.5 per cent annually during the Seventh Plan period (1985–90). For all the emphasis on industrialization, then, a relatively small number of people (compared, that is, with the vast numbers in agriculture) have gained by finding employment in factories. This is not surprising given the capital intensive nature of much factory industry and the inappropriateness to conditions of over-abundant labour of a great deal of imported technology. One fears that liberalization and even more modern technology, for all the arguments for them, will do little to bring redress unless redoubled efforts are made to increase employment.

Small-scale industries (defined in terms of plants employing less than fifty persons if power is used, less than one hundred if it is not) have in recent years become highly dynamic and productive, employing a rapidly-increasing work-force, partly at least because of the official allocations to it of specified items of manufacture.[70] The sector, however, is not without its problems of efficiency, and it remains to be seen how it will stand up to liberalization, especially if such allocations are reduced or removed. Village (that is, cottage) industries continue to produce, mainly in terms of traditional crafts, employing an unknown number.

It is also clear that, in spite of measures like industrial licensing and the establishment of trading estates for small-scale industries, modern manufacture at any rate is still largely confined to areas that had significant industry at independence: Calcutta, Hugliside and south-eastern Bihar; Bombay–Ahmedabad and Bombay–Pune–Nagpur; and Madras–Coimbatore and adjacent areas. This is not surprising, given the sectoral, rather than regional emphasis in Indian policy. More recently, however, there has been noteworthy industrial growth in Punjab–Haryana–Delhi and also around Bangalore.

Spatial aspects of development

Clearly, then, industrialization in India has not produced the 'balanced regional development', early declared to be an objective of Indian planning and given a chapter to itself (albeit a somewhat ambivalent one, lost in the plethora of sectoral material) in the Third Plan. Equally clearly, the 'green revolution' has tended to increase regional disparities. What, then, of action designed to reduce these disparities?[71] The decentralization of planning that followed the growth in the power of the states, vis-à-vis the Centre, was a far cry from objectively planned 'balanced regional development'. States have varied widely, too, in action to reduce intra-State disparities.[72] A review in 1982 showed that a number of States (Bihar, Haryana, Himachal Pradesh, Orissa, Punjab and West Bengal) had taken the politically-easier course of visualizing the all-round development of *all* districts. Others did have policies of discriminating in favour of backward areas. Maharashtra, for example, was keen to disperse industry from Greater Bombay, while Andhra Pradesh was one of the first states to contemplate intra-State regional planning. The States have also engaged in the preparation of district and even block plans, which in theory at any rate could provide a means of redressing spatial imbalances.[73] But district and block-level planning have often been far from successful. Such programmes, one fears, tend to be no more than pious hopes in the face of the formidable social resistances of the dominant groups.

There have, however, always been Central schemes and projects with potential effects on the distribution of prosperity. Thus the three new steelworks of the early post-independence era were all located in green field (or green jungle) sites, whence it was hoped that development would diffuse to surrounding areas. Again the Centre has instituted transport subsidies for Jammu and Kashmir and for the north-eastern States to reduce the friction of distance, and its schemes for the resettlement of landless labourers took development of a sort into some remote wasteland areas.[74] 'Target group' schemes, like those for tribals and Harijans, are spatial in impact to the extent that the groups concerned are concentrated in backward regions.

One of the aims of the Industrial Policy Resolution of 1980 was more specifically concerned with the correction of regional imbalance in the location of industry. 'Backward districts' were to be designated in terms of relatively low industrialization and level of infrastructure; and lay in Andhra, Assam, Bihar, Jammu and Kashmir, Madhya Pradesh, Nagaland Orissa, Rajasthan, Uttar Pradesh, and the remoter Union Territories.[75] In the same year additional concessions became available to entrepreneurs wishing to locate in backward areas, and had some effect, mainly in terms of small-scale industries: in the early 1980s some 40 per cent of industrial licences went to backward areas (though few to really remote ones). But interest seems to be waning, and the number of relevant licences has been declining; liberalization and deregulation can hardly be expected to reverse the trend.

Finally, a further and different area in which planning has made some attempt to alter regional distributions is that of urbanization, a major problem given the apparently unstoppable inflow of migrants, many of them extremely poor, to all major cities and many smaller ones. Plans for major cities include those for Delhi–New Delhi, Calcutta, Bombay and Hyderabad.[76] A National Capital Regional Plan–2001 was finalized in 1988, extends from Delhi city and Union Territory into Haryana, Uttar Pradesh and Rajasthan, thus involving difficult relations with State governments, and proposes 'counter-magnets' to Delhi in places like Meerut, already in some cases becoming unmanageable agglomerations. The Union Territory of Delhi is projected to have a population of over 13 million by 2001 and the National Capital Region to contain over 32 million by that date. But all this urban planning is fraught with uncertainty, not least because of the interface with politics.

At the other extreme from the multi-million cities lie India's innumerable villages; and in between there are smaller urban settlements, ranging from small market towns to regional centres, though never in the nicely-ordered hierarchy that characterizes Britain or Western Europe. The hierarchical pattern is most completely approached in Punjab, Haryana and Tamil Nadu.[77] There has been some discussion in India on the desirability of supplying a more complete hierarchy of 'central places' between metropolitan city and village, on the dubious assumption that such central places would energize the countryside by the diffusion of innovations and the provision of employment. This has merged into the notion of 'growth poles', urban centres that should be foci for further desiderata like rural industrialization and the development of backward areas.[78] But the scope for government action, even if one is convinced of the general idea of building up central places as growth poles, is strictly limited: here a public sector industry or industrial estate, there a licensed market to build a small town into a larger. Barbara Harriss urged convincingly that the effects on the surrounding region would be limited and that regions get the central places that they deserve, that is, solutions lie in rural development (which by all means could include rural industry).[79]

Foreign trade

Since independence there have been very substantial changes in the volume, composition and direction of India's foreign trade, reflecting particularly economic development, government policy, and exogenous factors.[80] It is, however, important to emphasize that India, like other South Asian countries, still plays a relatively small part in world trade.

Exports remained relatively stagnant during the 1950s and early 1960s, when import substitution was, as we have seen, the order of the day. However, they showed stronger growth after 1970, while still disappointing some observers. Imports rose markedly in most years from 1953–4, owing largely to the needs of industrialization, tempered, however, by effects of import substitution. A growing gap between exports and imports has led to a continuing shortage of foreign exchange. Since 1970–1 there has been an even more vigorous upward tendency in imports, owing much till very recently to increased oil purchases at an enhanced price, and this in spite of mounting home production.

Over the years since independence there have been considerable changes in the composition of foreign trade: these have been most marked since the middle 1960s. There has been a relative decline in such long-standing exports as tea and jute manufactures, though cotton cloth has more nearly held its own, and a rise in such products of agriculture and animal husbandry as leather, leather manufactures, oil cake and cashew kernels. There have also been increased exports of iron ore and of products of heavy industry like iron and steel, engineering goods and chemicals. For the future much will clearly depend on competitiveness in price and quality.

Imports have included foodgrains in years of bad harvests (one hopes only in the past). Imports of consumer goods have declined with industrialization, as have those of capital goods, though some machinery and raw materials are still necessary. But imports of intermediate goods have held up.

Turning to the direction of trade, an outstanding feature is the decline in India's trading relationship with the United Kingdom and the complementary forging of links with other parts of the world.[81] From 1980–1 onwards the United Kingdom received under 6 per cent of India's exports, compared with 28 per cent in 1955–6, while the USA took from 11 to 15 per cent and the USSR from 10 to 18 per cent. (The future of trade with and aid from the USSR is, of course, now clouded with uncertainty.) By 1987–8 some 20 per cent of India's exports were going to (mainland) western Europe. As for imports into India, from 1975–6 to 1984–5 only some 5–6 per cent were coming from the UK, less than from West Germany in the latter year. But there is still relatively little trade with other Asian countries, apart from Japan and the oil-producers (over 7 per cent of India's imports came from Saudi Arabia in 1984–5).

Of other aspects of India's changing economy, enough has been said already about foreign aid in its several contexts and many complexities (see, for example, p. 123).[82] But a word must be added about tourism and overseas remittances. The former activity has developed greatly since the mid-1970s and become the second largest earner of foreign exchange (though most estimates take no account of extra imports related to tourist requirements). Delhi, Agra and Rajasthan are the main centres of attraction in the northern hemisphere winter, and Kashmir (in happier and more stable times) at other seasons. Some 1.2 million tourists came to India in 1989.

Remittances by Indians working overseas also grew to notable proportions, particularly those from the Middle East (and therefore latterly subject to disturbed conditions and indeed war, creating great problems, not least for the mainly poor workers involved).

In conclusion

The governments and peoples of India have many achievements to their credit as a result of their labours since independence. Foodgrain production has increased at a rate generally faster than population growth, itself very rapid. India is able to manufacture a wide range of capital, intermediate and consumer goods which, before independence, had to be imported. The rail and road networks have been improved. Exports have been diversified and destinations widened. And in terms of GNP per capita, the Indian economy grew by an annual average of 3.7 per cent in the period 1970–1 to 1985–6. There are also developments in school and university education, and, notably, the emergence of scholars, scientists and computer experts of international reputation.

But economic changes could have been greater and more beneficial: if agriculture had from the beginning received as much attention as industry (for example, if as much research had been devoted to rice and the millets as to wheat); if industrial policy had been oriented earlier to exports and also to labour intensiveness and the raising of living standards; if liberalization had come earlier; if . . . the list is endless.

'More beneficial'? The most crucial question to be asked of Indian economic development is 'Who benefits?' a question that assuredly cannot be answered by citing GNP figures. We have seen that whatever gains have accrued to industrialists and to urban upper and middle classes, and to farmers over a wider spectrum than is sometimes admitted by writers on agrarian change, many of the urban poor and of the much larger numbers of the rural poor have gained little if anything, and some are worse off. And let us not forget the plight of myriads of poor women, while the Mahatma's Harijans are still a most severely disadvantaged group.

At a deeper, yet more controversial level Frankel (1978) saw in India a contradiction between Nehru's two main aims: accommodative politics and radical social change.[83] On the one hand, the Congress party, in seeking to hold together a wide range of classes and interests, was bound to try and accommodate rural landed interests, which grew in power as time went on. Meanwhile the Government of India and its Planning Commission were formulating a number of policies that, if fully implemented, would have eroded the economic, social and political power of the rural dominant castes, to say nothing of the big industrialists. Here lay the contradiction. So far, except in Kerala and West Bengal, the power of the dominant landed interests is generally undiminished, if not augmented. The Nehru vision of a 'gradual revolution' to achieve his twin aims has faded, if indeed it is not outmoded.

By mid-1991 the Indian economy was in deep trouble on a number of fronts: most notably a severe foreign exchange crisis, dwindling currency reserves, budget deficits, and escalating prices to consumers. The reader will recognize the roots of these problems, not only in the imbalance between imports and exports and in the far-reaching consequences of the Gulf War, but also in recent political history (which brought some reckless fiscal policies). The minority government of Narasimha Rao formed in June 1991, with a distinguished economist, Manmohan Singh, as Finance Minister, acted swiftly by means of such measures as devaluation, an austerity budget, and an approach for large credits to the International Monetary Fund (which tends to impose tough conditions, resentment at which could well lead to political troubles).

If, in now turning to the other countries of South Asia, beginning with Pakistan, I proceed partly, or even largely by comparison with India, I hope that my friends in these other countries, or readers primarily interested in one or more of them, will not be hurt or disappointed. Certainly I do not wish to imply that India is in any way the norm against which the achievements and problems of other South Asian countries must be measured: far from it. It is merely that time's wingèd chariot hurries near, and that space is scarce.

PAKISTAN

Introduction

(The sections on Pakistan will, except where specific reference is made to East Pakistan (now Bangladesh) or where the historical context requires otherwise, refer only to the former West Pakistan.)

From early sections of this chapter it is clear that Pakistan at independence was even more of an agricultural country than India, and a landlord's country to boot. Although it inherited most of the great irrigated areas of the Punjab and all of those in Sind, it had large tracts of arid territory. It possessed but little mineral wealth or modern factory industry. Pakistan was also handicapped by the need to set up from scratch an administration above the provincial level. Clearly, too, Pakistan has had a disturbed political history: this has in many ways hindered or distorted economic development, and a high proportion of the budget and of GNP has gone on military purposes.

Economic strategies

Not surprisingly, government economic planning in Pakistan took some time to get off the ground; the first Five Year Plan did not emerge until 1955.[84] That there was such planning, and that it declared aims of 'social justice' as well as industrialization and economic growth, suggests parallels with India that are in fact misleading. At least, before the Bhutto era (1971–7), government was much less pervasive in economic affairs than in India. There were no great areas reserved for the public sector, and a much greater role, and much more latitude, were accorded to the private sector, whether in agriculture or in industry. In fact, the Pakistan Industrial Development Corporation (PIDC), an apparent exception to this policy, established industries that were handed over to private firms as they became viable. Development in Pakistan has also been more export-oriented than in India, while concepts of social justice were generally circumscribed.

Successive governments of Pakistan, moreover, generally placed much greater reliance than those of India on foreign, especially American, expertise and on foreign aid, and this served to reinforce capitalist tendencies. This reliance owed something to desperate need, but also reflected Pakistan's involvement in close relations with the United States, relations none the less with a somewhat chequered history (see pp. 101–2).

The Bhutto period, however, proclaimed 'Islamic socialism' and talked of nationalizing the 'commanding heights of the economy' and of showing greater favour to the public sector generally. It attempted more land reforms and attacked the concentration of industrial ownership. But after the overthrow of Bhutto in 1977 the earlier strategy was, generally speaking, restored, though with stronger Islamic overtones (for example, measures to abolish interest, and closer economic relations with the Middle East, involving substantial aid). In 1982 the military government promised to give a new impetus to private sector investment, and relaxing bureaucratic controls. Nevertheless, it was announced in 1988 that the Seventh Plan would pay special attention to the provision of non-farming jobs for the landless, and that, in spite of the unfavourable economic climate, the budget would have 'economic justice' as a principal aim. There was also discussion of the improvement of the education of women. Liberalization of the economy, however, continued. More recently have come political problems associated with the fall of Bennazir Bhutto's government and the fragility of its successor; to say nothing of the consequences of Middle East crises in terms of oil prices and loss of remittances. According to World Bank sources, Pakistan's GNP per capita in 1990 was, at US $380, slightly ahead of India's at US $350.

In 1992 Pakistan joined Turkey and Iran in reviving an Economic Co-operation Organization dating from 1985 and inviting the Central Asian Republics of the former Soviet Union to join them. Pakistan no doubt had an eye to the fact that Karachi is the nearest seaport for these Republics, albeit via Afghanistan.

Agriculture

Pakistan has recorded some notable increases in foodgrain production since independence (all figures in metric tons).[85] The production of wheat, by far and away the principal foodgrain, showed little general upward trend until the mid-1960s, and a great deal of fluctuation; overall, production was losing the race with population. But after 1965, with the introduction of HYVs, there was a remarkable 111 per cent increase between 1966 and 1976–7 to reach 12 million tons, according to official figures, and on to 14 million tons in 1989. Expansion in area played some part in this increase (Pakistan has its colonization areas, notably in the Thal, between the Indus and the Jhelum), but the main factor has been increase in yield. Rice is a less important crop than in India, of course, but, given irrigation and Pakistan's *kharif* sunshine, one that is less subject to the environmental problems that have hampered India's 'green revolution'. Yields have, however, only increased notably since the HYVs came in, rising by over 50 per cent between 1966 and 1976–7 to 2.6 million tons. But production in the 1980s appears to have stabilized at around 4.8 million tons (of paddy). In Pakistan the millets *bajra* and *jowar* are fodder rather than food crops. Maize is, however, basic to the rural economy of the northern hill country, and is increasing in importance. Production in 1989 stood at 4.5 million tons. Pulses are a main traditional source of protein, but are agronomically a somewhat neglected crop with fluctuating production. Of the oilseeds, cotton seed is the most prominent.

Cotton is the main commercial crop of Pakistan, and is largely concentrated in the canal-irrigated areas. Production grew from about 200,000 tons (as lint) at independence to over 700,000 tons in the early 1970s, but then declined to 569,000 tons in 1977–8, apparently because of competition from sugar-cane. But growth began again and in the late 1980s output stood at over 1.4 million tons.

Except for the era of Bhutto 'populism' (see p. 75), government policy towards agriculture in Pakistan has generally been more production-oriented and less concerned with rural development and the uplift of the villages and of their poor. Given the virtual stagnation of agricultural production in Pakistan until the mid-1960s, whatever government action there was has little to its credit. There was, however, once the country had settled down, an effort in agricultural research and extension, and a Village Agricultural and Industrial Development Programme (Village AID) which invites comparison with India's Community Development.[86] For there were to be village level workers, stimulation of self-help projects, and liaison with specialists in health and so on, all with much American assistance. But the main thrust was in terms of agricultural productivity. There was also a Rural Works Programme. Neither can claim great success, even in production terms.

B.L.C. Johnson says

> the scheme seems to have foundered on two rocks: . . . the quality of the village workers who tended to be college graduates with little real experience of village life . . . (and) the scheme trod on too many administrative toes by urging self-reliance, and perhaps excessive boldness in the under-privileged of the semi-feudal society.

In the mid-1960s, however, following measures to subsidize tubewells and fertilizer, successful efforts were made to popularize the new HYVs. With the brief Bhutto era there came in 1971 a People's Works Programme, and an Integrated Rural Development Programme (IRDP) recalling the old Village AID, and seeking to bring information, credit, inputs, and marketing to farmers.[87] Significantly, given the production orientation of Pakistan's efforts, this was launched by the Ministry of Food and Agriculture; and, for all Bhutto's rhetoric, was economic rather than social in its thrust. IRDP in fact was only implemented in a few pilot schemes. Also in the Bhutto period came the Ministry of Production's plan for 'agrovilles', small market towns to be established all over the country with the aim of energizing development (compare the Thana Development Centres in Bangladesh: see p. 156), and the conflation of central places and growth poles in some Indian thinking. According to Shahid Javed Burki, 'the agrovilles plan was given up after the launching of one project – Shabab near Lahore'.

In 1988 the Federal Minister of Food, Agriculture and Cooperatives foresaw a 'second green revolution' if an 'integrated approach' was made to ensure fuller participation by small farmers, while in the following year the Governor of Punjab emphasized the need for attention to rainfed areas.

It is surprising that, given the general bias thrust in economic policy in Pakistan, more use has not made of price incentives. In fact, and in the words of G.T. Brown of the World Bank, 'Export duties and bans and the government monopoly of raw cotton and rice exports kept domestic prices for many agricultural commodities far below world market levels'.[88] Associated with this monopoly of rice-exporting was the high relative price paid to the farmer for *basmati*, the scented rice popular in the Middle East: this has adversely affected adoption rates of higher yielding but less exportable varieties. However, in 1981 it raised procurement prices, while still preserving a differential for *basmati*.[89]

One area in which successive governments of Pakistan have been active is that of irrigation and drainage. The great canals inherited from the Raj have been maintained, aided by the new construction made under the Indus Waters Treaty (see pp. 50–1). The Thal area between the Indus and the Jhelum has been irrigated by a new canal system taking off from the Indus at Kalabagh, where in 1989 a new giant dam was planned (cf. pp. 9–10). Two additional dams were constructed lower down the Indus to help solve the considerable problems of Sind, but clearly the more water that is abstracted higher up the Indus system the greater those problems. Altogether, there has been a notable increase in the irrigated area: it is claimed that three-quarters of cropped land is now under irrigation. Government has addressed itself to the grave problems of interrelated waterlogging, salinity and alkalinity (see p. 130) in canal-irrigated areas of Punjab and Sind.[90] SCARP (Salinity Control and Reclamation Projects) involve drainage works and public tubewells to lower the water-table (and to irrigate if the water is suitable). (But tubewells, which perhaps contribute as much as 30 per cent of water for irrigated agriculture, are mainly, and increasingly, privately owned).

Agrarian structure

I have emphasized that Pakistan is a landlord's country with a highly unequal landownership pattern, though some tribal areas are an exception. Since in parts of Punjab there was considerable peasant proprietorship national aggregate figures conceal greater inequalities elsewhere. In 1962, it was estimated that there were 1.6 million marginal owner-cultivators (with less than 5 hectares), 750,000 tenants with at least 3 hectares, no fewer than 1.8 million tenants-at-will, and 550,000 landless labourers.[91] At independence *zamindari* tenure was strong in Punjab outside areas of peasant proprietorship and of 'government' tenures in the canal colonies. Sind was nominally a *raiyatwari* area, but *jagirdari* had evolved and most cultivators were sharecropping tenants, *haris*. In the years before 1958, Sind, Punjab and the North-West Frontier Provinces (NWFP) all promulgated land reforms, but these were half-hearted in conception and implementation. Ayub Khan enacted land reforms that abolished intermediaries: placed a (high) ceiling at 203 hectares of irrigated land or twice that level for unirrigated; and gave tenants (including the *haris*) freedom from ejection except for non-payment of rent, failure to cultivate properly, or subletting. But there were a list of exemptions from the ceiling legislation, and some built-in loopholes. Not surprisingly, Ayub's measure was ineffective, given the landholding interests of the ruling military and bureaucratic groups. But some bigger landowners did lose land, which was redistributed to no more than 200,000 families.

Given the only mildly reformed agrarian structure and the general agricultural policies of government, it is not surprising that initial adoption of HYVs of wheat and rice and extensive use of fertilizer was mainly limited to the bigger farmers who already had, or soon sank, tubewells and who had the capital, credit and influence to acquire fertilizers.[92] Tenants and small proprietors were absolutely, or, at any rate, relatively worse off, though some of them were adopters by the early 1970s. Alavi, however, writing from a Marxian standpoint, sees the situation at that time as inhibiting the growth of 'middle peasants', while Pearse (1980) (see note 57) stresses the rise of tractor-using 'entrepreneurial cultivators'.

Z.A. Bhutto initiated his own programme of land reform in 1972. This reduced the ceiling to 60 irrigated or 120 unirrigated hectares (40 hectares for public servants) with no compensation and no exemptions, but a bonus equivalent to 10 hectares of irrigated land for those who had bought tractors or sunk tubewells before 1971. Farmers with less than 5 hectares irrigated or 10 acres unirrigated were exempt from land revenue. Tenancy was subject to the same conditions as in Ayub's measures, except that land revenue became a responsibility of the landlord. There was much evasion by prior disposal. However, it is reported that, up to Bhutto's fall in 1977, 1.4 million hectares had been resumed by government under the ceiling provision, and something under half of this distributed free. But by 1977, Bhutto had become more dependent on landed interests.[93] The military government that succeeded Bhutto had priorities other than land reform and social change. There was ministerial advocacy of support for small farmers, actually during Benazir Bhutto's brief period of office (1988–90).

As for agricultural credit in Pakistan, commercial banks, the official Agricultural Development Bank, and co-operative societies have all functioned: their performance, especially for small farmers and share-croppers, has left much to be desired.

There has been an officially-sponsored programme for the consolidation of holdings, and for similar reasons. By 1974–5 nearly 7 million hectares had been covered.[94]

Mining and manufacturing

Pakistan, we have seen, had at independence very little factory industry. Such mineral wealth and power potential as it possessed remained relatively unexploited. True, coal was mined in the Salt Range of Punjab and elsewhere to produce some 250,000 tons annually; oil came in small quantities from the Attock and other fields; and there was some mining of chromite, which continues. But effective capacity for power generation was only about 40,000 kW, largely from thermal stations.[95]

However, by about 1970 annual coal production was over a million tons; oil production was sufficient to maintain several refineries; natural gas, discovered in 1955 at Sui in Sind was being sent by means of pipelines to principal centres and had become a main source of energy; and some 2.5 million MW of power were being produced from hydroelectric schemes in the hills.[96] Cotton-weaving had become a major factory industry, with an annual output of over 600 million metres of cloth; and cement manufacture was in full swing. Karachi and Hyderabad in Sind, and Lahore and Faisalabad (formerly Lyallpur) in Punjab, were the main factory locations. Here, then, is a substantial record of productive achievement.

Now, up to the time of Ayub Khan's coup in 1958, factory industry was dominated by refugee merchant groups who had settled mainly in Karachi and Sind (see remarks on the Mojahirs, p. 55). Initial efforts were mainly bent to import substitution, behind tariff barriers and with much foreign aid. Ayub is seen by Burki as the leader of a new middle class who aimed to reduce the power not only of the landed aristocracy but also of these merchant industrialists.[97] Fiscal measures encouraged export orientation, and a new group of industrialists broke the monopoly of the Karachi merchants. But their industrial power was concentrated in a very few families, twenty-two of them according to an opinion popular in the late 1960s.[98] During the brief Bhutto period of 'Islamic socialism' there was an attack on the twenty-two families, a burst of nationalization, and some initiatives in the public sector. (But before Bhutto fell private capital was already reasserting its position, and continues to dominate.)

The secession of Bangladesh and accompanying and subsequent events had a traumatic effect on the previously spectacular industrial progress: growth in production slackened, or even fell, in a number of sectors. Trade deficits and international debt mounted. Recovery was slow. By the late 1980s, however, and to choose one example only, annual coal production had climbed to 2 million tons. Moreover, a new steelworks had been built at Karachi with Soviet aid, and a number of plants, some with aid from the Middle East, were producing fertilizer using Sui gas as feedstock.

Meanwhile, small-scale and cottage industries continued to provide employment and to produce hand-woven fabrics, carpets and other goods.

Regional planning

Planning in Pakistan has been, as in India, predominantly sectoral; and, given the free rein allowed to private enterprise, it is not surprising that the growth areas for both agriculture and industry have been almost entirely those already relatively prosperous and urbanized: the irrigated agricultural areas of Punjab and Sind, the Karachi region and eastern Punjab for industry. Exceptions are to be found in newly-irrigated regions like the Thal. In 1988 and 1989, however, there were reports of 'master plans' for rural areas of Sind and of 'special projects' in the provinces, including Baluchistan, NWFP, and Azad Kashmir.[99]

Foreign trade

Comparison of the foreign trade of Pakistan up to the secession of Bangladesh with that in subsequent years is complicated by the fact that in the earlier period trade between West and East Pakistan was internal and so excluded from official statistics. The effects of inflation and devaluation also hinder ready interpretation of time-series. However, at independence, and for some time afterwards, the exports of (West) Pakistan reflected an unindustrialized economy, and consisted almost entirely of raw cotton and wool, cotton-seed, and hides and skins.[100] Raw cotton alone made up 84 per cent of exports in 1949–50. Imports in those early years comprised cotton yarn (for hand looms) and cloth, intermediate goods such as machinery and metal products, and other manufactures.

In 1971–2, on the other hand, cotton cloth and yarn made up 29 per cent of exports, clearly showing the effect of industrialization. By 1979–80 cotton cloth and yarn had fallen back to under 20 per cent of exports and raw cotton to 14 per cent; rice exports, 8 per cent of the total in 1971–2, had risen to some 18 per cent, a consequence of the production of *basmati* primarily for export; and petroleum products (reflecting refinery construction) to 7.5 per cent. Exports of carpets, wool, and hides and skins continued at modest levels, while a beginning had been made with the export of specialist manufactures such as sports goods and surgical instruments. Exports of raw cotton and of rice were badly hit by floods in 1988.

Imports into Pakistan since 1971–2 have been dominated by machinery and vehicles, and other manufactured goods, though the composition of the latter has changed as industrialization has got under way. In some years considerable imports of foodgrains have been necessary. Oil grew from 7 per cent of imports in 1971–2 to 23 per cent in 1979–80. 1974 was critical for Pakistan because of the hoist in oil prices in that year.

Pakistan has long suffered from an imbalance between exports and imports and so from a deficit in its balance of trade. This was especially alarming after 1974. Recourse has had to be made to foreign borrowing and to various forms of aid. Remittances from Pakistanis abroad (especially in the Middle East) were hit by the Gulf War. Tourism makes little contribution to Pakistan's economy; entrepreneurs have been slow to exploit the charms of hill stations like Murree.

As in the case of India, the United Kingdom as a market for exports and a source for imports has declined in importance over the years, to under 10 per cent of both exports and imports. Pakistan in fact now trades world-wide, though its trade with India is pitifully low for sad but obvious reasons. A notable feature over the years has been an increase in exports to and imports from the Middle East; imports consist, of course, largely of oil.

In conclusion

The economic development clearly provides interesting comparisons and contrasts with that of India, if only because of its greater reliance on private enterprise and on foreign advice and aid. Starting with many handicaps and with very little factory industry, the growth in GNP was, once it had settled down after partition, spectacular, and pleasing to advisers who saw development in just those terms. But that growth owed more to industry than to agriculture, which for some years failed to increase production of foodgrains at a rate sufficient to compensate for the rise in population, and the 'green revolution' was at first less spectacular in Pakistan's well-irrigated Punjab than across the border in India. India, however, for all its problems, did not suffer the trauma that befell Pakistan with the loss of Bangladesh, nor quite such grave trade imbalances.

In terms of distribution, whether spatially or class-wise, there is little achievement to record, and Pakistan remains a very unequal society, notwithstanding the rhetoric of the short Bhutto period.[101] Clearly there is no emerging contradiction in Pakistan between radical social and economic aims and political accommodation of the kind that Frankel saw in India, but there may well prove to be a contradiction between Islamicization and modernization in Pakistan's economic development.

BANGLADESH

Economic strategies

In the first years after secession in 1971 Bangladeshis and their friends were apt to complain, with a good deal of justification, that Pakistan's economic strategies and related policies from 1947 to 1971 bore unequally on the eastern wing: claiming, for example, that the foreign exchange earnings of jute exports, raw and manufactured, from the East were used by the central government for the benefit of the West, as was most foreign aid; that government revenues collected in the East were, in large measure, spent in the West; and that what development of jute and cotton manufactures took place in the East, under PIDC-encouraged private enterprise, was mainly in the hands of West Pakistanis, especially Punjabis; in fine, that a poverty-stricken, over-populated province was neglected and exploited by West Pakistan, and treated as a dependent colonial territory.[102] This picture needs, however, some modification. The government did develop hydroelectric power and natural gas resources.[103] A steel-rolling mill and an oil refinery were also, belatedly, set up at Chittagong, which grew into a major port. Agriculture, too, received some official support, though foodgrain production failed overall to keep pace with population increase.

Bangladesh started its independent statehood in 1971 with many handicaps: over and above its crushing poverty and population pressure, and the inadequacies and distortions of development under Pakistan, there was the devastation wrought during the struggle for 'liberation', though these were to some extent mitigated by the rallying-round of friends in the international community. A first priority was clearly rehabilitation, as became very clear to me during a visit in 1973.

The strategies and mechanisms of official planning during the early years of independence bore at least a superficial resemblance to Indian practice.[104] Thus a Planning Commission formulated a Five Year Plan to start in 1973, and assumed a mixed economy – seen as a stage in the transition to socialism. The commission was, however, more technocratic than India's, relying almost exclusively on talented Bangladeshi economists; and there was less interplay with politicians and bureaucrats. The Plan placed strong emphasis on agriculture and on employment. Some socialist policies, notably nationalization of industries, were implemented even before the Plan was finalized. The Plan itself soon ran into difficulties, not least because of declining morale in the public service and growing confusion and corruption (see p. 76). Planned targets were for the most part not achieved, and production actually fell in a number of sectors. Since 1975, in the context of recurrent coups, military rule, and much instability, socialism has gone by the board. There has been a general process of denationalization and privatization, with reduced direct investment even in irrigation. On the other hand, Ershad did in 1982 propose agrarian reforms to include 'a due share of crops to the landless'.[105] Moreover, the Planning Commission has survived, and produced further Plans in 1978, 1980 and 1985.[106] It remains to be seen what changes in strategy and policy will follow the political changes of 1971 and after. But it is difficult to feel hopeful.

Agriculture

Foodgrain production in Bangladesh has fluctuated considerably from year to year, with famine conditions in 1974.[107] Not surprisingly, massive food imports, often in the form of aid, were necessary in a number of years. Downward fluctuations in foodgrain production, apart from those during and just after 'liberation', mainly reflect the incidence of the cyclones, droughts and abnormal floods to which this unfortunate country is all too prone. (There were particularly severe floods in April–May 1991.) However, according to the FAO Food Production Yearbook aggregate, annual cereal production grew steadily from some 21.0 million tons in 1979–81 to 27.5 million tons in 1989 (measuring rice as paddy); and it has been claimed that growth in food production has, since independence, kept just ahead of population increase. This is not to say that nutritional needs have been satisfied: far from it.

Rice is by far and away the principal food crop, accounting for 26.6 million tons of the total cereal production in 1989 (again measuring rice as paddy). In Bangladesh rice is grown in three overlapping seasons. *Aus* paddy is sown with the pre-monsoon rains in March or April and harvested during the monsoon in July or August. *Aman* paddy, which may be broadcast in March/April or sown in July/August for transplanting, grows till November or December. *Aus* and *aman* varieties may, on some land, be sown mixed, as an insurance against one of the crops failing; while *aman* varieties include the broadcast, low-yielding deep water rices able to grow in flood-water up to 20 feet deep. *Boro* is the dry-season crop, grown between November and May either in low land with natural moisture or, increasingly, under irrigation.

Much of the growth in rice production has so far come in the *boro* season because of the increased use of low-lift irrigation pumps, mainly diesel-powered, in association with HYVs and fertilizer. In early 1992 drought in some sixteen districts compounded problems created by a shortage of diesel fuel. *Boro* yields per acre have more than doubled since 1965. But there has been some adoption of (different) HYVs and other improved varieties in *aus* and transplanted *aman*, even in areas flooded to a moderate depth. But to improve the yields of the deep-water rices is a difficult and intractable problem.

Wheat production in the dry season grew from almost nothing to over a million tons in 1989, given the possibility of irrigation and the introduction of HYVs, with notably early adoption in the north-west of the country.

Other food crops include various pulses and oilseeds (generally also dry-season crops; their production has tended to stagnate), and sugar-cane. The principal commercial crops are tea and jute; the latter competes with *aus* paddy in certain topographical situations, and loses to *aus* when this is grown by transplanting. Jute production fluctuates, but stood at about 800,000 tons in 1989. Jute is fighting a losing battle with synthetic substitutes in world markets.

Given the semi-aquatic environment of Bangladesh, it is not surprising that fish form a prominent part of the diet, and provide protein (as do pulses, oilseeds and vegetables). These are not always within the reach of the poor; nor, for that matter, are cereals.

What of government efforts to stimulate agricultural production? Before 'liberation', and as in West Pakistan, the strategy was predominantly production-oriented; and, even in those terms, of limited impact. The provision and encouragement of pump, tubewell and other irrigation did, however, supplement traditional methods and provide the infrastructure for the adoption of HYVs of rice and wheat in *boro*. And agricultural research was maintained. Moreover, in the early 1960s a notable and generally successful experiment in rural development, which attracted considerable attention internationally, was begun in Comilla District. This involved co-operatives for credit and marketing, irrigation, training, rural works, and an attempt at popular participation through the establishment of 'development councils' at *thana* (subdistrict) level. The Comilla recipe was applied to other districts and fed into the Integrated Rural Development Programme (see p. 148).

Independent Bangladesh continued to spread the Comilla recipe, with the help of various aid agencies, and under the aegis of the Bangladesh Rural Development Board and its system of co-operatives. This rural development programme, with its more participatory, less bureaucratic, approach, can take some of the kudos for the adoption of HYVs, for a marked increase in co-operative credit, and for the spread of pump and tubewell irrigation to complement direct government construction (a total of over 2 million hectares were reported irrigable in 1989). It was government policy to subsidize irrigation pumps and fertilizers (whose use greatly increased). But from the late 1970s, and in tune with changing ideology, government agencies have tended to withdraw from direct construction and even from subsidization and to rely on private development of shallow tubewells, with adverse effects on the provision of irrigation, not least in terms of equity. Some groundwater potential, in fact, still remains untapped.

However, government organizations like the Bangladesh Rice and Jute Research Institutes continued their good work. And let us not forget the initiative and skill shown by individual cultivators who, in the immemorial tradition of the subcontinent, have continued their work, come coup, come counter-coup (I was told of some who went to India by train to buy HYV rice seedlings not available in their own area).

156

It will be clear that much remains to be done, however, in Bangladesh agriculture (and it must not be forgotten that there are regional and local disparities that there is no space to discuss here). Self-sufficiency in foodstuffs at adequate nutritional levels is still not forthcoming, and this is not wholly unrelated to the fact that there has been insufficient special effort to spread innovations, and what it takes to innovate, to the small farmer. This leads us on to considerations of equity.

Agrarian structure

The agrarian structure of East Pakistan in 1947 was highly unequal. It was also a land of *zamindari* tenure;[108] but many of the *zamindars* were Hindus who fled to India. This facilitated the land reforms of 1950 and 1957 which abolished intermediaries and provided for the occupier of land to pay revenue direct to the state. A ceiling was placed at 33 acres on land held for self-cultivation by ex-*zamindars*. There was further legislation under Ayub, placing a general ceiling, not lower, but higher at 100 acres. These measures brought little benefit to tenants and less to share-croppers. Land reform was prominent in the programme of the Awami League but actual measures were feeble, though in 1972 the general ceiling was lowered back to 33 acres (but few holdings exceeded this area), and land revenue was abolished on holdings below about 9 acres. But little more was done under Mujib, and little has been achieved since. There were gross inequalities in agricultural land holding in 1978, as is shown by Table 6.4.

It is not possible to update these figures (themselves of unknown accuracy) reliably and comprehensively, partly because, it has been said, of a lack of committed officials, and partly because of the unwillingness of cultivators to reply truthfully to questions (a trait not unknown elsewhere in South Asia – and more widely).[109] But it does seem that the distribution of land is becoming ever more skewed and the numbers of very small holdings, of tenants (often even more disadvantaged here than in India and Pakistan), and of the landless all increasing. And poverty, much of it desperate, and pressing particularly on women and young children, is

Table 6.4 Size-distribution of total owned land in rural Bangladesh, 1978

Acres	Percentage of total households
Zero	14.69
0.01–1.00	44.68
1.01–5.00	32.14
5.01–10.00	5.82
10.01–15.00	1.51
Over 15.00	1.16

Source: Derived from Jannuzi and Peach (1980), op. cit. (note 108), p. 107.

growing alarmingly. The 'green revolution' has had some beneficial effects for other than the bigger farmers by direct, if delayed adoption of HYVs by small cultivators, and by some increase in labour demand (for example, by increased *boro* cropping and by the effect of higher yields on workloads during and after harvest). On the other hand, replacement of jute by paddy reduces the labour requirement. Government policy under Ershad favoured the bigger farmers, among whom his power base lay, and who have grown more exacting in their relations with poorer people, not least in terms for credit.

A radical land reform that might tackle this situation does not appear likely, unless a post-Ershad government unexpectedly finds both the political will and the administrative means. But even then it would face many formidable obstacles. For the time being, and in addition to the good work being done by voluntary agencies, perhaps the only possible policy for a government, however well-intentioned, is one that has its advocates, namely, an agriculture-led development strategy, with employment- and income-generating schemes for the rural poor. It can be argued that an increase in income so generated will become necessary to provide a market for growing and perhaps diversified agricultural production. But manifestly there are no easy solutions.

Mining and manufacturing

Bangladesh has little mineral wealth, and hardly any of it was tapped in 1947. Since the early 1950s, however, natural gas has been exploited in a number of places in the east of the country, and forms its most important source of energy as well as providing feedstock for fertilizer plants. There are pipelines to Dhaka and Chittagong, and to these plants. So far no oil has been found, but a little is condensed from gas. Coal exists, again in the east, much of it too deep to mine economically. A hydroelectric station operates in the Chittagong hills (displacing many tribal people: see p. 54). Power supply is, however, absent from much of Bangladesh, and where it does exist shortage is endemic.

Modern factory industry was almost non-existent in 1947. By 1971, however, some 30 jute-mills and a number of cotton-mills had been developed, albeit largely by Punjabi entrepreneurs. These industries were hit by much disturbance during 'liberation', which was followed by hasty nationalization and, later, inept privatization. But by 1984 there were 40 additional jute-mills, and a total of over 50 cotton-mills, subject, however, to fluctuating output. There were also cement works and paper-mills, and an oil refinery at Chittagong, as well as the fertilizer plants just mentioned. But modern industries only account for a small proportion of GDP and of employment, and barely affect regions beyond Dhaka–Narayanganj and Chittagong, despite talk of 'spatial equity' in the First Plan. Nurul Islam has highlighted the inefficiency, excess capacity and unprofitability of many of them.[110]

Cottage industries were not unimportant in 1947, or for that matter in 1971, and there has been much talk of expanding them because they are labour-intensive. But progress in both cottage and small-scale industry has been disappointing, though not negligible. Products include textiles, leather goods and *bidis* (small cigars).

Foreign trade

For reasons already mentioned, separate evaluation of the imports and exports of Bangladesh from 1947 to 1971 are not easy to make. Between 1970 and 1979 imports grew by 0.6 per cent while exports declined by 4.1 per cent.[111] These figures speak eloquently of the difficulties facing the new-born country in its international trading relations. A trade imbalance has been a persistent feature, and has emphasized the need for aid of various kinds. This is associated in the case of some of the sources with a rising burden of debt. Exports by the late 1980s consisted of primary products (mainly jute and tea); textiles and clothing which rose to some 50 per cent of exports (in some lights a remarkable figure); and other manufactures. Exports have not been helped by certain official policies, notably an overvalued currency, but rather more vigorous promotion has more recently been evident. Imports comprised food, machinery and transport supplies and, most notably, oil (whose rise to over 25 per cent of the value of imports mounted even higher with price rises and the Gulf War). As in the case of other South Asian economies, some help was earlier given by remittances, especially from Bangladeshis in the Middle East, in closing the gap between imports and exports that remained after aid was taken into account, but this source has of course been severely hit, for the time being at any rate. Not surprisingly, tourism makes a negligible contribution, though there are charming rural scenes that justify the old title *shona Bangla*, 'golden Bengal'.

The direction of trade, as elsewhere in the region, has seen a decline in relations with the UK, and later with the US, but relatively little trade with other South Asian countries.

The external economy of Bangladesh presents, then, as many difficulties, and actual and potential crises, as its environment, its population growth, and its internal economy – all, of course, interrelated.

In conclusion

What more can one say in summary of the economic development of Bangladesh? Clearly one is here dealing, sympathetically one hopes, with a chronic case of underdevelopment compounded of an agrarian economy with but little industry so far; of enormously heavy pressure of population still rising very rapidly, so that it is hard enough for production to keep pace with population growth, let alone to improve living standards of the tens of millions of very poor people in villages and towns; of severe lack of capital and of government revenue for developmental investment and also, it would appear so far, of adequate entrepreneurial and administrative talent; of gross and growing inequalities in wealth and income; and of hydra-headed corruption and recurrent political crises and coups (of which we have probably not seen the last). Yet behind this sombre picture lie resourceful cultivators whom one cannot fail to admire if one gets out into the villages, where great ingenuity is using every scrap of land as many times annually as it will stand: cultivators who have survived and laid hold, when they can, of the new varieties and technology (sometimes the product of Bangladeshi research) and introduced their own innovations – for example, by trans-planting traditionally broadcast crops; albeit in the context of an increasingly skewed distribution of land and income. For the 'Bangladesh village is no rural idyll; and the powerful dominate it'.

SRI LANKA

Economic strategies

We have seen (pp. 109–10) that Sri Lanka had at independence what was essentially a colonial export economy, with little industrialization, and imported most of its manufactured goods from the United Kingdom. Largely as a result of the productivity of its export sector, it had a GNP per capita approximately twice that of India and Pakistan. Already, however, steps were being taken to modify its economy, especially after internal self-government came in 1931.[112] The new ministers were interested, for example, in peasant agricultural colonization in the Dry Zone, and in modest industrialization. The First World War and the depression of the 1930s had shown the dangers of reliance on food imports and underlined the need for diversification; and population was growing fast, as was landlessness in the Wet Zone and hills.

Independence at first brought little alteration in economic objectives: with the ruling United National Party (UNP) there was no commitment to socialism, no Gandhianism, to supply an ideology of change. But the traumatic general election of 1956 brought an alternative party, the Sri Lanka Freedom Party (SLFP), to government. When for some years successive general elections brought these two main parties and their allies alternately to power, there were corresponding oscillations in economic policy: more conservative and pragmatic under the UNP, more left-of-centre under the SLFP. But there were also important continuities, many of them in welfare policies such as to justify the claim that Sri Lanka was some sort of welfare state. Thus all governments maintained a policy of Dry Zone agricultural colonization, like the complementary 'village expansion' schemes aimed largely at the relief of landlessness. Governments of both complexions operated guaranteed price schemes, which, with input subsidies and the non-collection of irrigation dues, constituted a distributive measure for agricultural producers. Rice rations were also subsidized. And all governments maintained what was, for a Third World country, a high level of expenditure on health and education; so that in the 1960s Sri Lanka rated high in terms of the 'Physical Quality of Life Index' (PQLI), narrowly based as it was on life expectancy; the inverse of infant mortality; and literacy.[113] The PQLI for Sri Lanka was in fact higher than that for Washington, DC. But many of these infancy-surviving, long-lived, literate Sri Lankans were unemployed, perhaps two-thirds of those in the 15–29 age-group.

The continuities in 'welfare' policies owed something to populism related to a long history of adult franchise, with a politicized electorate; and to the tendency for parties out of power to seek to outbid parties in power as elections approach.

Another continuity concerns the plantation sector: most governments, whatever their colour, submitted this sector to relative neglect for reasons that were a mixture of rather crude dependency theory under which the plantations, whatever the nationality of their ownership, were seen as 'imperialist enclaves'; of lack of political punch on the part of estate owners; and of even less punch on the part of the disenfranchised estate labourers (see p. 88).

But over and above these continuities there were further oscillations in economic policy: first, in attitudes to planning. Before 1956, there was really no strategic planning. The first UNP government did set up a Planning Secretariat, but the Six-Year Programme of Investment, 1954–5 to 1959–60 was really no more than a set of colonial-style departmental estimates. But Bandaranaike, on coming to power in 1956, set up a planning machine based on the Indian model, and its Ten Year Plan emerged in 1959.[114] This presented a coherent strategy: to avoid headlong industrialization, especially in terms of heavy industry, given the country's lack of natural resources and the smallness of its internal market; but rather to achieve suitable industrialization progressively by importing capital goods, to be paid for initially by increasing traditional exports. The Plan soon became a dead letter, for it was overtaken by foreign exchange crises related largely to difficulty in expanding exports, though parts of its strategy can be discerned as a thin thread running through later years.

A SLFP government produced a more radical Plan for 1972–6, seeking amongst other things to involve 'the people in the formulation and execution of development projects at the local level'. It was the post–1977 UNP administration, however, which appointed District Ministers with wide functions, each to chair an elected development council. It will not surprise the reader that the operation of this apparently liberal and participatory organization has been met with allegations of corruption and undue influence.

Industrial policy played a relatively minor part in early UNP days, though in the early 1950s such public sector plants as a hydroelectricity station and a cement plant were opened. But the SLFP governments of 1956 and later initiated a number of such industries in rapid succession; restricted imports; and encouraged private sector consumer goods industries. There were no very marked changes of industrial policy during UNP rule from 1965 to 1970; but when that party came back to power in 1977 there was a more pronounced move away from whatever was seen as socialistic in SLFP policy. For example, industries were privatized; a Free Trade Zone was established north of Colombo; and efforts were made to develop an open economy and to attract foreign firms on the capitalist model of Singapore.

Land reform is another field in which the SLFP was more enthusiastic than the UNP. True, under the latter a Paddy Lands Act was enacted in 1952, but it was limited to the ineffective regulation of tenancy in two districts. The SLFP's act of the same name passed in 1958 was ostensibly more thoroughgoing, involving security of tenure and maximum rent for tenants island-wide, and elected Cultivation Committees to manage agriculture at village level. More spectacular and far-reaching was the SLFP government's ceiling legislation of 1972, which affected mainly commercial crops grown by local companies and individuals: surplus land really was collected. An amendment of 1975 effectively nationalized foreign-owned estates. These land reforms have not been reversed by later UNP governments, though operation of many estates (though not ownership) has been privatized and (in the 'peasant' sector) Cultivation Committees abolished.

As for other and more recent developments, it will be clear that Sri Lanka lies in the midst of a sea of troubles, especially those related to Jatika Vimukti Peramune (JVP) insurrections and to civil war springing from Sinhalese–Tamil tensions. Government spending on defence has rocketed upwards and adversely affected the balance of payments, also hit by the crises in and emanating from the Middle East and the former USSR. One can readily understand that in these circumstances tactical considerations may overshadow thought on strategy; though it is commendable that public-spirited individuals continue to give of their best in looking ahead for their country.

Agriculture

It is conventional, but misleading, to recognize two distinct sectors in the agriculture of Sri Lanka, a peasant sector devoted to rice and other locally-consumed food crops, and an export sector producing for overseas markets: misleading if only because in the Wet Zone many 'peasants' grow export crops on small holdings in addition to food crops.

In the production of rice Sri Lanka has achieved noteworthy increases in production and in yield, though both fluctuate from year to year with rainfall: from some 300,000 tons (as paddy) annually at independence to over two million tons in the late 1980s. This greatly raised the contribution of local production to national supplies. After about 1965, in fact, production was gaining on population increase. It was in about the same year that national yields began to increase quite steeply, as a result first of locally-bred long-strawed hybrids but later of short-strawed HYVs, crosses between International Rice Research Institute (IRRI) varieties and local strains. Governments of both complexions paid attention to agricultural extension and to fertilizer subsidies as well as to plant breeding. But what distinguishes Sri Lanka from other South Asian countries is the great part played by increased area under paddy, largely as a result of Dry Zone colonization schemes. Since independence, in fact, the paddy area harvested has more than doubled, while gross area irrigated has increased by over 50 per cent. But, as a number of enquiries has shown, colonization is generally an expensive process, primarily because of the costly irrigation works involved.[115] Yet massive schemes like those on the Mahaveli Ganga continue to be developed. Finally, rice production in the Dry Zone has been adversely affected by the civil war.

Also characteristic of the Dry Zone, and in some areas disturbed by the civil war, is *chena* cultivation: this was originally the growing of a variety of crops in clearings made in the forest, which were abandoned to natural regeneration after a few years. But in all too many areas, nowadays, forest is destroyed or reduced to scrub and cultivation has become more or less permanent, but often with inadequate application of fertilizers to substitute for natural regeneration.

Efforts are being made to encourage a variety of food crops on some categories of paddy land.

Turning to the principal export crops, tea production increased to an annual average of 222,000 tons for 1964–5 to 1968–9; but since then there has been a more or less steady decline to some 200,000 tons for 1979–80 to 1983–4. In the case of rubber, annual production rose slowly after independence to the early 1960s, after which there was a sharp increase up to the early 1970s; since then it has declined to 135,000 tons for 1979–80 to 1983–4. Coconut production is more difficult to quantify with any accuracy, but appears at best to be static. The reasons for the recent stagnation or decline in production (and productivity) in the export sector are a matter of some controversy, but include taxation, adverse weather and prices, and neglect by owners in anticipation of land reform, or otherwise; but G.H. Peiris concluded in 1975 'the possibility that the institutional transformation is also responsible ... cannot be ruled out' and cited the alienation of former estates to peasants in small units; the delays in converting estates into co-operatives; the history of non-profitability in the State Plantations

Corporation, which took over many estates; and corruption and general inefficiency.[116] Now, while successive governments supported export agriculture by subsidizing replanting schemes, and while there are research institutes for each of the three principal crops, nevertheless there was an underlying record of relative neglect of the export sector. Diversification of crops has also been insufficiently attempted, for instance, by encouraging the cultivation of oil palm, as has been done so successfully in Malaysia. After 1977 the UNP government, with its different ideological slant, sought to improve incentives to producers of export crops and to move to privatization of management.

Sea fisheries, it should be mentioned, are of considerable importance in Sri Lanka.

Agrarian structure

In spite of the land reforms already sketched, and in spite of long-standing measures of agricultural colonization and village expansion, it appears that average landholdings in the peasant sector are growing smaller and more unequal. Especially does this apply to paddy land. In many colonization schemes, notwithstanding conditions of tenure that forbid fragmentation, either original holdings have become broken up, or descendants of the original allottee have moved off to encroach with small parcels on the waste, or become landless. Indeed, some of the most deplorable rural poverty is to be found in and around older schemes.[117] In 1982, for the peasant sector as a whole, some 42 per cent of holdings were said to have covered less than one acre, whereas 22 per cent held more than 3 acres.[118] Share-cropping was, and is, widespread. Moreover, as already hinted, cultivation committees (now abolished) did little to undermine the power of the 'big men', who, with tractorization and other changes incident to the 'green revolution', have tended to grow in influence: 'a new feudalism of technology' in the telling phrase of C.N. Jayaweera.[119] Even more recent developments do not seem to have worked in the direction of greater equity. The Land Commission that reported in 1990 notably recognized many of these problems and recommended a number of new policies and appropriate legislation.

Turning to the estate sector, we have already seen that 'surplus' land was collected; that foreign-owned estates were nationalized; and that a variety of structures were at first employed in farming the resumed land. What were the equity effects? Richards and Gooneratne concluded in 1980: 'The major comment on land reform is that despite its extent the rural social and economic structure was hardly changed' . . . because popular participation was discouraged in favour of indirect participation through, and direct control by, political representatives, and because village groups had no say in the disposal of estate land and may have suffered where, for example, new managements forbade grazing by cattle that had been countenanced by former owners.[120] It may be that it was the politicians and their clients who did best out of 'land reform'; and that this state of affairs continues, though with changed ideology and actors. And the Indian estate labourer certainly has benefited not at all.

Mining and manufacturing

Sri Lanka has little mineral wealth beyond limestone for cement-making, china clay, graphite, gemstones and mineral sands. There is considerable potential for hydroelectric power, some already harnessed, and the Mahaveli Ganga scheme will add substantially to this, though at the cost of displaced communities and of fears on environmental grounds.

Since independence industry has grown in importance from about 5 per cent of GNP to 27 per cent in 1989.[121] Industries include textiles (about 20 per cent of national value added by manufacture), petroleum refining, ceramics, salt-making, chemicals, and producers of a range of consumer goods. Many of these industries were originally controlled by state corporations, and aimed at import substitution; they earned a reputation for inefficiency and gross overmanning (though the felt need to reduce unemployment must not be forgotten). The growth rate of manufacturing production was 6.2 per cent for 1965–80 and nearly double that figure for 1980–9, an increase that owes something to continuing efforts to develop an open, export-oriented economy and to attract foreign capital, and which was achieved in spite of destruction during the 1983 communal riots and the troubles more generally.

Craft industries survive and, indeed, benefit from tourists, who are attracted by Sri Lanka's beaches and incomparable scenery and, in the case of the more discerning, by its antiquities, but severely reduced in numbers and mobility during the troubles.

It is a characteristic, of course, of an underdeveloped country, that it has a large primate city, a triton among the minnows, and Colombo is no exception. Nevertheless, economic activity in Sri Lanka is not so concentrated in the capital as in some Third World countries, for reasons that include the existence of unused or underused land in the Dry Zone, the scene not only of agricultural colonization but also of spontaneous settlement and other development, and the tendency of tourism to spawn hotels in many scattered coastal and inland locations.[122] Most private sector industries have, however, located in or near Colombo, and it may well be that the Free Trade Zone and other developments under the UNP government will, if circumstances permit, lead to increased polarization of industry on the capital city.

Foreign trade

Sri Lanka at independence had, I have emphasized, a colonial export economy, and trade still remains of greater significance to it than to other

South Asian countries. In 1950, 96 per cent of exports were made up of tea, rubber and coconut products.[123] By 1978, the three principal agricultural exports were still forming 73 per cent of total exports. By the late 1980s, however, all primary products together were forming under 50 per cent of total merchandise exports; just over 50 per cent were industrial products, two-thirds of them textiles.

Over 30 per cent of imports in 1950 consisted of food grains, mainly rice; this, as a result of increased home production, had fallen to under 20 per cent by the late 1980s. Over the same time span petroleum products had increased from 2.3 to 17.2 per cent. By the late 1980s, 27 per cent of merchandise imports consisted of machinery and transport equipment, and some 46 per cent of other manufactures.

A major characteristic of Sri Lanka's economy since independence has been the emergence of a wide gap in most years between export earnings (which fell in the early 1970s) and the cost of imports. This was particularly the case between 1966 and 1975. By 1984 there was some improvement, a contribution having been made by remittances from the Middle East (later, of course, greatly diminished), by aid (especially after 1977) and by tourism.

As might be expected, the United Kingdom has fallen from its position as the dominant trading partner of Sri Lanka, taking 25 per cent of exports and supplying 20 per cent of imports in 1950. By 1978, Sri Lanka's exports to Pakistan, the US, and China were all of the same order of magnitude (at 7–9 per cent of total exports) and there was a long list of countries taking from 2 to 6 per cent. Sources of imports were also highly diversified, Saudi Arabia and Iran, as oil suppliers, being prominent.

In conclusion

Here, then, is a small country with an economy and a recent history of economic development different in a number of important respects from those of other South Asian countries. Because of welfare policies more or less consistently pursued, it has much to its credit in education, health services, infant mortality and life expectancy; and, some might add, in lowering its birth-rate (see p. 116). The effects of industrialization are by no means negligible. But great inequalities, much poverty and frighteningly high unemployment persist. Moreover, and while one does not wish to re-enthrone GNP, there is the fact that GNP per capita, nearly twice India's at independence, was in 1989 only some 25 per cent above India's. Whatever may be true of welfare measures, then, growth has been relatively low (though higher than India's in 1989). The question arises, therefore, whether the welfare measures are responsible, in whole or in part, for the absorption of resources available to the government that might otherwise have gone to growth-oriented development. Richards and Gooneratne conclude, fairly I believe, that 'it is problematical to single out welfare policies as leading to slow growth'.[124] Clearly Sri Lanka has difficulties arising from lack of mineral resources, small size and colonial heritage, that do not in the same way affect India and Pakistan. But it is also possible to point to such shortcomings as the relative neglect and mishandling of the export sector and misplaced and expensive policies, some of which we have underlined, and also, unfortunately, to political failures and problems.

THE ECONOMIC DEVELOPMENT OF NEPAL, BHUTAN AND THE MALDIVE ISLANDS

Nepal

Nepal is one of the poorest countries of the Third World. Devotees of the dependency school of underdevelopment may see it as the periphery of a periphery, a dependency of India which is in turn a dependency of the world capitalist system; while within Nepal the valley around Kathmandu acts as the core within the periphery of a periphery to even more peripheral and remote rural areas.[125] Readers of pp. 91–4 may, however, wonder whether Nepal *is* such a dependency of India, given the history of relations between the two countries and the way in which modern Nepal has skilfully secured economic aid from all and sundry. But on the other hand, there were what may be seen as the high-handed Indian actions in relation to the Trade and Transit Treaty (see Chapter 5).

Nepal has one of the frustrating characteristics of the least-developed countries, a paucity of accurate and comprehensive statistical data; though there is now more by way of partial and qualitative information than was the case a few years ago. But the statistics that follow still carry the health warning 'According to official sources . . .'.

Over 90 per cent of Nepal's labour force are engaged in agriculture, growing rice in the plains of the Tarai and, with maize and wheat, on terraces in the hills. Paddy production has increased slowly, from 2.2 million tons in 1964–5 to around 3 million tons in the late 1980s.[126] Over the same period the production of maize reached about a million tons and of wheat some 800,000 tons, all reflecting the rather pale 'green revolution' in Nepal. In the hills most production is for subsistence or local sale; but some farmers in the Tarai are able to produce for a wider market, helped by the roads that aid donors press on the willing recipient government. Irrigation apparently covers some 10 to 20 per cent of the cropped area, the higher figure if stream-fed hill terraces are included.

After 1960 the government set up various research stations, community development schemes, and extension agencies, some on Indian models and many in the framework of the hierarchical *panchayat* system (see Chapter 4). The impact of these institutions seems to have been limited. It remains to be seen what developments will accompany changed constitutional arrangements. There are also government agencies designed to administer the official colonization of the Tarai, but much more land is cleared by independent settlers (including those from India).

In the hills high pressure of population on land has built up, and has been doing so in many areas for a long time.[127] Sedentary agriculture has replaced shifting cultivation and pastoralism, and has in turn extended on to steeper and steeper slopes so that, in spite of terracing, soil erosion has set in. Some authors therefore see Nepal's agrarian economy in a crisis that is already at or near catastrophe level.[128] On the other hand, it has been cogently argued that, while there is a crisis, and one which demands careful study and effective action, there is not yet a catastrophe because of the conservational effects of traditional terracing. A study that promises to supply valuable and objective data in this context was initiated north of Kathmandu in 1990 under a British aid programme and is operated jointly by the Institute of Hydrology and the Royal Geographical Society.

The Tarai, and remittances sent home by emigrants, including Gurkhas serving in the Indian and British armies, act as temporary safety valves for population pressure in the hills. So far little relief has been afforded by industrialization. True, there are many rice and oil mills and sugar factories in the Tarai, while of recent years there has been a limited amount of private industrial development, particularly in textiles, the work of Indian entrepreneurs selling mainly to their home market.

Nepal has a formal planning machine and has produced a series of Five Year Plans, all very much on the Indian model (even unto words about regional balance and equity) but without Indian resources, though with massive aid from various quarters. Indeed, aid per capita is six times that received by India.

What, then, of equity? There are great disparities of wealth and income in this poor country. True, some of the grossest inequalities were tackled in 1960, when 'vast land grants made during the last century to nobles, successful generals, and other favoured state functionaries were abrogated' and limited land reforms instituted.[129] But there are still landowners (many absentees) and wealthier peasants who employ the labour of others, or use scantily-protected share-croppers. Landlessness is growing. Since 1977 there have been schemes specifically to help small farmers, but once again with limited impact.[130]

Nepal's foreign trade is even harder to quantify than internal aspects of its economy, for so much can pass unrecorded across the long frontier with India; and the same applies to the smaller volume of traditional trade over the Himalayan passes and by the modern road to Tibet.[131] It is clear, however, that textiles now form the most important export to India, that rice passes in the same direction, that oil fuel makes up more than 10 per cent of imports, and that there is a wide trade deficit which is, however, reduced by aid and by tourism (there is, however, concern about the environmental impact of excessive numbers in the Himalayas).

Given then, the state of affairs in the hills, the generally undeveloped and unequal state of the economy, and the limited gains made by aid and government agencies and by private industry so far, Nepal gives but little ground for optimism, not least about the present and likely future of the poor of both sexes and all ages.

Bhutan

Bhutan is in a number of respects a smaller version of Nepal, for example in terms of physiography (though the Duars in its plains are narrower than the Tarai), and dominance of agriculture, with maize, and rice where there is water.[132] But some of Nepal's features are exaggerated in Bhutan: an even greater lack of reliable information; even greater dependence on India; remoteness and lack of communications in the mountainous interior; and an almost total lack of industry. On the other hand, Bhutan seems to have suffered less environmental degradation so far, and its people (mainly owner-cultivators) less extreme poverty. Government efforts, within the framework of Indian-style plans, are being made to balance imports (which include rice) by increasing agricultural exports of the local type of cardamoms (with adverse effects on forests) and potatoes (with adverse effects on soil). New HYVs of cereals are being introduced accompanied by those baleful insignia of the visiting 'expert', insufficient attention to local conditions and crop varieties, and to the sound, sustainable basis of traditional agriculture. Clearly, then, Bhutan has an environmental rod in pickle, and will suffer Nepal's problems unless great care is exercised and close monitoring practised.

The Maldive Islands

The Maldive Islands are, of course, very different, though also a tiny economy within the Indian sphere of influence.[133] Agriculture is little practised, though yams and vegetables are grown; and more could be done, for example, to produce fruit for tourists. There are, of course, coconut palms a-plenty, and their produce, such as copra, is important. But the great traditional Maldivian occupation is fishing, whose produce with copra figures large in exports. A wide range of imports is necessary. The only significant industry is shipbuilding. Tourism, with over 200,000 visitors annually, is a valuable economic activity, helping to bridge the trade gap; though there is anxiety about its long-term sustainability, particularly given the effects of pollution on the coral on which the islands stand. (For the catastrophe that may overwhelm the Maldives through a rise in sea level, see Chapter 2).[134]

ENVOI

In completing one man's view of a complex and rapidly changing South Asian scene, I recognize with gratitude how much I have learnt, not only from other authors and research workers, but also from South Asian people at all levels from senior government officers to cultivators in their fields and 'tribals' in their forests. It is one man's view that is, I hope, broad enough to take in the scene as perceived by observers with widely differing values and theoretical and ideological stances; for there is much that is controversial about South Asia.

It would be presumptuous to look over the horizon and to forecast the future. Let it just be said that there are grounds for both sadness and hope as one contemplates what that future might be: sadness, because all the chapters of this book have given grounds for pessimism, or at any rate caution in predicting a bright future. To one with western liberal values there can only be sadness at the present and likely future plight of the Harijans in many parts of India, of the tenants of Sind, or of the landless in Bangladesh, or of many people in Sri Lanka; sadness, too, at the political instability and periods of autocracy that in Pakistan and Bangladesh have blighted the bright hopes held out for democracy at independence; at the manipulation of the system by vested interests of various kinds in India and at the heightened violence associated with unrest in a number of parts of that country. There are those who look for a revolutionary solution to these ills; but a revolution, even if well intentioned, could not fail to do great damage. Again, the international scene gives little ground for hope that the South Asian subcontinent and the ocean around it will be left to settle its affairs in peace. Current uncertainties of several kinds make one veer further to pessimism.

On the other hand, and if one compares South Asia with many other parts of the Third World, then there are grounds for hope rooted in achievement since independence. This is particularly, though not exclusively, the case with economic development, making all due allowance for problems and inefficiencies and backward areas, for the adverse effects of exogenous factors, and for the failure of benefits to trickle down to many of the disadvantaged. For increases in production in a number of sectors have been notable, and must be seen against the background of the first signs, in some areas at any rate, of slackening in the rate of population increase. And South Asia assuredly does not lack men and women of great ability and of high principles, some of whom will, I hope, read this book which, for all its criticisms, strives to be sympathetic to the people of the subcontinent as they face formidable problems, and appreciates such bright spots as the freedom of the Indian press, and the quality and irrepressibility of the intelligentsia.

NOTES

2 THE ENVIRONMENTS OF SOUTH ASIA NATURAL AND SOCIAL

1 For this section see Spate, O.H.K. and Learmonth, A.T.A. (1967) *India and Pakistan*, 3rd edn, London; *The Times Concise Atlas of the World* (1982), especially pp. 8–9; and Bradnock, R.W. (1989) 'Land', in Robinson, F. (ed.) *The Cambridge Encyclopaedia of India, Pakistan, Bangladesh and Sri Lanka*, Cambridge, pp. 12–38. See also Farmer, B.H. (1974) *Agricultural Colonization in India since Independence*, London, p. 36; and, for a map of forest cover in Sri Lanka, Gelbert, M. (1988) *Chena Cultivation and Land Transformation in Sri Lanka*, Zurich.

2 Farmer, B.H. (1979) 'The "green revolution" in South Asian ricefields: environment and production', *Journal of Development Studies* 15: 311.

3 Kipling, R. (1964) 'The conversion of Aurelian McGoggin', in *Plain Tales from the Hills*, London: St Martin's Library Edition.

4 For flooding in Bangladesh more generally see Brammer, H. (1990) 'Floods in Bangladesh', *Geographical Journal* 156: 12–22, 158–65. For floods and other hazards in Pakistan see Johnson, B.L.C. (1979) *Pakistan*, London.

5 See, for example, Vohra, B.B. (1990) *Managing India's Water Resources*, New Delhi.

6 See particularly Gourou, P. (1953) *The Tropical World*, 1st edn, London.

7 *Our Common Future: Report of the World Commission on Environment and Development* (1987), Oxford. See also Adams, W.M. (1990) *Green Development: Environment and Development in the Third World*, London and New York. For Sri Lanka see Fernando, R. and Samarasinghe, S.W.R. de A. (1989) *Forest Conservation and the Forestry Master Plan for Sri Lanka*, Colombo.

8 See Ives, J.D. and Messerli, B. (1989) *The Himalayan Dilemma: Reconciling Development and Conservation*, London and New York.

9 Béteille, A. (1977) *Inequality among Men*, Oxford, p. 130. See also 'Caste and class in India', *Economic and Political Weekly* 14 (1979); Low, A. (1981) *Dominant Peasant: Intimations from Asia*, Adelaide. Desai, I.P. (1984) 'Should "Caste" be the basis for recognising backwardness?', *Economic and Political Weekly* 19: 1106–1; and Brass, P.R. (1990) *The Politics of India since Independence* (Cambridge) *passim*, especially pp. 210–19.

10 Dumont, L. (1970) *Homo Hierarchicus: The Caste System and its Implications*, London.

11 Roberts, M. (1981) *Caste Conflict and Elite Formation: the Rise of a Karava Elite in Sri Lanka, 1500–1931*, Cambridge.

12 Imtiaz Ahmad (ed.) (1973) *Caste and Social Stratification among the Muslims*, New Delhi; Ahmad, S.S. and Chakravarti, A.K. (1981) 'Some regional characteristics of Muslim caste system in India', *GeoJournal* 5: 55–60; McLeod, W.H. (1974) 'Ahluwalias and Ramgarhias: two Sikh castes', *South Asia* 4: 78–90; and Kaufmann, S.B. (1981) 'A Christian caste in Hindu Society', *Modern Asian Studies* 15: 203–34.

13 Srinivas, M.N. (1967) 'The cohesive role of Sanskritization', in Mason, P. (ed.) *India and Ceylon: Unity and Diversity*, London.

14 Bailey, F.G. (1961) '"Tribe" and "caste" in India', *Contributions to Indian Sociology* 5: 7–19. See also Haimendorf, C. von F. (1982) *The Tribes of India: The Struggle for Survival*, Berkeley, and (1985) *Tribal Populations and Cultures of the Indian Subcontinent*, Leiden.

15 Srinivas, M.N. (1976) *The Remembered Village*, Berkeley; and see Harriss, J. (1982) *Capitalism and Peasant Farming: Agrarian Structure and Ideology in Northern Tamil Nadu*, Bombay, pp. 40–9 for a careful study of caste in a village.

16 Hill, P. (1980) 'Joint families in rural Karnataka, South India', *Modern Asian Studies* 14: 29–36 and Bhardwaj, S. (1973) *Hindu Places of Pilgrimage in India: a Study in Cultural Geography*, Berkeley.

17 Béteille, A. (1979) 'Homo hierarchicus, homo equalis', *Modern Asian Studies* 13: 529–48. See also Parry, J. (1974) 'Egalitarian values in an hierarchical society', *South Asian Review* 7: 95–121.

18 Thorner, D. (1966) 'Marx on India and the Asiatic mode of production', *Contributions to Indian Sociology* 9: 33–66. See also Breman, J. (1979) *The Shattered Image*, Amsterdam.

19 Béteille, A. (1967) 'Elites, status groups and caste in modern India', in Mason, P. (ed.) *India and Ceylon: Unity and Diversity*, London, p. 17.

20 See *A Social and Economic Atlas of India* (1987) Oxford and New Delhi, pp. 42–4; and Shackle, C. (1989) 'Religions', in Robinson, F., op. cit.

21 Liddle, J. and Joshi, R. (1986) *Daughters of Independence: Gender, Caste and Class in India*, London; and Nesmith, C. (1991) 'Gender, trees and fuel: social forestry in West Bengal', *Human Organization* 50: 337–48.

22 Shackle, C. (1989), 'Languages', in Robinson, F., op. cit., which has been an invaluable source for this subject. See also Shackle, C. (ed.) (1985) *South Asian Languages: a Handbook*, London; and *A Social and Economic Atlas of India*, (1987), op. cit., pp. 16–58, *passim*; and Brass, P.R. (1990), op. cit., 135–60.

23 Morris-Jones, W.H. (1967) 'Language and region within the Indian Union', in Mason, P. (ed.) *India and Ceylon: Unity and Diversity*, London; Cohn, B.S. (1971) *India: the Social Anthropology of a Civilization*, Englewood Cliffs, NJ, Chapter 4.

24 Spear, P. (1961) *India: a Modern History*, Ann Arbor.

3 THE BRITISH PERIOD, THE COMING OF INDEPENDENCE AND PARTITION

* In the parts of this chapter concerned with the period before independence it is more appropriate to use 'Ceylon' instead of 'Sri Lanka'; while 'India' means the whole area that became the British Indian Empire, unless the context requires otherwise.

1 Stokes, E. (1978) *The Peasant and the Raj: Studies in Agrarian Society and Peasant Rebellion in India*, Cambridge, Chapter I, especially p. 26; Marshall, P.J. (1991) '"A free though conquering people": Britain and Asia in the eighteenth century', an inaugural lecture, London; Kumar, D. (ed.) (1982) *The Cambridge*

Economic History of India, vol. 2, Cambridge; and, especially, Bayly, C.A. (1988) *Indian Society and the Making of the British Empire*, Cambridge (a masterly study).

2 Schwartzberg, J.E. (ed.) (1978) *A Historical Atlas of South Asia*, Chicago and London, pp. 125–6, 247–8; Murphey, R. (1977) *The Outsiders: The Western Experience in India and China*, Ann Arbor, pp. 109–11.

3 Whitcombe, E. (1982), 'Irrigation', pp. 677–737 in Kumar, D., op. cit.; and Stone, I. (1984) *Canal Irrigation in British India: Perspectives on Technological Change in a Peasant Economy*, Cambridge.

4 Farmer, B.H. (1974) *Agricultural Colonization in India since Independence*, London, pp. 10–15.

5 Blyn, G. (1966) *Agricultural Trends in India, 1891–1947: Output, Availability and Productivity*, Philadelphia and London; Islam, M.M. (1978) *Bengal Agriculture, 1920–1946: A Quantitative Study*, Cambridge; and Heston, A. (1982) 'National income: agriculture,' p. 387 in Kumar, D., op. cit.

6 Hardy, P. (1972) *The Muslims of British India*, Cambridge, pp. 42–50; Stokes, E. (1978), op. cit.

7 Kumar, D. (1965) *Land and Caste in South India* and (1982), op. cit., Chapter 2, part 4.

8 Fukazawa, H. (1982) 'Western India: agrarian relations', p. 286 in Kumar, D., op. cit.; also a later study, Charlesworth, N. (1985) *Peasants and Imperial Rule: Agriculture and Agrarian Society in the Bombay Presidency, 1850–1935*, Cambridge.

9 Farmer, B.H. (1957) *Pioneer Peasant Colonization in Ceylon*, London, pp. 81–2, 109–12; and Meyer, E. (1992) 'From landgrabbing to land hunger: high land appropriation in the plantation areas of Sri Lanka during the British period', *Modern Asian Studies* 26: 321–61.

10 Morris, M.D. (1982) 'The growth of large-scale industry to 1947', Chapter 7 in Kumar, D., op. cit. Also Macpherson, W.J. (1972) 'Economic development under the British crown, 1858–1947' in Youngson, A.J. (ed.) *Economic Development in the Long Run*, London; and Harnetty, P. (1991) 'Deindustrialization revisited: the handloom workers of the Central Provinces, c.1800–1947', *Modern Asian Studies* 25: 455–510.

11 Farmer, B.H. (1957), op. cit., Chapter 4; Snodgrass, D.R. (1966) *Ceylon: an Export Economy in Transition*, Homewood, Ill.; and De Silva, K.M. (1981) *A History of Sri Lanka*, London.

12 Spear, P. (1972) *India: A Modern History*, 2nd edn, Ann Arbor.

13 Seal, A. (1968) *The Emergence of Indian Nationalism: Competition and Collaboration in the Later Nineteenth Century*, Cambridge, Chapter 2.

14 De Silva, C.R. (1977) in De Silva, K.M. (ed.) *Sri Lanka: A Survey*, London, p. 405; and De Silva, K.M. (1981), op. cit., especially Chapter 24.

15 Schwartzberg, J.E. (ed.) (1978), op. cit., p. 104.

16 Stokes, E. (1978), op. cit., Chapter 1; also his (1959) *The English Utilitarians in India*, Oxford; and Mill, J.S. (eds Robson, J.L. *et al.*) (1990) *Writings on India*, Toronto and London.

17 Bayly, C.A. (1988), op. cit., Chapter 5.

18 Farmer, B.H. (1963) *Ceylon: A Divided Nation*, London.

19 Macfarlane, A. (1976) *Resources and Population: A Study of the Gurungs of Nepal*, Cambridge.

20 Spear, P. (1961) *India: A Modern History*, Ann Arbor, p. 341.

21 Spear, P. (1961), op. cit., pp. 353–6; and De Silva, K.M. (1981), Part 4.

22 Stokes, E. (1978), op. cit., pp. 269–70; Seal, A. (1968), op. cit.; Johnson, G. (1973) *Provincial Politics and Indian Nationalism: Bombay and the Indian National*

Congress 1880–1915, Cambridge; Bayly, C.A. (1973) 'Patrons and politics in northern India', *Modern Asian Studies* 7: 349–88; Baker, C.J. (1976) *The Politics of South India 1920–1937*, Cambridge; Washbrook, D.A. (1976) *The Emergence of Provincial Politics: The Madras Presidency 1870–1920*, Cambridge; Baker, C.J. et al. (eds) (1981) *Power, Profit and Politics*, ten papers in *Modern Asian Studies*, 15: 355–721; Sisson, R. and Wolpert, S. (eds) (1988) *Congress and Indian Nationalism*, Berkeley; Ramusack, B.N. (1988) Chapter 17 in Sisson, R. and Wolpert, S. (eds), op. cit.; and Robb, P.G. et al. (1989) 'British imperialism and Indian nationalism', pp. 116–47 in Robinson, F. (ed.) *The Cambridge Encyclopaedia of India, Pakistan, Bangladesh and Sri Lanka*, Cambridge.

23 Stokes, E. (1978), op. cit., p. 63.

24 De Silva, K.M. (1977) in De Silva, K.M. (ed.) *Sri Lanka: A Survey*, London; Roberts, M. (1981) *Caste Conflict and Elite Formation: The Rise of a Karava Elite in Sri Lanka, 1500–1931*, Cambridge.

25 Hardy, P. (1972), op. cit.; Robinson, F. (1974) *Separatism among Indian Muslims: The Politics of the United Provinces Muslims 1860–1923*, Cambridge; Moore, R.J. (1983) 'Jinnah and the Pakistan demand', *Modern Asian Studies* 17: 529–61; and Jalal, A. (1985) *The Sole Spokesman: Jinnah, the Muslim League and the Demand for Pakistan*, Cambridge. For a pro-Pakistan (and especially pro-Jinnah) account, see Rushbrook Williams, L.F. (1966) *The State of Pakistan*, London.

26 See the very detailed work by Jalal, A. (1985), op. cit., especially Chapters 5–7; and compare with Shaikh, F. (1989) *Community and Consensus in Islam: Muslim Representation in Colonial India, 1860–1947*, Cambridge, with its stress on the 'normative prescriptions of a religious and political tradition'.

27 Jalal, A. (1985), op. cit., p. 241.

28 Spate, O.H.K. and Learmonth, A.T.A. (1967) *India and Pakistan*, 3rd edn, London, pp. 129–30.

4 POLITICAL DEVELOPMENTS WITHIN SOUTH ASIA SINCE INDEPENDENCE

1 Spear, P. (1972) *India: a Modern History*, rev. edn, Ann Arbor, 424–7; Schwartzberg, J.E. (ed.) (1978) *A Historical Atlas of South Asia*, Chicago, pp. 75–7. See also Morris-Jones, W.H. (1982) 'The transfer of power, 1947', *Modern Asian Studies* 16: 1–32. For the Kashmir problem see Lamb, A. (1991) *Kashmir: a Disputed Legacy, 1841–1990*, Hertingfordbury, which incorporates much recent research.

2 Rushbrook Williams, L.F. (1966) *The State of Pakistan*, 2nd edn, London; and Michel, A. (1967) *The Indus Rivers: a Study of the Effects of Partition*, New Haven, pp. 195–340.

3 Farmer, B.H. (1974) *Agricultural Colonization in India since Independence*, London, pp. 36–42.

4 Ibid., pp. 280–9.

5 Stephens, I. (1968) *The Pakistanis*, London, p. 1.

6 Rushbrook Williams, L.F. (1975) *Pakistan under Challenge*, London, pp. 14–16.

7 Stephens, I. (1968), op. cit., p. 95.

8 In Ziring, L. et al. (eds) *Pakistan: the Long View*, Durham, NC, pp. 271–300, especially pp. 286–8.

9 Rushbrook Williams, L.F. (1975), op. cit., pp. 92–3. See also Ziring, L. (1981) *Pakistan: The Enigma of Political Development*, Folkestone, Chapter 6; and

Ataur Rahman, 'Pakistan: unity or further divisions?', pp. 197–221 in Wilson, A. Jeyaratnam and Dalton, D. (eds) (1982) *The States of South Asia: Problems of National Integration*, London.

10 For separatism in India generally see Brass, P.R. (1990) *The Politics of India since Independence*, Cambridge. For north-east India see Chaube, S. (1973) *Hill Politics in Northeast India*, Bombay; Venkata Rao, V. (1976) *A Century of Tribal Politics in North-East India*, New Delhi; and Singh, B.P. (1987) *The Problem of Change: A Study of North-East India*, Delhi. See also Taylor, D. and Yapp, M. (eds) (1979) *Political Identity in South Asia*, London; and Rustomji, N. (1983) *Imperilled Frontiers*, Delhi.

11 Farmer, B.H. (1974), op. cit., pp. 13–15, 56–9.

12 Weiner, M. (1962) *The Politics of Scarcity: Public Pressure and Political Response in India*, Chicago, pp. 41–3; and Corbridge, S.E. (1988) 'The ideology of tribal economy and society', *Modern Asian Studies* 22: 1–42.

13 Farmer, B.H. (1974), op. cit., pp. 272–4.

14 Grey, H. (1971) 'The demand for a separate Telangana State in India', *Asian Survey* 11: 463–74 and (1974) 'The failure of the demand for a separate Andhra State', *Asian Survey* 14: 338–49.

15 Parthasarathy, G., Ramana, K.V. and Dasaradha Rama Rao, G. (1973), 'Separatist movement in Andhra Pradesh', *Economic and Political Weekly* 18: 560–3.

16 Kothari, R. (1970) *Politics in India*, Boston, Mass., p. 7.

17 Some of the principal books on politics in India are: Hardgrave, R.L. (1975) *India: Government and Politics in a Developing Nation*, New York; Kothari, R. (1970), op. cit; Kothari, R. (ed.) (1971) *Caste in Indian Politics*, New Delhi; Mellor, J.W. (ed.) (1979) *India: A Rising Middle Power*, Boulder, Colo.; Taylor, D. and Yapp, M. (eds) (1979) *Political Identity in South Asia*, London; Morris-Jones, W.H. (1987) *The Government and Politics of India*, 3rd edn with Epilogue, Huntingdon; Kohli (ed.) (1988) *India's Democracy*, Princeton; Graham, B. (1990) *Hindu Nationalism and Indian Politics*, Cambridge; and, very important., Brass, P.R. (1990) *The Politics of India since Independence*, Cambridge.

18 Morris-Jones, W.H. (1987), op. cit.

19 Low, D.A. (1991) 'Emergencies and elections in India', pp. 148–63 in his *Eclipse of Empire*, Cambridge.

20 Morris-Jones, W.H. (1987), op. cit.

21 Ibid., p. 120.

22 Hardgrave, R.L. (1975), op. cit., p. 156. See also Hart, H.C. (ed.) (1976) *Indira Gandhi's India: A Political System Reappraised*, Boulder, Colo.

23 Mendelsohn, O. (1978) 'The collapse of the Indian National Congress', *Pacific Affairs* 51: 41–66, especially pp. 47–8.

24 Blair, H.W. (1980) 'Mrs Gandhi's Emergency, the Indian elections of 1977, pluralism and Marxism', *Modern Asian Studies* 14: 237–71.

25 Farmer, B.H. (1974), op. cit., London, pp. 255–6.

26 For example, Brass, P.R. (1965) *Factional Politics in an Indian State*, Berkeley.

27 For example, Ram Reddy, G. and Seshadri, K. (1972) *The Voter and Panchayati Raj*, Hyderabad; and Seshadri, K. and Jain, S.P. (1972) *Panchayati Raj and Political Perceptions of the Electorate*, Hyderabad. On populism versus vote banks see conclusion to Harriss, J. (1992) 'Does the depressor still work', *Journal of Peasant Studies* (forthcoming).

28 Maneshwari, A.C. (1980) 'Uttar Pradesh: rigging in practice', *Economic and Political Weekly* 15: 99–100; and Nalini Singh (1980) 'Elections as they really are', *Economic and Political Weekly* 15: 909–15.

29 Blair, H.W. (1980), op. cit., referring to Morris-Jones, W.H. (1971) *The*

Government and Politics of India, 3rd edn; Hardgrave, R.L. (1975), op. cit.; and Kothari, R. (1970), op. cit.

30 Some of the more important general works on the politics of Sri Lanka are: Wriggins, W.H. (1960) *Ceylon: the Dilemmas of a New Nation*, Ithaca, NY; Wilson, A.J. (1974) *Politics in Sri Lanka, 1947–1973*, London; De Silva, K.M. (ed.) (1977) *Sri Lanka: a Survey*, London, especially Chapters 12–15; Moore, M. (1985) *The State and Peasant Politics in Sri Lanka*, Cambridge; and Manor, J. (1989) *The Expedient Utopian: Bandaranaike and Ceylon*, Cambridge.

31 For example, Woodward, C.A. (1974–5) 'Sri Lanka's electoral experience: from personal to party politics', *Pacific Affairs* 47: 455–71.

32 Lerski, G.J. (1970) 'The twilight of Ceylonese Trotskyism', *Pacific Affairs* 43: 384–93. See also Blackton, C.S. (1974) 'The Marxists and the ultra-Marxists of Sri Lanka since independence', *Ceylon Journal of Historical and Social Studies*, new series, 4: 126–33.

33 Obeyesekere, G. (1974) 'Some comments on the social background of the 1971 insurgency in Sri Lanka (Ceylon)', *Asian Studies* 33: 367–84; Spencer, J. (1990) 'Collective violence and everyday practice in Sri Lanka', *Modern Asian Studies* 24: 603–23.

34 Farmer, B.H. (1963) *Ceylon: a Divided Nation*, London; Wilson, A.J. (1982) 'Sri Lanka and its Future: Sinhalese versus Tamil', pp. 295–313 in Wilson and Dalton, op. cit.; de Silva, C.R. (1982) 'The Sinhalese-Tamil rift in Sri Lanka', pp. 155–74, in Wilson and Dalton, op. cit.; Tambiah, S.J. (1986) *Sri Lanka's Ethnic Fratricide and the Dismantling of Democracy*, London; and Manogaran, C. (1987) *Ethnic Conflict and Reconciliation in Sri Lanka*, Hawaii.

35 For politics in Pakistan see especially Rushbrook Williams, L.F. (1966), op. cit. and (1975), op. cit.; Stephens, I. (1963) *Pakistan*, London, especially Chapters 18 and 19; Ziring, J. *et al.* (eds) (1977), op.cit.; and Burki, S.J. (1989) 'Politics: Pakistan', pp. 203–18 in Robinson, F. (ed.) *Cambridge Encyclopaedia of India, Pakistan, Bangladesh and Sri Lanka*, Cambridge.

36 Rushbrook Williams, L.F. (1966), op. cit., p. 196.

37 Rushbrook Williams, L.F. (1966), op. cit.; Anwar H. Syed, 'The Pakistan people's party', in Ziring, L. *et al.* (eds) (1977), op. cit., Chapter 4; and Burki, S.J. (1988) *Pakistan under Bhutto*, 2nd edn, London.

38 Ahmed, Akbar S. (1983) *Religion and Politics in Muslim Society*, Cambridge; and Khan, A. (1985) *Islam, Politics and the State: the Pakistan Experience*, London.

39 Hardy, P. in a lecture at the Centre of South Asian Studies, University of Cambridge, 3 March 1980.

40 For politics in Bangladesh see, in particular, Maniruzzaman, T. (1980) *The Bangladesh Revolution and its Aftermath*, Dhaka, and (1989) 'Politics: Bangladesh', pp. 216–22 in Robinson, F. (ed.), op. cit.; Franda, M.F. (1982) *Bangladesh: The First Decade*, New Delhi; Baxter, C. (1984) *Bangladesh: A New Nation in a New Setting*, Boulder, Colo.; and O'Donnell, C.P. (1985) *Bangladesh: Biography of a Muslim Nation*, Boulder, Colo.

41 Rose, L.E. and Scholz, J.T. (1980) *Nepal: Profile of a Himalayan Kingdom*, Boulder, Colo.; Rose, L.E. (1989) 'Politics: Nepal', pp. 229–31 in Robinson (ed.), op. cit., and Shaha, R. (1990) *Politics in Nepal, 1980–1990*, New Delhi.

42 Rose, L.E. (1977) *The Politics of Bhutan*, Ithaca; and 'Politics: Bhutan' (1989) pp. 231–2 in Robinson, F., op. cit.

43 Adeney, M. and Carr, W.K. (1975) 'The Maldive Republic' in Ostheimer, J.M. (ed.) *The Politics of the Western Indian Ocean*, New York; and Reynolds, C. (1989) 'Politics: Maldives', pp. 228–9 in Robinson, F. (ed.), op. cit.

5 SOUTH ASIA: INTERNATIONAL RELATIONS

1 See, for example, Nayar, K. (1972) *Distant Neighbours*, Delhi, and Gupta, S. (1966) *Kashmir: a Study in Indo-Pakistan Relations*, Bombay, for Indian points of view; Choudhury, G.W. (1968) *Pakistan's Relations with India*, London, for the view of a Pakistani who was close to Ayub Khan; and Barnds, W.J. (1972) *India, Pakistan and the Great Powers*, Durham, NC. See also Ziring, J. *et al.* (eds) (1977) *Pakistan: the Long View*, Durham, NC. and Bradnock, R.W. (1990) *Indian Foreign Policy since 1971*, London, Chapter 5. For Kashmir see Lamb, A. (1991) *Kashmir: a Disputed Legacy*, Hertingfordbury.

2 Wriggins, W.H. (1977) 'The balancing process in Pakistan's foreign policy', in Ziring, L. *et al.* (1977), op. cit.

3 Onkar Marwah (1979) 'India's military intervention in East Pakistan', *Modern Asian Studies* 13: 549–80, especially 552–3.

4 Ziring, J. (1974) 'Bhutto's foreign policy, 1972–3', in Korson, J.H. (ed.) *Contemporary Problems of Pakistan*, Leiden.

5 Barnds, W.J. (1977) 'Pakistan's foreign policy; shifting opportunities and constraints', in Ziring, L. *et al.* (1977), op. cit.

6 Quoted by Choudhury, G.W. (1968), op. cit., p. 227.

7 Wriggins, W.H. (1977), op. cit., p. 576.

8 Barnds, W.J. (1977) in Ziring, L. *et al.* (1977), op. cit., p. 373.

9 Bradnock, R.W. (1990), op. cit., Chapter 5.

10 Barnds, W.J. (1977), op. cit., pp. 379–81.

11 Burke, S.M. (1973) *Pakistan Foreign Policy: an Historical Address*, London, pp. 381–3. See also Sawvell, R.D. (1978) 'Crisis on the Ganges: the barrage at Farakka', *Geography* 63: 49–52 (with map); and Brammer, H. (1990 & 1991) 'Floods in Bangladesh', *Geographical Journal* 156: 12–22, 126–65.

12 See Wriggins, W.H. (1960) *Ceylon: Dilemmas of a New Nation*, Princeton, NJ, especially part 3; Kodikara, S.U. (1965) *Indo–Ceylon Relations since Independence*, Colombo; Wilson, A.J. (1974) *Politics in Sri Lanka 1947–1973*, London, especially Chapter 6; Samaraweera, V. (1977) 'Foreign policy', in De Silva, K.M. (ed.) *Sri Lanka: A Survey*, London, Chapter 14; and Bradnock, R.W. (1990), op. cit., Chapter 5.

13 Panikkar, K.M. (1945) *India and the Indian Ocean*, London, especially p. 84.

14 Quoted by Wriggins, W.H. (1960), op. cit., p. 399.

15 See Farmer, B.H. (1963) *Ceylon: A Divided Nation*, London.

16 Kodikara, S.U. (1965), op. cit., p. 11.

17 Bradnock, R.W. (1990), op. cit.

18 See Kavic, L.J. (1967) *India's Quest for Security*, Berkeley, *passim*; Mihaly, E.B. (1965) *Foreign Aid and Politics in Nepal*, London, and Rose, L.E. and Dial, R. (1969) 'Can a ministate find true happiness in a world dominated by protagonist powers? The Nepal case', *Annals of the American Academy of Political and Social Science* 386: 89–101 for varied western viewpoints; Jha, B.K. (1973) *Indo–Nepalese Relations (1951–1972)*, Bombay; Jha, S.K. (1975) *Uneasy Partners: India and Nepal in the Post-Colonial Era*, New Delhi; Ramakant (1976) *Nepal–China and India (Nepal–China Relations)*, New Delhi, for Indian views; and Shaha, R. (1978) *Nepal's Politics Retrospect and Prospect*, Delhi, Chapters 3, 4 for the views of an experienced Nepali politician. See also Banskota, N.P. (1981) *Indo–Nepal Trade and Economic Relations*, Delhi.

19 Quoted by Mihaly, E.B. (1965), op. cit., p. 16.

20 See Jha, B.K. (1973), op. cit., Chapter 5.

21 For Bhutan see Rose, L.E. (1977) *The Politics of Bhutan*, Ithaca. For the Maldives see Reynolds, C.H.B. (1989) 'Maldives', in Robinson, F. (ed.) (1989) *Cambridge*

Encyclopaedia of India, Pakistan, Bangladesh and Sri Lanka. For SAARC See Rose, L.E. (1989) 'Foreign relations', in Robinson, F., op. cit., and Bradnock, R.W. (1990), op. cit., pp. 81–3.

22 See Murphey, R. (1977) *The Outsiders: The Western Experience in India and China*, Ann Arbor.

23 Fisher, M.W. *et al.* (1963) *Himalayan Battleground: Sino–Indian Rivalry in Ladakh*, London, p. 82.

24 For the border dispute and Chinese incursion of 1962 see, for example, Kirk, W. (1962) 'The inner Asian frontier of India', *Transactions of the Institute of British Geographers* 31: 131–68; Fisher, M.W. *et al.* (1963), op cit.; Lamb, A. (1964) *The China–India Border*, London; Maxwell, N. (1970) *India's China War*, London; Woodman, D. (1969) *Himalayan Frontiers: a Political Review of British, Chinese, Indian and Russian Rivalries*, London; and Barnds, W.J. (1977), op. cit., Chapters 7–9 and *passim*. For Indo–Chinese relations more generally see Bradnock, R.W. (1990), op. cit. and Rose, L.E. (1989) 'India and its neighbours in the region', in Robinson, F., op. cit.

25 Varkey, O. (1974) *At the Crossroads: The Sino–Indian Border Dispute and the Communist Party of India*, Calcutta.

26 Woodman, D. (1969), op. cit., p. 303.

27 Miller, K.J. (1981) 'The international Karakoram project, 1980', *Geographical Journal* 147: 153–63, especially 156–8 (with map).

28 Ayoob, Mohammed (1990) *India and Southeast Asia*, London.

29 See Barnds, W.J. (1972), op. cit. and (1973) 'India and America at odds', *International Affairs* 49: 371–84; Burke, S.M. (1973), op. cit.; Ziring, L. (1977) *et al.*, op. cit.; Mellor, J.W. (ed.) (1979) *India: a Rising Middle Power*; Bradnock, R.W. (1990), op. cit.; Duncan, P.L.S. (1989) *The Soviet and India*, London; Light, M. (ed.) (forthcoming) *The Soviet Union and Third World Friends* and Duncan, P.L.S. 'The Soviet-Indian model from Brezhnev to Gorbachev', in Light, M., op. cit.

30 Lipton, M. and Firn, J. (1975) *The Erosion of a Relationship: India and Britain since 1960*, London.

31 Palmer, N.D. (1977) 'Pakistan: the long search for foreign policy', in Ziring, L. *et al.* (eds), op. cit., Chapter 14, especially p. 424.

32 See, for example, a number of the contributions in Mellor, J.W. (ed.) (1979), op. cit. See also Bradnock, R.W. (1992) 'India in détente', pp. 154–81 in Palmier, L. (ed.) *Détente in Asia*, Oxford.

6 ECONOMIC DEVELOPMENTS IN SOUTH ASIA SINCE INDEPENDENCE

1 Spate, O.H.K. (1954) *India and Pakistan*, 1st edn, London, contains good accounts of the economy in general, and of agriculture in particular, as they were at about the time of independence.

2 See Potter, D.C. (1964) *Government in Rural India*, London.

3 Bhagwati, J.N. and Desai, P. (1970) *India: Planning for Industrialization*, London, Chapter 3.

4 Ibid., pp. 19–24, 48, 50.

5 Ginsburg, N. (1961) *Atlas of Economic Development*, Chicago.

6 See Spate, O.H.K. (1954), op.cit., and his (1947) 'The partition of the Punjab and of Bengal', *Geographical Journal* 110: 201–22 and (1948) 'The partition of India and the prospects of Pakistan', *Geographical Review* 38: 5–29.

7 See Farmer, B.H. (1974) *Agricultural Colonization in India since Independence*, London, *passim*, especially pp. 56, 87–8 and 107–0.

8 Compare Snodgrass, D.R. (1966) *Ceylon: an Export Economy in Transition*, Homewood, Ill., and Ponnambalam, S. (1981) *Dependent Capitalism in Crisis: The Sri Lanka Economy, 1948–1980*, London. See also Wickremeratne, L.A. (1977) 'The economy in 1948', in De Silva, K.M. (ed.) *Sri Lanka: A Survey*, London, pp. 131–43. See also Farmer, B.H. (1957) *Pioneer Peasant Colonization in Ceylon*, London.

9 Ginsburg, op. cit.; and see Karan, P.P. and Jenkins, W.M. (1963) *The Himalayan Kingdoms*, Princeton, NJ.

10 See, for example, Frankel, F. (1978) *India's Political Economy, 1947–1977: the Gradual Revolution*, Princeton, NJ; but see the review by Brass, P.R. (1981) 'Class, ethnic group and party in Indian politics', *World Politics* 33: 449–67 at pp. 466–7.

11 See Cassen, R.H. (1978) *India: Population, Economy, Society*, London, pp. 5–6; and compare Macfarlane, A. (1976) *Resources and Population: A Study of the Gurungs of Nepal*, Cambridge; Miranda, A. (1982) *The Demography of Bangladesh*, Bergen; Bose, A. (1991) *Demographic Diversity of India: 1991 Census*, Delhi; and World Bank (1991) *World Development Report 1991*, Oxford.

12 Planning Commission, Government of India (1961) *Third Five Year Plan*, New Delhi, p. 22.

13 Robinson, E.A.G. (1974) 'The economic development of Malthusia', *Modern Asian Studies* 8: 521–34.

14 Rao, V.K.R.V. (1981) 'Inter-state variations in population growth and population policy', *Economical and Political Weekly* 16: 2105–8, and Bose, A. (1991), op. cit.

15 Crude birth and death rates from World Bank (1991), op. cit., Tables 26 and 27; Cassen, R.H. (1978), op. cit.; Balakrishnan, N. and Gunasekara, H.M. (1977) 'A review of demographic trends', in De Silva, K.M. (ed.), op. cit. and Bose, A. (1991), op. cit. (crude birth and death rates are those actually recorded, unadjusted for the age composition of the population). See also Clarke, J.I. (1985) 'Islamic populations: limited demographic transition', *Geography* 70: 118–28; Gopal Krishan (1989) 'Fertility and mortality trends in Indian States, *Geography* 74: 53–6; and Baldwin, M.F. (ed.) (1991) *Natural Resources of Sri Lanka: Conditions and Trends*, Colombo.

16 Fernando, D.F.S. (1972) 'Recent fertility decline in Ceylon', *Population Studies* 26: 445–53 and (1975) 'Changing nuptiality patterns in Sri Lanka', *Population Studies* 29: 179–90.

17 For projections for India on various assumptions see Cassen, R.H. (1978), op. cit., pp. 127–43.

18 World Bank (1991), op. cit., Table 27.

19 Cassen, R.H. (1978), op. cit., Chapter 3. See also Blaikie, P.M. (1975) *Family Planning in India: Diffusion and Policy*, London, and Bose, A. (1991), op. cit.

20 See, for example, Ponnambalam, S. (1980) *Dependent Capitalism in Crisis: The Sri Lankan Economy 1948–1980*, London, p. 61.

21 Mamdani, M. (1972) *The Myth of Population Control: Family, Caste and Class in an Indian Village*, New York, and Corbridge, S.E. and Watson, P.D. (1985) 'The economic value of children: a case study from an Indian village', *Applied Geography* 5: 273–95. See also Bondestam, J. and Bergstrom, L. (1980) *Poverty and Population Control*, London, and Cassen, R.H. (1978), op. cit., p. 67.

22 Of the multitude of general works on economic development since independence the following may usefully be cited here: Streeten, P. and Lipton, M. (eds) (1968) *The Crisis of Indian Planning: Economic Planning in the 1960s*, London;

Bhagwati, J. and Desai, P. (1970), op. cit.; Mellor, J. (1976) *The New Economics of Growth: A Strategy for India and the Developing World*, Ithaca and London; Chaudhuri, P. (1978) *The Indian Economy*, London and (1989) 'Economies' and 'The colonial legacy', in Robinson, F. (ed.) *The Cambridge Encyclopaedia of India, Pakistan, Bangladesh and Sri Lanka*; Frankel, F. (1978), op. cit.; Jha, L.K. (1981) *Economic Strategy for the Eighties*, New Delhi; and Bagchi, A.K. (1982) *The Political Economy of Under-development*, Cambridge, pp. 227–36.

23 See Frankel, F. (1978), op. cit., p. 67; Bhagwati, J.N. and Desai, P. (1970), op. cit., p. 140; and Farmer, B.H. (1974), op. cit., pp. 30, 96–8 and 202–3.

24 Bhagwati, J.N. and Desai, P. (1970), op. cit., pp. 140–1.

25 Farmer, B.H. (1974), op. cit., especially pp. 56–9, 87–8, 102 and 108.

26 See Bhagwati, J.N. and Desai, P. (1970), op. cit., Chapter 13 for a critical review of licensing policy.

27 Little, I.M.D., Mazumdar, D. and Page, J.M. (1987) *Small Manufacturing Enterprises: A Comparative Analysis of India and Other Economies*, New York.

28 See, among many examples that might be cited, Streeten, P. and Lipton, M. (eds) (1968), op. cit.; Myrdal, G. (1968) *Asian Drama*, Harmondsworth, vol. 1, Chapter 7; Mellor, J. (1976), op. cit.; Chaudhuri, P. (1978), op. cit.; Frankel, F. (1978), op. cit.; and Toye, J. (1981) *Public Expenditure and Indian Development Policy, 1960–70* Cambridge.

29 For aid inflows (and foreign exchange reserves), 1950–1 to 1970–1 see Toye, J. (1981), op. cit., p. 44; and Bradnock, R.W. (1992), 'India in détente'.

30 USAID administrator in New Delhi quoted in Frankel, F. (1978), op. cit., p. 286.

31 Streeten, P. and Lipton, M. (eds) (1968), op. cit., pp. 10–11; and Frankel, F. (1978), op. cit.

32 For example, Patel, I.G. (1987) 'On taking India into the twenty-first century (New Economic Policy in India)', *Modern Asian Studies* 21: 209–31.

31 Shroff, M. (1990) 'Liberalisation of the economy: the Indian experience', *South Asia* 13: 1–18; and Corbridge, S.E. (forthcoming) 'The poverty of planning or planning for poverty', *Progress in Human Geography*.

33 For an introduction to South Asian agriculture generally see Harriss, B. and Harriss, J. (1989) 'Agriculture', in Robinson, F. (ed.) (1989), op. cit.

34 See Potter, D.C. (1964), op. cit.

35 In Farmer, B.H. (ed.) (1977) *Green Revolution? Technology and Change in Rice-growing Areas of Tamil Nadu and Sri Lanka*, London, p. 136 and Chapter 11.

36 Frankel, F. (1978), op. cit., pp. 274–92.

37 See Shanmugasundaram, V. (ed.) (1972) *Agricultural Development of India: A Study of Intensive Agricultural District Programme*, Madras, and Desai, D.K. (1972) 'Intensive agricultural district programme', in Chaudhuri, P. (ed.) *Readings in Indian Agricultural Development*, London.

38 See also Toye, J. (1981), op. cit., pp. 46–7.

39 Of the great volume of literature on the 'green revolution', some of it controversial, the following may usefully be cited here: Frankel, F.R. (1971) *India's Green Revolution: Economic Gains and Political Costs*, Princeton, NJ; Etienne, G. (1973) 'India's new agriculture', *South Asian Review* 6: 197–213; Sen, B. (1974) *Green Revolution in India: a Perspective*, New Delhi; Dasgupta, B. (1977) *Agrarian Change and the New Technology in India*, Geneva; Farmer, B.H. (ed.) (1977), op. cit.; (1979) 'The "green revolution" in South Asian ricefields: environment and production', *Journal of Development Studies* 15: 304–19; (1986) 'Perspectives on the "green Revolution" in South Asia', *Modern Asian Studies* 20: 175–99; Lipton, M. (1989) *New Seeds and Poor People*, London; Bayliss-Smith. T. and Wanmali, S. (eds) (1984) *Understanding Green Revolutions:*

Agrarian Change and Development Planning in South Asia, Cambridge; Harriss, J. (1987) 'Capitalism and peasant production: the green revolution in India', in Shanin, T. (ed.) *Peasants and Peasant Societies*, Oxford; and Hazell, P.B.R., Ramasamy, C. *et al.* (1991) *The Green Revolution Reconsidered: The Impact of High-Yielding Rice Varieties in South India*, Baltimore and London.

40 For irrigation in India see Spate, O.H.K. and Learmonth, A.T.A. (1967) *India and Pakistan*, 3rd edn, London, pp. 230–3, and Johnson, B.L.C. (1983a) *India*, 2nd edn, London, Chapter 4. For agriculture without irrigation see Hill, P. (1982) *Dry Grain Farming Families*, Cambridge.

41 Farmer, B.H. (1974), op. cit., p. 41, and Clay, E.J. (1982) 'Technical innovation and public policy: agricultural development in the Kosi Region, Bihar, India', *Agricultural Administration* 9: 189–210.

42 See, for example, Madduma Bandara, C.M. (1977) 'Hydrological consequences of agrarian change', in Farmer, B.H. (1977), op. cit., Chapter 21.

43 See, for example, Murthy, Y.K. (1976) 'Utilization of irrigation facilities', in Indian Society of Agricultural Economics, *Role of Irrigation in the Development of India's Agriculture*, Bombay, pp. 16–30. See also Vohra, B.B. (1989) 'The case against big dams', *Indian Express* 20 May and (1990) *Managing India's Water Resources*, New Delhi; and Lewis, D. (1991) 'Drowning by numbers', *Geographical Magazine* 63: 34–8.

44 See Johnson, B.L.C. (1983b), *Development in South Asia*, Harmondsworth, and (for examples), Farmer, B.H. (1974), op. cit., pp. 163–4.

45 Clay E.J. (1982), op. cit., pp. 197–200. See also Pant, N. (1981) 'Utilisation of canal water below outlet in Kosi irrigation project', *Economical and Political Weekly*, 16: A.78–88 and (1982) 'Major and medium irrigation projects: analysis of cost escalation and delay in completion', *Economics and Political Weekly* 16: A34–43; and Chambers, R. (1989) *Managing Canal Irrigation: Practical Analysis from South Asia*, Cambridge. For the inadequacies of soil surveys in India in the 1960s, see Farmer, B.H. (1974), op. cit., pp. 144–6.

For control of irrigation by cultivators see Wade, R. (1988) *Village Republics: Economic Conditions for Collective Action in South India*, Cambridge.

46 Tarlok Singh (1945) *Poverty and Social Change: A Study in Economic Reorganisation of Indian Rural Society*, London; (1969), 2nd edn, with a reappraisal, Bombay. See also Farmer, B.H. (1974), op. cit., pp. 92–8.

47 See Frankel, F. (1978), op. cit., pp. 68–70, and Warriner, D. (1969) *Land Reform in Principle and Practice*, Oxford, pp. 150–6.

48 See Farmer, B.H. (1974), op. cit., pp. 252–6.

49 Quoted by Warriner, D. (1969), op. cit., p. 136. There is a vast literature on land tenure and land reform in India. See, in particular, Warriner, D. (1969), op. cit., Chapter 6; Frankel, F. (1978), op. cit., *passim*; Bagchi, D. (1981) 'India', in Mushtaqur Rahman (ed.) *Agrarian Egalitarianism: Land Tenures and Land Reforms in South Asia*, Dubuque, Iowa; Herring, R.J. (1983) *Land for the Tiller: the Political Economy of Agrarian Reform in South Asia*, New Haven and London; Kohli, A. (1987) *The State and Poverty in India*, Cambridge; Boyce, J.K. (1987) *Agrarian Impasse in Bengal*, Oxford, especially Chapter 7; and Harriss, J. (1992) 'Does the "depressor" still work? Agrarian structure and development in India – a review of evidence and argument', *Journal of Peasant Studies* (forthcoming).

50 Lipton, M. (1989), op. cit.

51 Harriss, J. (1982) *Capitalism and Peasant Farming: Agrarian Structure and Ideology in Northern Tamil Nadu*, Bombay, pp. 115–8.

52 Warriner, D. (1969), op. cit., p. 171; see also Bagchi, D. (1981), op. cit.

53 Planning Commission, Government of India (1981) *Sixth Five Year Plan*, New Delhi, pp. 114–15; see also Bagchi, D. (1981), op. cit., p. 102; and Jones, S. *et al.* (ed.) (1982) *Rural Poverty and Agrarian Reform*, New Delhi, Introduction and Chapter 4.
54 See Bagchi, D. (1981), op. cit., p. 115 and Farmer, B.H. (1974), op. cit., pp. 252–60.
55 See Farmer, B.H. (1974), op. cit., especially Chapter 6.
56 See Farmer, B.H. (1960) 'On not controlling subdivision in paddy-lands', *Transactions, Institute of British Geographers* 28: 225–35.
57 Farmer, B.H. (1977), op. cit. and (1986), op cit.; and Pearse, A. (1980) *Seeds of Plenty, Seeds of Want*, Oxford.
58 See Farmer, B.H. (1977), op. cit., especially Chapter 8; and Lipton (1989), op. cit.
59 See, for example, Frankel, F. (1978) op. cit., pp. 336–9, and Harriss, B. (1981) *Transitional Trade and Rural Development*, New Delhi.
60 See Farmer, B.H. (1977), op. cit., p. 114, and Harriss, J. (1982), op. cit., pp. 185–98.
61 See Dasgupta, B. (1977), op. cit., pp. 293–313.
62 See Raj, K.N. (1969) *Investment in Livestock in Agrarian Economies*, Delhi (originally in (1969) *Indian Economic Review* 4); (1967) 'The cow: a symposium', *Seminar* 9: 10–55; and Chakravarti, A.K. (1985) 'Cattle development problems and programmes in India: a regional analysis', *GeoJournal* 10: 21–45.
63 Crotty, R. (1982) 'EEC surplus contributes to India's hunger', *Geographical Magazine*, 54: 338–40; and Baviskar, B.S. (1984) 'Operation flood and social science research', *Economic and Political Weekly* 19: 94–6.
64 See Kohli, A. (1987), op. cit., and Basant, R. (1987) 'Agricultural technology and employment in India: a survey of recent research', *Economic and Political Weekly* 22: 1297–1308 and 1348–64.
65 For aid from the USSR see Duncan, P.J.S. (1989) *The Soviet Union and India*, London and New York.
66 For Indian industry see especially Bhagwati, J.N. and Desai, P. (1970), op. cit.; Chaudhuri, P. (1978) *The Indian Economy: Poverty and Development*, London, especially pp. 147–76; and Johnson, B.L.C. (1983a), op. cit.
67 *Sixth Plan*, p. 259. See also Ahluwalia, I.J. (1985) *Industrial Growth in India: Stagnation in the Mid-Sixties*, Delhi; Eapen, M. (1985) 'The new textile policy', *Economic and Political Weekly* 20: 1072–3; and Shroff, M. (1990) 'Liberalisation of the economy: the Indian experience', *South Asia* 13: 1–18.
68 See Jha, L.K. (1980), op. cit., and Chaudhuri, P. (1978), op. cit., p. 154; and, for fiscal policy, Toye, J. (1981), op. cit.
69 Bhagwati, J.N. and Desai, P. (1970), op. cit., p. 31; *Sixth Plan*, p. 218; and Chaudhuri, P. (1978), op. cit., p. 152.
70 See Little, I.M.D. *et al.* (1987), op. cit.; and *Social and Economic Atlas of India* (1987), Delhi.
71 See in particular Misra, R.P., Sundaram, K.V. and Prakasa Rao, V.L.S. (1974) *Regional Development Planning in India*, Delhi; Sundaram, K.V. (1977) *Urban and Regional Planning in India*, New Delhi; and (1983) *Geography of Under-development: The Spatial Dynamics of Underdevelopment*, New Delhi, Chapters 1, 9.
72 As reported in (1982) *The Hindu: International Edition*, 5 June. See also Wanmali, S. (1983) *Service Centres in Rural India: Policy, Theory and Practice*, New Delhi, for regional development in Andhra Pradesh.
73 See Sundaram, K.V. (1983), op. cit., pp. 210–11.
74 Farmer, B.H. (1974), op. cit., pp. 100–1 and 111–17.

75 See Little, I.M.D., *Social and Economic Atlas of India* (1987), op. cit., p. 200.
76 See Sundaram, K.V. (1977), op. cit., pp. 6–12; Prakasa Rao, V.L.S. (1983) *Urbanization in India: Spatial Dimensions*, New Delhi.
77 See Chapman, G. and Wanmali, S. (1981) 'Urban–rural relationships in India: a macro-scale approach using population potentials', *Geoforum* 12: 19–43.
78 See Harriss, B. (1976) 'The Indian ideology of growth centres', *Area* 8: 263–9 and references there cited.
79 Harriss, J. (1991) 'Agriculture/non-agriculture linkages and the diversification of rural economic activity', pp. 429–57 in Breman, J. and Mundle, S., *Rural Transformation in Asia*, Delhi; and Hazell, P.B.R., Ramasamy, C. *et al.* (1991), op. cit.
80 On India's trade see, for example, Mellor, J. (1976), op. cit., Chapter 8; Chaudhuri, P. (1978), op. cit. pp. 70–5; and (1989) 'Trade and tourism', pp. 310–15 in Robinson, F. (ed.) *The Cambridge Encyclopaedia of India, etc.*, op. cit.; Little, I.M.D., *Social and Economic Atlas of India*, (1987), op. cit., pp. 235–54; and Bradnock, R.W. (1992).
81 See Lipton, M. (1975) *The Erosion of a Relationship: India and Britain since 1960*, London.
82 Little, I.M.D., *Social and Economic Atlas of India* (1987), op. cit., pp. 203–8.
83 Frankel, F. (1978), op. cit.
84 Although Pakistan has not attracted as much economic analysis and writing as India, there is nevertheless a considerable literature, partly because of the involvement of American economists. This includes: Andrus, J.R. and Mohammed, A.F. (1966) *Trade, Finance and Development in Pakistan*, Karachi; Mahbub Ul Haq (1963) *The Strategy of Economic Planning: A Case Study of Pakistan*, Karachi; Brecher, I. and Abbas, S.A. (1972) *Foreign Aid and Industrial Development in Pakistan*, Cambridge; Griffin, K.B. and Khan, A.R. (eds) (1972) *Growth and Inequality in Pakistan*, London; Moin Baqai and Brecher, I. (eds) (1973) *Development Planning and Policy in Pakistan, 1950–1970*, Karachi; Rashid Amjad (1974) *Industrial Concentration and Economic Power in Pakistan*, Lahore, and (1982) *Private Industrial Investment in Pakistan, 1960–70*, Cambridge; Ziring, L. *et al.* (eds) (1977) *Pakistan: The Long View*, Durham, NC, especially Chapters 6–8; Johnson, B.L.C. (1979) *Pakistan: a Geography*, London, and (1979), op. cit.; Ahmed, V. and Rashid Amjad (1984) *The Management of Pakistan's Economy 1947–1982*, Karachi; Burki, S.J. (1980) *Pakistan under Bhutto, 1971–1977*, New York, and World Bank (1992) *World Development Report 1992*.
85 Johnson, B.L.C. (1983b), op. cit. and FAO (1989) *Food Production Yearbook*.
86 See Andrus, J.R. and Mohammed, A.F. (1966), op. cit., pp. 42–4 and Johnson, B.L.C. (1979), op. cit., pp. 155–6.
87 See Brown, G.T. (1977) 'Pakistan's economic development after 1971', in Ziring, J. *et al.* (eds), op. cit., especially p. 189, and Burki, S.J. (1980), op. cit., pp. 139–41.
88 Brown, G.T. (1977), op. cit., p. 203.
89 *Dawn Overseas Weekly*, 16–22 October 1981.
90 Johnson, B.L.C. (1979), op. cit., p. 83 and (1983b), op. cit., Chapter 5.
91 See King, R. (1977) *Land Reform: A World Survey*, London, pp. 303–8; Johnson, B.L.C. (1979), op. cit., pp. 102–5 and (1983b), op. cit., Chapter 6; Sanderatne, N. (1974) 'Landowners and land reform in Pakistan', *South Asian Review* 7: 123–36; and Herring, R.J. (1983), op. cit., Chapter 4.
92 There is a considerable, and not uncontroversial literature on the equity effects of the 'green revolution' in Pakistan. See, for example, Alavi, H.A. (1970) 'Elite farmer strategy and regional disparities in the agricultural development of West

Pakistan', in Stevens, R.D., Alavi, H.A. and Bertocci, P. (eds) *Rural Development in Pakistan*, Honolulu; Rashid Amjad and Sen, A. (1977) *Limitations of a Technological Interpretation of Agricultural Performance: A Comparison of East Punjab (India) and West Punjab (Pakistan)*, South Asia Papers, South Asia Institute, Lahore; and Herring, R.J. (1980) 'Zulfikar Ali Bhutto and "eradication of feudalism" in Pakistan', *Economic and Political Weekly* 15: 599–64.

93 Burki, S.J. (1980), op. cit., p. 193.
94 Johnson, B.L.C. (1979), op. cit., p. 155.
95 Andrus, J.R. and Mohammed, A.F. (1966), op. cit., Chapter 1.
96 Johnson, B.L.C. (1979), op. cit., Chapter 1.
97 See Burki, S.J. (1980), op. cit., Chapters 6 and 7, and Weiss, A.M. (1980) *Culture, Class and Development in Pakistan*, Boulder, Colo.
98 See Rashid Amjad (1974), op. cit. For the industrialization of Pakistan see Brecher, I. and Abbas, S.A. (1972), op. cit.
99 *Pakistan Times Overseas Weekly* 2–8 April and 16–22 October 1981.
100 See especially Johnson, B.L.C. (1979), op. cit., pp. 36–41.
101 See, for example, Bergan, A. (1972) 'Personal income distribution and personal savings in Pakistan', in Griffin, K.B. and Khan, A.R. (eds) op. cit., Chapter 8.
102 See, for example, Khan, A.R. (1972) *The Economy of Bangladesh*, London; and Johnson, B.L.C. (1982) *Bangladesh*, 2nd edn, London.
103 See Qazi Kholiquzzaman Ahmad (1978) 'The manufacturing sector of Bangladesh – an overview', *Bangladesh Development Studies* 6: 385–416.
104 For post-'liberation' economic development in Bangladesh see, in particular, Faaland, J. and Parkinson, J.R. (1976) *Bangladesh: the Test Case for Development*, London; Nurul Islam (1977) *Development Planning in Bangladesh*, London, and (1978) *Development Strategy of Bangladesh*, Oxford; Stepanek, J.F. (1979) *Bangladesh – Equitable Growth?*, New York; Johnson, B.L.C. (1982) *Bangladesh*, 2nd edn, op. cit.; and Bangladesh Planning Commission (1989) *Food Strategies in Bangladesh: Medium and Long-Term Perspectives*, Dhaka.
105 Reported in *Bangladesh Today*, London, 16–30 June 1982.
106 See *Bangladesh Today*, 15–28 February, 1–14 March and 15–31 March 1981.
107 Johnson, B.L.C. (1982), op. cit., bears the stamp of an authority on Bangladesh agriculture who knows his subject intimately from field experience. See also Stepanek, J.F. (1979), op. cit.; Farmer, B.H. (1979), op. cit. and (1986), op. cit.; and Rafiqul Huda Chaudhury (ed.) (1980) 'Food policy and development strategy', *The Bangladesh Development Studies* 8. See also Amartya Sen (1981) *Poverty and Famine* Oxford; Mahabub Hossain and Jones, S. (1983) 'Production, poverty and the co-operative ideal: contradictions in Bangladesh rural development policy', in Lea, D. and Chaudhuri, D.P. (eds) (1983) *Rural Development and the State: Contradictions and Dilemmas in Developing Countries*, London, Chapter 6; Bangladesh Planning Commission (1989), op. cit.; FAO (1989) *Food Production Yearbook*, op. cit.; and Brammer, H. (1990) 'Floods in Bangladesh', *Geographical Journal* 156: 12–22 and 158–65.
108 See, *inter alia*, Zaman, M. (1975) 'Bangladesh: the case for further land reform', *South Asian Review* 8: 97–115; Clay, E.J. and Sekandar Khan, M. (1977) *Agricultural Employment and Under-Employment in Bangladesh: The Next Decade*, Dacca; Nurul Islam (1978), op. cit., pp. 30–40; Iqbal Ahmed (1978) 'Unemployment and underemployment in Bangladesh agriculture', *World Development* 6: 1281–96; Jannuzi, F.T. and Peach, J.T. (1980) *The Agrarian Structure of Bangladesh: An Impediment to Development*, Boulder, Colo.; and Herring, R.J. (1983), op.cit.

109 See Bangladesh Planning Commission (1989), op. cit.
110 See Nurul Islam (1978), op. cit., Chapter 3, especially pp. 55–62; Johnson, B.L.C. (1983b), op. cit.; and Humphrey, C.E. (1990) *Privatization in Bangladesh*, Boulder, Colo.
111 World Bank (1992) *World Development Report 1992*, New York.
112 See Snodgrass, D.R. (1966) *Ceylon: An Export Economy in Transition*, Homewood, Ill., especially Chapter 4; also Farmer, B.H. (1957) *Pioneer Peasant Colonization in Ceylon*, London, especially Chapters 5–7.; Samarasinghe, S.W.R. de A. (ed.) (1977) *Agriculture in the Peasant Sector of Sri Lanka*, Peradeniya; De Silva, K.M. (ed.) (1977) *Sri Lanka: Land, People and Economy*, London; Ponnambalam, S. (1980) *Dependent Capitalism in Crisis: The Sri Lankan Economy, 1948–1980*, London; Johnson, B.L.C. (1983b), op. cit.; Gelbert, M. (1988) *Chena Cultivation and Land Transformation in the Dry Zone of Sri Lanka*, Zurich; Chaudhuri, P. (1989) 'Economies', in Robinson, F. (ed.), op. cit.; and, as an example of recent commendable thinking, Panabokke, C.R. (1991) 'Irrigated Agriculture in the Year 2000', *Economic Review* (Colombo) 16: 3–6 & 37.
113 For the PQLI see Morris, M.D. (1979) *Measuring the Condition of the World's Poor: The Physical Quality of Life Index*, New York.
114 See Farmer, B.H. (1961) '*The Ceylon Ten-Year Plan, 1959–1968*', *Pacific Viewpoint* 2: 123–36; Johnson, B.L.C (1983b), op. cit.; and Oberst, R.C. (1985) *Legislatures and Representations: the Decentralization of Development Planning in Sri Lanka*, Boulder, Colo.
115 For agriculture generally see Johnson (1983b), op. cit.; Harriss, B. and Harriss, J. (1989) 'Agriculture', in Robinson, F., op. cit.; and FAO (1989) *Food Production Yearbook*. For irrigated colonization see Farmer, B.H. (1957), op. cit., Chapter 16 and Government of Ceylon (1970) *Report of Gal Oya Project Evaluation Conmittee*, Sessional Paper no. 1 of 1970, Colombo.
116 See Peiris, G.H. (1975) 'The current land reforms and peasant agriculture in Sri Lanka', *South Asia* 5: 78–89; and (1978) 'Land reform and agrarian change in Sri Lanka', *Modern Asian Studies* 12: 611–28. See also Herring, R.J. (1983), op. cit., especially pp. 55–77 and 138–47.
117 Farmer, B.H. (1957), op. cit., pp. 289–91 and (1960), op. cit.; V. Samarasinghe and S.W.R. de A. Samarasinghe (1984) in Bayliss-Smith, T.P. and Wanmali, S., op. cit., pp. 173–93; and *Report of the Land Commission, 1987* (1990), Sessional Paper no. 3 of 1990, Colombo.
118 See Herring, R.J. (1983), op. cit.
119 Farmer, B.H. (1977), op. cit., especially pp. 370–7 and Chapter 12.
120 Richards, P. and Gooneratne, W. (1980), *Basic Needs, Poverty and Government Policy in Sri Lanka*, Geneva, pp. 98–9.
121 Johnson, B.L.C. and Scrivenor, M. Le M. (1981), *Sri Lanka*, Chapter 6; Johnson, B.L.C. (1983b), op. cit. and *World Development Report* (1991).
122 See Samarasinghe, V. (1977) 'Some spatial aspects of agricultural development in Sri Lanka', in Samarasinghe, S.W.R. de A. (ed.) (1977), op. cit., Chapter 1.
123 There is a useful treatment of foreign trade in Johnson, B.L.C. and Scrivenor, M. Le M. (1981), op. cit., pp. 30–5.
124 Richards, P. and Gooneratne, W. (1980), op. cit., pp. 163–76.
125 See Blaikie, P.M., Cameron, J. and Seddon, D. (1980) *Nepal in Crisis: Growth and Stagnation at the Periphery*, Delhi; Johnson, B.L.C. (1983b), op. cit.; Chaudhuri, P. (1989) in Robinson, F. (ed.), op. cit., and *World Development Report* (1991).
126 See Blaikie, P.M. *et al.* (1980), op. cit., p. 50; Kansakar, V.B.S. (1985) 'Land

resettlement policy as a population distributive strategy in Nepal', pp. 111–12 in Kosinski, L.A. and Elahi, K.M. *Population Redistribution and Development in South Asia*, Dordrecht; Harriss, B. and Harriss, J., 'Agriculture', pp. 213–5 in Robinson, F., op. cit.; FAO (1989) *Food Production Yearbook*, and Shrestha, N.R. (1990) *Landlessness and Migration in Nepal*, Boulder, Colo.

127 See Macfarlane, A. (1976) *Resources and Population: A Study of the Gurungs of Nepal*, Cambridge.

128 See Blaikie, P.M. *et al.* (1980), op. cit.; Blaikie, P.M. (1988) 'Explaining soil degradation', Chapter 4 in Blaikie, P.M. and Unwin, T., *Environmental Crisis in Developing Countries*, London; and Ives, J.D. and Messerli, B. (1989) *The Himalayan Dilemma: Reconciling Conservation and Development*, London.

129 Blaikie *et al.* (1980), op. cit., p. 47. See also Regmi, M.C. (1976) *Landownership in Nepal*, Berkeley.

130 Blaikie, P.M., Cameron, J. and Seddon, D. (1979) *The Struggle for Basic Needs in Nepal*, Paris, p. 88.

131 Johnson, B.L.C. (1983b), op. cit. and Chaudhuri, P. (1989), 'Trade', p. 292 in Robinson, F., op. cit.

132 Misra, H.N. (1988) *Bhutan: Problems and Policies*, New Delhi; and Young, L.J. (1991) 'Agricultural Change in Bhutan', *Geographical Journal* 157: 172–8.

133 Chaudhuri, P. (1989) p. 260 in 'Economies', in Robinson, F., op. cit. and Dupuis, J. (1974) 'Les Maldives', *Cahiers d'Outre Mer* 27: 5–21.

134 Morrison, D. (1992) 'Blue lagoon's ill tidings', *The Guardian*, 28 August.

INDEX OF SUBJECTS

189

INDEX OF PLACES, COUNTRIES AND AREAS

INDEX OF PERSONS